confessions of a guilty freelancer

break away books

INDIANA UNIVERSITY PRESS

Bloomington & Indianapolis

confessions of a guilty freelancer

William O'Rourke

This book is a publication of

INDIANA UNIVERSITY PRESS
601 North Morton Street
Bloomington, Indiana 47404-3797 USA

iupress.indiana.edu

Telephone orders 800-842-6796
Fax orders 812-855-7931

∞ The paper used in this publication meets the minimum requirements of the American National Standard for Information Sciences – Permanence of Paper for Printed Library Materials, ANSI Z39.48-1992.

Manufactured in the United States of America

Library of Congress Cataloging-in-Publication Data

O'Rourke, William.
Confessions of a guilty freelancer / William O'Rourke.
p. cm.
Includes index.
ISBN 978-0-253-00181-8 (pbk. : alk. paper)
ISBN 978-0-253-00185-6 (e-book)
I. Title.
PS3565.R65C66 2012
814'.54 – dc23

2012014828

1 2 3 4 5 16 15 14 13 12

FOR MAGGIE

AND JOE

AND MY COLLEAGUES AT NOTRE DAME

In our age there is no such thing as "keeping out of politics." All issues are political issues, and politics itself is a mass of lies, evasions, folly, hatred, and schizophrenia. When the general atmosphere is bad, language must suffer.

George Orwell, "Politics and the English Language," 1946

Contents

Preface

The first confession I have to make is that *Confessions of a Guilty Freelancer* is misnamed. Technically, I haven't been a freelancer all these years; I've been a moonlighter. Since 1974, I have been employed by one institution of higher learning or another. *Mea culpa.*

But, in the world of words, moonlighter hasn't been much used, if at all, when it comes to those who write for the public prints. That "freelancer" has been the designation universally used is not an adequate excuse, of course. One of the first writers I ever knew personally, Edward Dahlberg (1900–77), used to thunder at me: "All excuses are perjuries!" and I certainly believe that.

But, in all my years of writing what is loosely called journalism (literature in a hurry, according to Matthew Arnold [1822–88]) I have never "worked" for any of the publications that have published me. In that way, I am solidly freelance. Freelancing has never been a pretty word, bringing to mind, as it does, medieval sport, jousting, and the general aggressiveness required to wield a pen for hire. I have never been a pen for hire. It is not so much for high-horse reasons, or that I was entirely above that sort of thing; it was because I didn't have a talent for it, pitching story ideas, interesting eager editors at the glossy magazines in New York City about trends and celebrities. Friends of mine who did have that talent went on to much more remunerative work in Hollywood. I left New York City, and returned to the Midwest, to teach at the University of Notre Dame, where all of the contents of this book have been written.

In the essay that ends this volume's first section, the title essay, you will find the line, "It is hard to overestimate the low esteem freelancing inspires in the regularly employed." After the article appeared, I was sent a note by a Chicago press critic, one who had never taken public notice of me during the five years I wrote a weekly political column for the *Chicago Sun-Times,* saying that the line had struck him and he wanted to apologize for never mentioning me, though he read my column regularly. Being freelance is similar to being single at a certain age, a suspect category.

We currently are experiencing an unsettling transitional time in journalism. I was paid, to write for the *Sun-Times,* a freelance rate of $150 a column. (None of those columns are found herein; but you can find them at www.theviewfromthecouch.com.) When the column ended, I presumed my demise was about money and space. I was the canary in the journalistic coal mine and was the first to go as the latest recession hit newspapers early. Steve Huntley, the editorial page editor of the *Sun-Times,* the man responsible for my being a five-year fixture there, had once told me, "No," when I asked him if he wanted to write columns. The unsigned editorials were more to his liking. Shortly after I was cut loose, the *Sun-Times* began to use more wire service copy and Huntley, himself, turned up as a regular columnist. The cutbacks had forced less original copy being used, while, at the same time, sweating those on staff who were permanently employed to produce more.

Looking over my table of contents, I see that about half of the contents was written "for free." (And those that were remunerated fetched mostly paltry sums.) Recall your Boswell, quoting Samuel Johnson:

"No man but a blockhead ever wrote, except for money." Well, we have created a generation of blockheads, and more to come.

The internet has turned writers into content providers, most often working for free. The word freelance is now becoming literal, at least the "free" part – why? lots of reasons: higher education, for one. Just as there used to be clear distinctions between "commercial" and "literary" fiction (and nonfiction), distinctions that, over time, have become decidedly blurred, there are fewer distinctions separating the work of what professors do in order to retain their jobs. Scholarship must be created: scholarship, which, in the past, did not necessarily pay enough to provide a celebration dinner, but which was necessary to keep the maker employed, and, thank the Lord, eventually tenured.

The growth in the academic world of the creative writing MFA over the last thirty or so years (increasing from a handful of such programs in 1970 to nearly three hundred in 2010) has dragged hundreds of writers, novelists, poets, nonfiction writers into the same world the dedicated scholar inhabits: publish or perish. And the changes that circumstance has brought about are easy to see. For one, check the back of any volume of, say, *The Best American Short Story* volume, pre 1945. You will find one or two pages listing the publications from whence the stories have been picked. More than half were high paying journals, the long-gone slicks, many defunct or empty now of fiction.

Now, there are thirty pages of journals listed in the 2010 volume, with only a handful of high paying publications included. Most are subsidized journals, existing because of universities or the ample pockets of a few rich people. Other than in advertising, the short form of both nonfiction and fiction is largely a non-remunerative form, except for a fortunate few.

I am not a member of the chorus of MFA program-bashers. I don't believe we have an oversupply of writers; if anything, we have an undersupply of readers. Reading literary nonfiction and fiction is not part of the popular culture; it is an activity of the unpopular culture, but, nonetheless, it is still alive.

In the volume at hand, you will find essays that address that problem. But, in the unpopular culture, the literary one, the current situation is not healthy. When Barnes & Noble and Borders began, such large stores were considered predators, out to eliminate the mom-and-pop bookstore business; but, it quickly became obvious, the big-box outlets were turning books into objects to be looked at. The stores were galleries of books (and coffee shops); now, even the big-boxes are imperiled, teetering toward bankruptcy.

The literate culture supposedly demolished the oral culture a couple of centuries ago, making literacy an elite and dominating bastion. But, the oral culture now has come back with a vengeance. Technology has led the way: the internet, the web, communication in general (cell phones and the like), operate in a volatile mixture of oral and loosely written speech, but a medium that requires typing, or "texting." The latest form of half speech and half prose, from Twitter, the tweet, has not ushered us into a new golden age of the brilliant aphorism. We now see, we now look, and occasionally hear; but fewer read, except for what can fit on a screen. (And writers played a foreshadowing role, once they abandoned their typewriters and began to stare at their work magically materializing on a screen when they adopted computers as "word processing machines.") Recently, I saw a picture in a major newspaper of grandparents giving a Kindle to their eight-year-old grandchild; when grandparents play that role, goodbye book culture.

In our largely aural-visual culture, we have reached an odd place in the pernicious division – not just of income, the gap between rich and poor – but of literacy. There is now a slice, not that much bigger than the one percent of the population, that controls so much wealth (though, of course, not the same people), which can be called hyperliterate. These are the people who used to read the book reviews that have now disappeared from so many newspapers.

The division of literacy and money continues to echo the economic distribution our country now lives with. The top ten percent of the income distribution are certainly the book buyers, the book buyers of so-called "better books." For the non-buyers, there are the libraries, always under siege by government budget cutters.

But libraries have taken over the distribution of the aural-visual popular culture, too, as well as the unpopular culture of literary fiction and nonfiction. And, then, like the poor, there are many who read almost nothing, or nothing like books. The poor may have flat-screen TVs, but not yet Kindles.

I don't mean to be apocalyptical, but, since this collection of short nonfiction pieces of various lengths has been written over a span of seventeen years (1993–2010), I am prone to taking the long view. The old days of freelancing, when writers tried to make a living cobbling together cash from diverse publications, is certainly over, though, in the way of the wild man in the woods, one or two such people may be still doing it. But many writers are writing for free (especially those who do it as a second job), just as college graduates the last few years find themselves working as unpaid interns post degrees.

And the ascendancy of the memoir over the past two decades, and its fast and easy relationship with the truth, has contributed to the general diminishment of literary judgment. The lack of trust begets confusion, which, in turn, lessens the status of the endeavor.

Our winner-take-all society operates in the literary world as fiercely as in the rest of the world. More and more power is given over to the gatekeepers that remain; book reviews are shutting down, even as the number of "books" published each year continues to rise (if you just go by ISBN numbers.) The *New York Times Book Review* rules over a kingdom that now exists mostly of abandoned villages and crumbling castles of departed nobles and their former duchies. But its power remains considerable. The setting of fashion is a high capital operation. The *New York Review of Books* remains, most likely because its lack of any competition. The rarest thing for most contemporary writers is to have their work written about beyond a 700-word limit.

And occasionally even fashion setters are upended. In a society where even the self-declared tastemakers do not know who are the best writers any more, once in a blue moon, outside agitators (usually judges of a few powerful prizes, themselves high capital operations – the Pulitzer Prize, the National Book Award, etc.) can shake up things.

In my precursor volume to this one (*Signs of the Literary Times* (Albany: SUNY Press, 1993), I wrote of the case of Larry Heinemann's novel *Paco's Story,* which was nominated for the National Book Award for the best novel of 1986, but was passed over for review by the *New York Times Book Review* until the nomination. The NYTBR testily reviewed it after the nomination, but took a defensive tone because its own judgment had been questioned on who-was-who and what-was-what, even after the novel won the prize.

And, it happened again, in 2010, when Jaimy Gordon's *Lord of Misrule* was nominated (and then won) the National Book Award for fiction. This time, the *Times* eventually ran a review and an article and the *Book Review* mentioned it, too, in a news column, though not a review, but the paper wasn't as pugnacious about its oversight as it was in Heinemann's case. It seemed to have learned a lesson. Humility is in order these days when no one, evidently, is able to keep up with all that is happening.

Even an Edmund Wilson couldn't keep track of the literary world today. And, at least, that is being acknowledged, if only begrudgingly. But, as any writer of books knows, there are three things one hopes for: to be published, to be reviewed, and to turn up in bookstores. What one learns is one of those must happen (publication), but it is even more difficult to capture all three.

In commercial journalism, what is happening is easier to see, since it is being played out in the popular culture on flat-screen televisions. The phenomenon of political consultants and operatives becoming television journalists continues unabated and the cult of celebrity dominates the news, both in its coverage and its production. The paradox of niche journalism that cable TV can offer (entire shows on pet veterinarians, or people who hoard things, etc.), still thirsting after large audience numbers in order to be economically viable, thereby becoming dumber and dumber, continues. Small "journals of opinion" struggle, even when backed by families flush with excess capital. But writers still long for readers, which is a perennial reason they will work for free. These days there are fewer calls for "public intellectuals." It is a job category I always wanted to fill, but there is not much demand at the moment, even less than there was two decades ago. Those that thrive are corporate intellectuals, hosted and promoted by the largest media outlets (primarily television) in the land.

I have divided this volume into three sections. When you are collecting a variety of articles over a long span of time, some sort of order begins to emerge. Given that I am part of the Vietnam-era generation, the sixties generation, I heard often enough in my youth the slogan "the personal is political."

I didn't need to be convinced back then; it was already part of my jejune analysis. As you will be reading, why Bill Clinton betrayed my (his) generation was that he forgot that simple nostrum. His dalliance with Monica Lewinsky ended, for a while, the rise of the meritocracy in politics, and handed presidential succession back to America's royal political families. Clinton should have known better. Though a segment of his defenders said then (and now) that what a person does in private has nothing to do with what a person does in public, no one from the sixties generation really believes that.

The first set of essays in the volume is the most personal. My fiction has been the major outlet for this sort of writing, but some experiences have found their way to the short and shorter forms of nonfiction. The essay that begins the collection is an account of my heart attack, which eventually became the first chapter of my book, *On Having a Heart Attack: A Medical Memoir* (Notre Dame: University of Notre Dame Press, 2006).

I did not rush to write the essay; the incident itself wasn't necessarily something I cared to revisit. But, after I had a heart attack I read what I could find about the event. I was surprised to see that the accounts by either victims or practitioners described the actual heart attack in a sentence or two, or, at most, a paragraph. I decided to rectify that hole in the literature and describe the event, the heart attack, at length.

As I have gotten older, writer friends of the generation ahead of mine have died, and two deaths, Richard Elman and Grace Paley's, prompted tributes. When I was a young writer the idea of generation had a lot of power in the literary culture, the notion of writers connected to each other, influencing one another. But the academy, for the last couple of decades, has more or less abandoned the idea of generational links, labeling such mere chronology and coincidence unfashionable. But writers still are interconnected and in the literary world, it matters. But, along with connection, there comes exclusion, and there is sufficient intellectual dishonesty afoot in the literary community to overlook other writers when so inclined.

Also included in the first section are a few short pieces about my family and the long concluding title essay contains a good bit of my own literary and personal autobiography.

The second section is "The Personal and the Political," where both subjects vie more equally for notice and attempt to show how inseparably they are combined.

The third section fuses all three concerns, the personal, the political and the literary. Many of those pieces are book reviews and review-essays, now an endangered species which, perhaps in the future, will likely only be preserved in the wildlife virtual habitat of the internet; certainly they will not play the same role in the general life of readers of journals and newspapers, given how those venues have been pruned.

Henry Kisor, who was the book review editor at the *Chicago Sun-Times,* enlisted me in a last burst of ample review space at that paper and kept assigning me political and history books to review, shortly before he retired and the pages given over to book reviews shrunk. And any close reader of this volume will notice in the assortment of reviews reprinted here the paucity of discussion of women writers (as well as a few repetitions – forgive, too, my fondness for my phrase "reverance for the rich"). In my defense, I can say that all of the books under consideration were assigned by others. Book reviewing I have always seen as community service in the literary world. In the *Notre Dame Review,* which I co-edit, I have given notice to many women writers, but, alas, not here.

This volume, of course, is an attempt to make available some of my writing that, thus far, only a select few have yet to sample, the readers of the somewhat obscure publications (with a few exceptions) where they first appeared. The *Sun-Times* and the *Chicago Tribune,* obviously have readers, but a much smaller percentage of those read the book reviews and the op-ed pieces, rather than, say, the sports pages. The purpose of bringing all these shorter nonfiction pieces together is to provide a new audience for them.

I am polemical, something of a complainer, a writer who values the role of curmudgeon, who attempts to unsettle, as well as inform. Unlike most short story writers, who, I find, rarely exercise much range (in form or length, that is), I write nonfiction in all lengths, as do many nonfiction writers. Collected they offer both a political and literary portrait of our country during the last two decades, the age of Clinton, Bush, ending at the doorstep of the age of Obama. One literary trend has definitely mirrored the political: globalization has affected everything. Examination of the recent O. Henry Prize volumes and *The Best American . . .* series will show almost as many stories set abroad as in the U.S.A. We are all post-colonial writers now.

Freelancers, guilty or not, are at the mercy and good graces of editors; someone has to like what you do before it gets published. It's a free press as long as you own one, etc. (H. L. Mencken 1880–1956). Some writers find they can't live with editors, but no writer can live without them. (Except, perhaps, the writer branded with a word as ugly as freelancer, the blogger.) Most of the essays in this volume, not all, are the longer, original versions I wrote, not the shorter versions that often ran; almost no editor will publish everything that I write on any one subject, for both good and bad reasons. But, nonetheless, this volume would not exist without them.

South Bend, IN
August 2011

confessions of a guilty freelancer

part one

the personal

Here's Mine

I was home in South Bend, Indiana, in my attic office, working on a novel involving coal miners, set against the backdrop of the 1984–85 National Union of Miners strike in England. The phone rang and it was Eric Sandeen, the oldest child of my friends, Eileen and Ernie Sandeen. Eric, a professor of American Studies at the University of Wyoming, was in town to go to the Notre Dame-University of Southern California football game. His father was an emeritus professor of English at the university and Eric was using his tickets. And he had an extra one for the game that was to start in about an hour, which he offered to me. I had donated my tickets to some good cause. It was October 26th, 1991, and the fall weather was only fair: but the gray, overcast sky wasn't supposed to turn into rain.

My day's work writing was about over, in any case: the cold, wet atmosphere of the novel's English pit towns had seeped into me and the idea of getting outside was appealing. My novel, for a number of reasons, had been hard going. I decided to abandon it and attend the game.

I went downstairs and told my wife I was leaving. She was working at her computer, preparing testimony for an appearance as an expert witness (she is an economist) and looked at me skeptically, but bid me adieu. She said, "I'm so worried about Monday my heart hurts."

Our fifteen-month-old, Joe, was downstairs with a babysitter, whom we had retained for three hours, so both my wife and I could get some work done. Eric was impatient to get into the stadium (he was an alum and wanted to bask in the pre-game show), so I was rushing to get there so as not to delay him any further.

The coal miners of Great Britain would have to wait. I said good-bye to everyone in the house and took off. What going to the game meant was that Teresa would have to take care of Joe by herself after Maria, the babysitter, left. I had planned to watch the game on television, which would have left me able to look after Joe. We were attempting to divide looking after our boy fifty-fifty, which amounted in these modern arrangements to doing it seventy-five-seventy-five. Teresa's father had been an all-American football player at Berkeley, but she was not a fan. Football was the bane of fall weekends for her as a new mother, just as it was when she was a young girl.

We lived near the campus, but on a football weekend the university becomes a sports franchise and for me get to the closest parking available required a circuitous route, through South Bend's downtown and then approaching the campus obliquely from the south, parking in a poor neighborhood adjacent to the campus.

South Bend isn't a college town and the university always has been separate from it, especially back in the heyday of the town, when the Studebaker car company was the city's biggest employer. But now Notre Dame is the largest employer and, though the campus is still on its edge, it is central to the business interests here. I parked my old Volvo near Notre Dame Avenue, by the first house I owned when I first moved to the town, about six blocks from campus.

It is a neighborhood of student rentals and African American households, and a few junior faculty, which is what I had been when I lived there. Notre Dame Avenue is a wide street that goes straight into the heart of the campus. It is wide because there are railroad tracks beneath layers of asphalt, tracks of the South Shore Railroad, since in the halcyon days of the midcentury, the era of Ronald Reagan as the Gipper, the South Shore Line used to come into the campus, as well as going straight through the middle of downtown South Bend.

After parking, I walked quickly to the stadium. It was about a half-hour before kickoff. There were stragglers on the periphery of the campus, but most of the 60,000 people were either in or around the stadium, tailgating in the pay parking lots, swarming around the brick edges of the stadium like ants around a morsel. I met Eric beneath the entrance he specified and he gave me a ticket. It was a good seat, better than my own season tickets provided.

Eric rushed in and I told him I'd join him after I got something at the concession stand. I hadn't eaten lunch, so I wanted a hot dog. I stood in line, put in my order for a Polish kielbasa, the thicker sort of hot dog, and a Diet Coke.

As I walked away with my refreshments I felt something peculiar. It was so strange it stopped me mid-step. I was forty-five years old and I had felt many things, but never before this particular feeling: I felt a click deep inside. The image the sensation produced in my mind was of a BB, a small round piece of copper-colored lead, falling into a socket. It was a very clear image. A BB is tiny, but the one I imagined felt infinitesimal, microscopic. Yet I felt it, a click, metal on metal. Like an expensive, microscopic gear had slipped, some exquisite piece of machinery falling out of alignment. Some medieval example of craftsmanship, a gyroscope, something intricate, needing fine balance. The feeling, the event, was located in my chest, below my left breast. It was thoroughly interior, as if a signal had been sent and registered, what those giant satellite dishes are poised waiting for, a transmission from deep space.

I continued on into the stadium to find my seat and join Eric. They were great seats, practically on the fifty-yard line. And they were real seats, with backs, not just a slab of lumber to sit on as I was used to, and we were only a few rows from the field.

The seat was so good someone was sitting in it. A woman, it turned out, who had misread her ticket's row number. After she moved I sat down and thought about eating my large hot dog. But I began to feel sick to my stomach. Since I hadn't eaten for a few hours I couldn't understand why. But I did feel nauseous. So much so I put my head between my legs to bring myself some comfort, to get some blood to my head, I supposed. Then I felt something electric, part tingle, part buzz, traveling down through my left arm.

I'm not sure how long I was bent over. I heard Eric say something along the lines of, "Are you all right?"

I replied, "I'm not sure." I began to feel cold and clammy.

I jerked myself up. It seemed that the temperature had dropped thirty degrees. My shoulders were up and my neck compressed down as if I was freezing. The electric feeling in my arm was creeping up my shoulder into my neck. I felt sweaty. I looked at my right hand. It was blazingly white. My left hand still had the hot dog in it. I put the hot dog in the pocket of my coat.

I heard Eric then say, from what sounded like a long way away, "Do you think it has to do with your heart?" I heard that, but I didn't react to it. It was as if I saw someone I thought I knew, but couldn't actually remember who it was. The question just hung there.

I am not sure how much time had passed. Three minutes? Five? But it took me at least that long to admit to myself what was going on. I was having a heart attack. I had read and heard the list of symptoms enough times. It seemed a classic case: nausea, tingling in the arm, sweat, the tightness of my neck and shoulders. I considered none of it pain: I had been hurtled forward into another state, one I had never been in, as if I was in outer space without a suit.

I knew there was a first aid station in the stadium. I needed to get there, but I didn't know where it was located in relation to these unfamiliar seats. I looked about and there seemed to be a mist in the stadium: a fog – one that transmitted color. Some USC players were on the field in front of me. They moved slowly, silently. The gold and red of their uniforms glowed incandescently.

I swung my head back around and looked for an usher. He would know. I told Eric I was going to the first aid station and I heard him get up behind me. There, at the end of the row, was a frail old man with an usher's cap on. "He must be near ninety," I thought. I asked him where the first aid station was and he looked at me with concern, took my arm, and led me through a tunnel to the concourse below the stands. This was familiar. I did not resist his help, though I thought it must look strange, a man twice my age helping me along. People parted before us, rubbernecking pedestrians, most staring with curiosity and alarm. Just who looked older or frailer at that moment, me or the usher, I cannot say.

Even in my distress, I thought us a strange sight, though I had seen one dying person walking before. It was 1981 and I was visiting my closest friends, Robert and Inez Kareka in Boston, right before I came out to the Midwest to start teaching at Notre Dame.

Inez had been fighting cancer for two years and her battle was almost over. In the middle of the night noise had awakened me. I saw Robert helping Inez to the bathroom. She had been asleep in the living room and had opened the refrigerator door, thinking it was the bathroom and had backed into it, crashing its contents. He was leading

Inez to the actual bathroom and she looked transformed; she was in her late fifties then and had always been a looker, in the style of Marilyn Monroe, from whose generation she was.

But that night her dyed blonde hair was wildly askew. Her hair's black roots framed her thinned face, her now stick-like limbs were held akimbo, and her expression was fixed in a muted scream, as if she wanted to say something but had lost the language to do so. She looked exactly like an eighteenth-century engraving of death I had seen. And that morning she went into a coma she never came out of until she died a week later.

In the stadium, dragging my legs and waving arms as I walked along with the ancient usher I thought I, too, must look like death.

We got to the door of the first aid station and, upon entering, the silence that had seemed to surround me vanished. There was a TV on tuned to the pre-game show. People were animated, talking. Eric stayed by the door.

"Is there a doctor here?" I asked. A few people in the room came toward me quickly. "Here, get his coat off." I was wearing an expensive Barbour coat I had bought in England. It had the hot dog in the pocket. I sat down and someone began to unbutton my shirt. Another hand had grabbed my wrist and I heard a voice say, "I can't find a pulse."

He said it to a slightly older man, but not that much older than me. "Oh, you're probably just hyperventilating," the man, who was addressed, said.

"He must be the doctor," I thought. "I'm a professor here," I said, "I've taught for over ten years and I've never hyperventilated in my life. If I'm hyperventilating, put a bag over my head."

No one was going to say what was obvious: I was having a heart attack. Not even me. But I did feel better saying something forceful; that I had some force. Eric (who is very tall) was looming by the doorway.

The doctor said, "We'll get you to the hospital just to be safe." There was more motion around the room.

Eric said something about him going to the hospital and I said, "No, stay, enjoy the game." He had come a long way to go to the game. I thought I heard him say he would call Teresa.

My shirt hung, unbuttoned, loose around me. My coat was gone. A gurney was produced near the doorway and I was led to it and helped up to lie down on it. Straps were put over me and I was wheeled down the concourse. I was now staring upward and would see the occasional face looking down at me, again with a mixture of alarm, curiosity and concern. I was a spectacle. The game hadn't yet begun. An ambulance was parked near one of the stadium's gates. I had seen it there before and took little notice. The gurney's legs were collapsed and it was picked up by two men wearing similar coats and rolled into the ambulance. One of the men hopped into the ambulance's narrow cabin and began to attempt to put an intravenous line into the skin above my left hand. They wanted to drip something in. He kept sticking me, trying to get a good purchase on a vein, but seemed not to be having much luck. His attempts didn't hurt. I seemed to have a surface numbness. I was just unhappy he wasn't succeeding. It seemed like a lot of time was passing and nothing was going on. Finally, he stopped trying and left the needle inserted in whatever fashion it was and taped it. More minutes seemed to pass and finally the doors of the ambulance closed.

I could picture where the ambulance was going, after it finally started to move. Though I was wearing a watch, I wasn't looking at it to check how much time had passed. Time was both elongated and slowed. Here was the now; I was in it. The ambulance needed to part the waters; there were still crowds around the stadium and there was no direct way out. It twisted and turned and finally I felt it speed up as it hit city streets. It turned out they were going straight up Notre Dame Avenue. Lying down on the gurney I was a mass of resistance; my shoulders continued to rise as my neck and head attempted to retract into my body, turtle-like. The sensation in my arm and neck was no longer an electrical buzz; it was molecular, an ethereal feeling, as if I was being transported somewhere – and not just my body being ferried in an ambulance. Its siren was on, but it didn't seem loud. Turning my head, I saw the roof of my former house go by; here, literally, was my life passing by. But what I was feeling was being erased. As if I was a stone on the surface of the water, about to be swallowed over, ripple-less. I felt, as clearly as I have ever felt anything, how everything in the world would go on without me.

Here and gone. Gone gone gone. Then, what I knew surfaced, how this ride up the empty street (because of the game there was no traffic on it) was so much like all the mythology I had ever read: Lethe, the river Styx, the voyage across, death's boatman, Charon at the wheel, the trip to Elysium. In the eerie quiet of the ambulance I was being taken away. Away. The ferrymen were riding up front. I was alone.

We arrived at the hospital. Doors opened and I was rolled out and in, ending up in an examining room, one of the ambulance attendants carrying the drip that he had attempted to hook up to me. I heard him say to a nurse he didn't think it was right. I was still on my back. A nurse took my hand and prepared another intravenous line. She left the one he put in in. Another drip was started through the new one.

Someone asked, "Are you from out of town?"

It seemed an odd question. Beyond the drip that had been started, nothing was happening. I was prone, making sounds that were between language and a moan.

I thought then of what they were looking at: a short, overweight, white male, in his mid-forties, with thinning hair, without a prosperous-looking face. I was wearing old work shoes, from Sears Roebuck with "Die Hard"(!) embossed on their soles. My khaki pants were close to twenty years old, as was the old, worn leather belt. The flannel shirt hanging loosely on me, though not twenty years old, was frayed and old enough.

"I'm a professor at Notre Dame," I said weakly.

I didn't hear a harrumph, but no one said anything. There continued to be some milling about. I lay there thinking someone should be doing something.

"I'm a professor at Notre Dame," I repeated more forcefully to no discernible affect.

Time passed. "Too much time," I thought, and, with some difficulty, I got myself to sit up. With my right arm and hand, the one that wasn't singing with molecular activity and didn't have a drip inserted into it, I awkwardly fished for my wallet. I laid it open on my thigh, and slowly thumbed through the contents until I found the thin and shiny Blue Cross card. I waved it above my head.

"Here's my insurance card," I proclaimed.

It was snatched from my hand and the room was immediately transformed into a beehive of activity. My shirt was removed, and an oxygen necklace was draped around my face. I was given nitroglycerin to take under my tongue, and someone appeared with a clipboard to take more information. Questions were asked, names, addresses. An EKG machine was wheeled in, and I was hooked up to it. An intravenous line was inserted into my other hand.

I realized that had I been wearing my English Barbour jacket, someone would have recognized it as the costly thing it was, and made some judgment other than that I might be a derelict. I felt whatever had caused the inactivity was my appearance; I did not appear to be a man of substance until I produced my Blue Cross card.

Finally, someone I took to be a doctor came into the room; she appeared to be in her late twenties, dark haired, with a good haircut. She was thin, and had a stethoscope hung around her neck. She looked at the EKG printout and wandered out of the room.

I was still sitting up in my parody of a freezing posture, shoulder blades peaked, neck squashed. I noticed I was talking out loud to myself. I was saying what I was thinking, as if I thought I couldn't hear myself silently think and needed to say it out loud. Then, out loud, I asked, "Why am I talking to myself out loud?" And then I answered myself, "Because I'm scared."

The doctor walked back into the room. She didn't react to what I had been saying, though I wanted her to join the conversation, so I asked, "Did the EKG show any heart involvement?" Not waiting for an answer, I said, "The doctor earlier at the stadium said he thought I was hyperventilating." Why I was still offering that bit of wishful thinking, I don't know, but I presumed it had to do with being scared. She responded with only one word, "Yes," and I knew it was the answer to the heart question. "You should try to relax," she said, and walked out again.

"Relax! Are you nuts?" I thought, but, this time, didn't say aloud. She had said it reproachfully, standing a few feet from me. "Oh, sure, I'm going to try to relax. I'm having a heart attack. If I could make my shoulders look less like Mount Kilimanjaro I would. Relax."

I was being silent, though. Not talking aloud to myself anymore.

An old man appeared at the door, wearing what looked like a highway hazard jacket, as if he was in the street, directing traffic. He was as old as the usher and looked like there might be a family resemblance, which made his orange and red hazard jacket seem even more incongruous.

"Your son is out in the waiting room and wants to see you," he said.

"Ahhh," I wailed. "He can't be out there! It's not my son. He's only fifteen months old!"

I felt as if I was keening, though I'm not sure what it sounded like. A sorrow deeper than despair hit me. I wondered if I was hallucinating. My son was waiting for me. For a fleeting second I wondered if that could possibly be true. Had Eric called anyone? Hadn't I asked him to call Teresa? Didn't he volunteer?

Nonetheless, I felt overcome, but I swallowed the sob. I was born. I finally had a child, a son. Then I died. My job was done.

A nurse wheeled in another bag, fussed with the intravenous line, attached an access joint to it and began another drip. "Morphine," she said. "That should help."

As I tried not to think about my son waiting outside for me, I realized I should call Teresa, my wife. The woman doctor had come back into the room (doubtless to see if I had "relaxed") and had again turned her back to me while looking at some papers.

"Could you call my wife, please? And tell her I'm here," I said, and told her the number. The doctor complied and I heard her speak softly into the receiver, though I couldn't make out the words. The hospital was less than ten minutes from our home.

I was breathing the fresh oxygen, thinking it must be for my brain cells. I continued to remain upright and I wondered what the morphine was doing to me, for me. I didn't feel any "pain." Morphine is for pain, isn't it?

I was already feeling utterly transformed, pushed into another dimension, a state hitherto unknown. Pain, in my lexicon, was being sliced by glass, or some other such calamity. No, I wasn't in pain. I was somewhere else. Not ecstasy, certainly. But I realized I was beginning to feel somewhat out of body: *ex stasis*. Looking down on myself. Perhaps, I thought, that's why people who are near death often report themselves floating around, looking at the operating table, or people in the room. That must be the morphine, I considered. I seemed to be disassociating. I still wasn't sure how much time had passed; but too much, I thought, without something crucial happening.

Then I saw my wife rush by the doorway, and then start to come back toward it and was intercepted by the doctor. She was telling her, "You've got to get him to relax." That I heard very clearly – the relaxation cure.

My wife walked into the room, her brown eyes wide.

"I'm hyperventilating," I said. "They say I'm hyperventilating."

Why I offered her the same nonsense the first aid room doctors offered me, I know not. Then I said, much more to the point, "I'm sorry."

She knew what I was sorry for. I was sorry for having a heart attack.

"They want you to relax."

"I know. I'm trying," I said, knowing I wasn't succeeding.

I was expecting her to come up to me, to touch me. But, at first, she stayed in the same spot the doctor had occupied, near the wall, near a counter, as if a magnet held people there. Or, perhaps, the sight of me created a force field. Looking at someone having a heart attack mustn't be attractive. It would have been reassuring to be touched, other than to have needles inserted. She finally came forward and grasped my ankle; my legs were the only extremities without tubes or wires attached. But that kept her a few feet from me.

It still felt as if it was thirty-below all around me.

It must have been at least an hour since I felt the click, the tiny ball falling out of the socket. It became clear that everyone must be waiting for something and it wasn't for me to start relaxing. A doctor. They were waiting for a doctor, capital D. The young woman must be an intern. Do heart attacks just go on and on? That was frightening, though I was already past frightened. Physically, the morphine wasn't making the sensations I felt any different, except that I seemed to continue to separate from them. My consciousness had become slippery.

My wife and the young doctor (who I had turned into an intern in my mind) were conferring again in the hallway. A nurse came in and adjusted the drips. I had two, lidocaine and heparin. I was also on oxygen, and I had been given nitroglycerin, a tablet under the tongue. I wasn't sure of its effects, but I knew it was a standard treatment. I was given more.

My wife was telling someone that I had just walked a couple miles with her the day before and hadn't been short of breath.

I didn't know what angina felt like, since I never had it. It seemed, given the questions, some sort of decision remained, loomed, needed to be made.

The clot of people in the hallway thickened. After the ambulance duo had left, and the odd ancient messenger looking for some son's father, everyone in attendance had been female. Now, there was a new arrival who was male, short, dark-haired, thin, from the Third World.

It was a great time to have a heart attack – early Saturday afternoon. Where were all the cardiologists? on the golf course? at the football game? I now realized that when I had answered earlier whom my doctor was, and had given the name of my allergist, that those had been important questions. They must have tried to contact my doctor first, I presumed, some chain of command, responsibility, protocol in the land of referrals. Who was going to take charge? It appeared to me it was this guy, standing next to me, asking me what happened. I knew it was a test: of lucidity, of my condition, my state. And what I said might have something to do with what he chose to do next.

I was at the football game, I told him, and then was hit with symptoms: nausea, tightness, odd feelings in my arm up to my neck, clamminess, sweat. I got to the first aid station, was told I was hyperventilating, was taken to the hospital, here I am. My wife was listening, too; most of it was news to her. The doctor seemed satisfied. He said to increase the amount of morphine I was getting, and, once more, that I should try to relax. He also said that I should be administered tPA, a clot-busting drug.

"Do you have it?" he asked. "Is it prepared? A bolus." I fastened on that word, since it was from a different vocabulary, a medical term. I began to picture a bolus, a golf-ball-sized something, another sphere, shiny, silver, bigger than a BB. My wife was quizzing him on what it was: the tPA may eat through the clot that was causing the heart attack. I caught that much even though the morphine was messing with my concentration.

Time passed, clipboards were consulted, the bolus was prepared. Finally, a nurse came in with a hypodermic. The doctor said, "All right. Give it to him." It was said casually, but the folk in the room had seemed to have acquired my tenseness. Now, everyone had become stiff. The nurse inserted the needle into a junction in the intravenous tube and delivered the hypodermic's contents into it, then into me.

The doctor, responding to a question from my wife, had told her that the tPA had a sixty percent chance of breaking up the clot.

"You mean," she said, alarmed, "it has a forty percent chance of not working?"

She is an economist. A scientist. They call economics the dismal science, and that was a dismal statistic. There was a bustle of hands around me. I was to be taken up to cardiac intensive care.

I was now reclining and someone was pushing the gurney out the room's door. A blonde nurse I had seen, one who had not done much, but who had reacted to remarks that had been made, one who seemed the most emotional of the nurses, meaning she had showed some emotion, an underlying discontent, a kind of anger – she seemed to be mad at the heart attack itself, what it was doing to me – touched me on the arm and said as I was wheeled off, "Did anyone tell you that it will hurt more if that works?"

"No," I said, knowing what "that works" meant. The TPA. She seemed to be telling me a secret, or, at least, the truth.

The clanking, the rolling, the filling the elevator occur and I am taken upstairs, moved ("one, two, three, lift") onto a hospital bed, the drips are rearranged. The room has monitors, chairs, a television suspended, curtains that can be drawn around the bed. It is a single. It doesn't seem brightly lit; gray light comes in through a window. Transferred to a bed, lying down, I hope the morphine is working without me realizing it. But I feel under pressure, as if I am going to explode; it's a kind of writhing.

I finally realize what that means: the body writhes. I am moaning. My wife is standing near the foot of the bed. I can see her. There are a couple of nurses, both female. No one who appears to be a doctor has come along. Nurses say things, but my concentration is shattered. A nurse is applying cold compresses, wet washcloths, to my forehead, as if we're in a western at the turn of the century and there is nothing to do but apply a damp cloth for comfort.

I bolt upright.

"Now this hurts," I say aloud. The force of the experience has lifted me off the bed.

"Ah."

I think that "this" can't continue, whatever it is I'm feeling. Nothing I felt up to this point would I have called pain; this is intolerable. It is if I am being burnt alive while hurtling through space. I expect some reaction from the women around me, my wife, but they just stare. How long can this go on?

"Ahhh," I let out again, and drop backwards onto the bed.

It's over.

Slowly, it dawns on me: I now feel as I felt before I walked up to the concession stand to buy my hot dog. All at once, it seems that the drugs I've been given for the past hour or so take effect instantaneously, as if I had been suspended over a pool of morphine, held up above its surface by the thin wire of the heart attack, and that has snapped. And I feel myself falling into the silvery water, submerging, warmth around me. I pass out.

First appeared as "Y Me?" in *Indy Men's Magazine*, vol. 3, no. 6, February 2005.

Richard Elman

"Richard Elman, Novelist, Poet and Teacher, is Dead at 63," I read in the *New York Times* of January 2. My wife and child and I had just returned from a Christmas trip to California and there was a message on our phone answering machine from Richard's daughter, which had portended as much. He was in the hospital and things were bad. . . . I hadn't called her back yet, to hear what I thought must be terrible news. I picked up the Midwest edition of the *Times* and stumbled upon the obituary.

A few days earlier, I had sent Richard a string of garlic from Gilroy, California. He had said on the phone, before my family's trip, how much he liked a plate of mashed potatoes he had eaten. Despite the side effects of the chemo and radiation treatments, it was food he managed to keep down; it was ambrosia. Garlic would make the mashed potatoes even better. Hoping he would rebound from treatments, I sent the garlic. It wouldn't have yet arrived.

In the empty space shock made, I remembered another writer whose death was announced to me by the *New York Times* some twenty years previous: Edward Dahlberg, who had left New York and moved to Santa Barbara. I was riding the PATH train to Newark in 1977 to teach my class at Rutgers when I opened that page and saw his obituary, dead at 77. I recalled Dahlberg because he and Richard were both my teachers and both in New York when I was a student, both connected to Columbia University, though Dahlberg had been let go from Columbia before I arrived. (He failed Herbert Read's son, Piers Paul Read, the future author of *Alive*. Because of this and other transgressions there had been a student revolt against him.) Even Richard was skeptical of Dahlberg's social skills and wary of Dahlberg's influence on me.

Shortly after I graduated I published my first book, a work of nonfiction (*The Harrisburg 7 and the New Catholic Left,* 1972), and Richard said he was disappointed I hadn't dedicated it to him. "Why?" I asked, truly baffled.

"Because I was the one who turned you on to nonfiction," he replied. He was sounding quite like Dahlberg then (Dahlberg had only accused me of plagiarizing him.) I didn't realize it then, but Richard might have turned me on to nonfiction in so far as his own work, career, was a model; he had written book-length nonfiction early. Now, I can see his point; then, in my mid-twenties, I was only baffled. Around the same time I made a remark to him I've only recently regretted, never noticing until now how full of unconscious youthful blindness it was. I said, "I've met two geniuses in my life, Edward Dahlberg and Leonard Boudin." Boudin was a constitutional lawyer of great renown, the defender of Benjamin Spock, Philip Berrigan and others. One should never tell a friend, a man of letters, that he isn't a genius, even indirectly and unintentionally. I was full of pronouncements in my twenties (and am still not completely emptied of them).

Richard was only eleven years older than I was, whereas Dahlberg and Boudin were quite senior indeed. I saw them as a different generation, not certainly Richard's, and I was only applying genius as a label to someone at least in his sixties. And now, in my sixties, Richard is genius enough for me.

And he was a model, though one I haven't always had the courage to completely emulate.

In friendship he was exemplary: he was loyal. His politics, too, from my point of view, were exemplary: as a writer he dared to be unfashionable. And being unfashionable, not tacking with the cultural winds, has turned out to be unpopular and unremunerative politics in the eighties and nineties. His ground breaking reports from Central America (found in *Cocktails at Somoza's*, 1981, and fictionalized in *Disco Frito*, 1988) made both warring sides unhappy. He was a partisan without being partisan; he was no one's apparatchik. During the late seventies, Richard amassed a large manuscript describing contemporary Brahmin American literary figures involvements with the CIA and though never published in full, its existence did not make him popular. Peter Matthiessen, I recall, was especially unhappy. A couple of years ago Richard sent me a photograph taken in Paris of Richard Wright with Peter Matthiessen and Max Steele of the *Paris Review*, c. 1954, which Richard captioned, "Can you guess from this photo who was being spooked and who was the spook?" Back in the seventies being connected to the CIA was not necessarily a reputation polisher; in the nineties, of course, it would only lead to career enhancement.

During the eighties Richard gave acerbic, insightful commentary on NPR's *All Things Considered*. That gig ended when he launched a hilarious dissection of people voraciously collecting Krugerrands. I guess it offended too many NPR listeners and producers. He was out of step, again, with the times; the greed decade was galloping by him. Reverence for the rich was reasserting control.

And Richard, happily, lacked that sentiment: one of my earliest memories of him was when I was a student at Columbia in 1969 and we were part of a luncheon group honoring George T. Delacorte, a donor to the school (my scholarship was named for him, which was why I was there). Richard was the first to leave. "May your millions increase," he said to Delacorte upon exiting and George did not receive it as a compliment. Anyone who eschews fashion in the late twentieth century is on the right political side, and is always in danger of our culture's most potent weapon, neglect.

But Richard was tireless. He wouldn't let the bastards get him down (hard to do these days, since they are so good at what they do). When he was struck with his cancer it was a shock; he was not in the mood to die. That was the last thing on his mind. The suddenness of its onset and the rapidity of its progress was astounding, yet he went through those days with the courage that had accompanied him throughout his life.

He still wished to work and was still sending out work. His last novel published when he was alive (which he finished here at Notre Dame, when he was the visiting Abrams Chair in Jewish Studies), *Tar Beach*, 1991, was an act of literary resurrection, a hymn involving all the themes of his earlier work leached of rancor and made radiant. Now three books are to emerge in succession, alas, posthumously. Even as the disease and treatments took their toll, he wanted to be active, to have his mind focused. He wrote me in late fall, "If you know of somebody for whom I can write a review. . . ." Even that most thankless of journeyman tasks meant life to him: the chance to be who he was, honest, direct, generous in the service of literature. He closed that note with a quote from Karl Marx, prompted by my concern at the grim prognosis of his illness, "The invitation to abandon illusions concerning a situation is an invitation to abandon a situation that has need of illusions." Richard knew which illusions to have and which not to have. It's clear to me I've known more geniuses than two.

First appeared in the *Notre Dame Review*, no. 6, Summer 1998.

Grace Paley

Grace Paley's opening lines in her story "Wants" would always echo in my mind when I would see her walking up to me on Sixth Avenue, "Hello, my life." I was a young writer then, residing in Milligan Place around the corner from Grace and her husband Robert Nichols' apartment on Eleventh street. Donald Barthelme lived across the street from her building. Stanley Kunitz's townhouse was a block away. They're all dead now.

It was the early seventies and Milligan Place's gate swung open freely back then. These days it is locked and one needs to be buzzed into the small, precious courtyard. The seventies were a good time in New York City, paradoxically, since there was a recession going on. The reverence for the rich hadn't begun to fill the air yet. The rich were still there, but they weren't preening about in the 1970s. That bred a certain kind of equality, one that began to disappear in the eighties.

I had been told the three-story Milligan Place building that contained my one room apartment was once Theodore Dreiser's house. The Village was always a literary place. I had just published my first book and its subject, if not the book itself, was a favorite of Grace's; it was about the case of the "Harrisburg 7" – priests and nuns, anti-war activists, government oppression – all the usual topics that preoccupied her.

Jean Boudin had introduced us. I spent a lot of time with the Boudins, Leonard and Jean, during those years. They are gone, too. Often I would be standing outside the chichi grocery store next to Milligan Place on Sixth Avenue, where I had just bought a container of yogurt (my dinner) and Grace and Robert and I would chat. Of course, then, none of this seemed as extraordinary as it does now. Grace was literal. She was grace. Given my Catholic background, I put much stock in grace, not "gracious living," as it was called when I left the city to teach at Mount Holyoke, in South Hadley, Mass., but grace right out of the mysteries of the spirit, the lifting up, the filling up.

Grace was especially kind to young writers; she herself was empty of bitterness and radiant with hope and good fortune to come and share. The last time I saw her was at her place in Vermont, in the company of Jean Boudin who was staying at the MacDowell Colony. I was about to leave Mount Holyoke and return to the Midwest to take a teaching job at Notre Dame when Jean and I visited.

Departing, she wished me well, as she always had. My new novel wasn't so much to her liking. The title, *Idle Hands* (hers were never idle), certainly gave a rather jaundiced portrait of the women's movement of the seventies. Grace devoted so much of her life to making the world better, though what I thought more remarkable was how well she thought of it, letting no anger or disappointment sway her from her belief of the wonderfulness of the people who lived in it.

First appeared in *The Massachusetts Review*, vol. XLIX, no. 4, Winter 2008;

My Rap Problems—and Yours?

First off, I am an OAF, an older American father. I've considered creating an organization, OAFS USA, but I decided I didn't want to spend a lot of time with geezers like myself. I got married late, in my early forties; back then, my wife-to-be kept pointing out that less than ten percent of men had never been married by age forty. She is an economist, a fan of numbers. A few years after we were married we had a child, a boy, Joe.

Joe is now fifteen (and I am sixty) and he is overscheduled, which I don't mind, except that it makes me overscheduled. I often drive him around and he plays CD compilations consisting mainly of rap tunes on the car's player.

"I'm gonna get my gun!" Around our neighborhood here in South Bend, Indiana, young folks do often go and get their guns. We've had a number of black children gunned down by other black children.

I, of course, dislike Joe's taste in music, but can't keep from recalling that my parents abhorred my music: The Beatles? The Rolling Stones? Janis Joplin? So, I try to temper my criticism – I don't want to sound like too much of a hypocrite, or Bill O'Reilly. And I am aware while I'm putting up with Joe's rap music I am driving him to his trombone lesson where he will be playing Rimsky-Korsakov.

So, I let Joe listen to his music of choice. The sexual content and language of a lot of it shocks me – me, a child of the sixties! Petey Pablo's "Freek-a-Leek" is one of the worst offenders. But language from six- and seven-year-olds I heard in parks playing with Joe as he was growing up shocked me, too. (Of course, I never expected to see erectile dysfunction commercials on television, either.) We live in what's called an "urban" neighborhood, which translates into poor black people living within shouting distance of white college professors.

There's a lot of cultural and educational distance, though not much geographic. And what was I doing about it? Not much. Along with being an OAF, I am also a member of a few do-good organizations, but what I mainly am, is theoretical: though we occasionally do try to live what we preach.

Ironically, the anti-rap tirades Joe hears from me sound similar to the one made by Ludacris, a rap star playing a rap star, in the film *Crash*. In that scene, Ludacris's character sounds like Bill Cosby – or, for that matter, Bill O'Reilly – attacking rap for what it does to black culture. The irony is heightened because the speech is delivered shortly after he and his buddy have car-jacked a monster luxury SUV. I wondered, after *Crash* won the Academy Award for Best Film this year, whether a white screenwriter had penned that anti-rap monologue, or if a black writer had done it. In any case, the gangsta rap group Three 6 Mafia won the Oscar for best song, "It's Hard Out Here for a Pimp." Pick your irony.

Joe has forced me listen to Eminem and his band D12, and after a while I began to realize M&M (my preferred spelling) has some talent. He may even be the Bruce Springsteen of his generation, since they have had similar career trajectories: at first, great adulation, then backlash and a trough of neglect, then springing back as classic iconic figures.

But, most often, I just listen and think perennial parental thoughts: "What is the world coming to?" Joe had been getting the series of NOW CDs, "contemporary" hits, and, for the last couple of years, they have been dominated by rap artists – Snoop Dogg, Chingy, 50 Cent, anyone with a semblance of a hit. Joe would censor them for me, even though the NOW discs were already "censored." Joe will turn down the volume when there are words he doesn't want me to hear.

That may well sound cute to some, but I don't think it is – I do think it is life, though. Joe is an only child, so he gets a lot of attention – and slack. Taking him home from a Boy Scout meeting I encourage him to listen to the public radio jazz station (he is in a jazz band), but, no, he wants to listen to hybrids like Lincoln Park, Black Eyed Peas, and other rap-lite groups, which I criticize less.

But, everything is more of the same: when I was teenager, Norman Podhoretz made a splash with an essay he published in *Commentary* in February, 1963 entitled "My Negro Problem – and Ours," writing about the pervasive racism he and his white friends weren't able to shake, though they often denied its existence.

Here I was, some forty years later, denouncing rap music, being superior to all its parts, ranting on about how its commercialization was as cynical and as damaging as McDonald's diets to poverty-level blacks. My son's generation doesn't think like mine and whatever is racist in his cohort doesn't look like it did in the 1950s or sixties, even if the results might be the same for so much of black youth: separation of the races, lower test scores, higher dropout rates, and the chance of being jailed.

"I'm gonna get my gun!" bounces again from the car's CD player. Joe enjoys it. Nearby, one of Joe's high school classmates is charged with felony murder, since another high school youth he was with killed an off duty police officer during an attempted robbery in the parking lot behind the local Boy Scout Council's office.

When I was a kid, my father would have changed the station on the radio; I do shut off the CD player every once in a while when I can't stand it any longer. The technology made things a lot easier in the 1950s – and there was less to chose from. Now we all make our own music, and carry it with us. Instead of Joe listening alone on his iPod, I choose to listen along with him. His world: a mystery to me, his liking what he likes, as it makes him who he is, who he is to become.

First appeared in the *Chicago Tribune,*

Arming Yourself for the Outdoors

Having a national parks' gun-toting provision slapped onto credit card reform legislation isn't as odd as it might seem. It's all in the name of freedom. When credit cards went viral over the last three decades they turned individuals into mini-Feds. Anyone could be Alan Greenspan and print money! It's refreshing to have the money supply be set by your next-door neighbor. Counterfeiting took a big hit when printing cash became discretionary. Over the years I've kept the twenties' presses rolling. So, why not let freedom ring? Since individuals can print money, why can't they arm themselves at least as well as Third World militias, ready for whatever jihad that interests them? From my cold dead hands, etc.

My household (wife, child, me) went to Yellowstone last June. And when you go to Yellowstone in June, you get more than a summer vacation – you get a spring/winter vacation. Snow remains, both on the mountaintops and in the valleys. Our boy was seventeen at the time and wanted nothing but adventure, whereas I was just trying to keep up.

So we're climbing snow-capped peaks (Bunsen) at the tip of the park, way up on the northern edge, near Mammoth. Then we're searching for grizzlies, not an occupation I ever sought. There's a lot of wildlife around that you can see by car (by rent-a-car in our case). It is wonderful to see two grey wolves running alongside a river, or a pronghorn giving birth, bouncing on her thin legs to shake out her new offspring, or a moose resting in a grassy gully alongside the highway.

But it was the long hikes I tended to balk at and not for cardiovascular reasons. In Yellowstone you see this odd lemming-like crowd movement, the crowd made out of a variety of vehicles. A grizzly sighting! The roads in early June are not heavily traveled and one comes upon suddenly a clot of caravan grouped on a road. Cameras and binoculars are rife, all pointed at the animal or animals, but, as of last June, no rifles, shotguns, or Glocks.

The first bear we saw was a large black one playing around a tree. Later in the afternoon, a mother grizzly with a newborn, lopping down a hill. Isn't that cute! June in Yellowstone, since it's actually spring in Yellowstone, sees a lot of birthing. And you know how parents are when they have young to protect.

As I watch the people trying to get as close as they can for their picture taking (until a ranger shows up and shoos them back to the road) I think of Jeff Goldblum's lines in the second *Jurassic Park* movie. "First it's aahs and oohs and then it's screaming and running." He was talking about dinosaurs. It is, what? thrilling, to see a grizzly. That mother was large. Unfortunately for me, the hill she was running down was around the corner from our destination, the starting site for our long hike. But that wouldn't deter my wife and son.

So, we park at the trail head and walk. I had read the handouts. If you see "carcasses" when you're hiking you should be alerted to the presence of bears. When we reached a high plateau there was nothing but carcasses along the worn path. When we hit the halfway mark of the hike there was a very large carcass, not that old, in a nearby thicket. Maybe it had just dropped dead. Heart problems. The trouble with preserving wilderness in its "natural" state is that it remains wilderness. The centuries evaporate. This could be the nineteenth, but where was my buckskin and long rifle, or at least a big Bowie knife? Only an idiot would travel this landscape unarmed, I said to myself, long before I became aware the NRA wanted to equip me with a Kalashnikov for our next tour of the park.

Heading back to Grand Tetons and Jackson Hole, we did think of looking up Dick Cheney, a resident of sorts. It's nice to have an airport in a national park where the rich and well-armed can fly in. We had heard about Cheney and tales of his secret service detail from a river guide. He had to rescue a couple of them who got beached on an island in a stream. Cheney had scuba divers on hand in case he ever fell in the river while fishing. Cheney, an espouser of the thumb-screw way of life, of course, knows how to fire guns. And it won't be just him any longer packing heat in our magnificent national parks soon. Look out.

First appeared in the *South Bend Tribune,* June 6, 2009.

Two Midwest Meditations

REUNION AND REVOLUTION

On the day in 1983 I flew to my high school class's twentieth reunion in Kansas City, Missouri, three members of my generation were convicted in Goshen, New York, on multiple counts of murder and robbery. Two of them were part of the hardest-core of the white student revolutionary groups of the sixties, remnants of the Weather Underground (an offshoot of SDS); they, along with a few others, including black-nationalist confederates, had taken to "expropriating" money from the Brink's company and various banks. They also killed and wounded guards and police, including the only black policeman on the Nyack, New York police force.

Perhaps not all of the members of the Weather Underground had to miss their twentieth high school reunions, since some of them emerged through the late seventies and early eighties forsaking under- for above-ground life. The press had made much of these defections from the ranks of sixties' rebels: Jerry Rubin, Eldridge Cleaver, Jane Albert, Mark Rudd, and Weatherpeople: Bernardine Dohrn and Billy Ayers. There is something appropriate about the media demeaning the same folk they helped to elevate. Journalists would rather laugh at others than laugh at themselves. But the people from the Brink's job emerged from the underground in a wholly unacceptable fashion – it was obvious they certainly didn't want to be considered laughable.

And they missed their twentieth reunions. I wondered why I wasn't missing mine. When I left high school in 1963, the notion of returning for a twentieth reunion would have seemed ludicrous. I had the longest hair then and was the most superficially rebellious of my class. It still seems slightly ludicrous, coming back: one of those manufactured promontories of reflection, a vantage at once trivial and portentous – a lot like high school, itself.

1963 was a pivotal year in our country's culture. Look in any almanac and see just how many hinges fashioned then history still swings on: not just JFK's assassination, but Diem's too: Buddhist monk "barbecues" as Madam Nu called them; civil rights emerging not as a Southern problem, but a national disgrace; Bob Dylan singing "Blowin' in the Wind."

My class of '63 was the beneficiary of a great fear: the Russians launched Sputnik in 1957 and, for a short period, Americans set aside their native anti-intellectualism and education was supported and esteemed. Our class of '63 profited. It was just after 1963 that national SAT scores began their long decline. Not that we boys were aware of this circumstance at the time: like teenagers everywhere, we avoided learning as much as we could.

And so, when my closest friend from high school suggested that we both attend the reunion, I agreed. Rockhurst was an all-male school, staffed by Jesuits, and it was still, twenty years later, all male. The reunion would he less than half the fun of other schools', I supposed. I expected to see a collection of men in their late thirties who looked like the sort of men you see at airports waiting to take a plane somewhere.

I didn't do a scientific study, but my class of '63 seemed to conform to demographic expectations. My class climbed up and down the peaks of contemporary history: a couple of us died in Vietnam; a couple returned home from the war relatively unscathed; a member went into the Peace Corps; another committed suicide; two died of "natural" causes; one had been, and still was, institutionalized; a handful were divorced and remarried; a smaller handful not married at all (my group, then). News that was jovial was announced loudly to all; darker words went more privately into fewer ears: who abused drugs, beat wives and/or girlfriends, welched on business deals, drank too much. Only a third of the class showed up, which, I thought, was also what one would expect.

Those who came seemed to break down physically into two groups: half you recognized immediately – they had just become older, weathered, seasoned. The other half seemed altered, and until you heard a name and their younger selves stepped out of their older shells, they were not recognizable. I, alas, was in the latter group. It seemed to have to do with hair – the loss of it, and weight – the acquiring of it. Two teachers of our time were present and shocked me by looking younger now than they had seemed to me then. I did realize that youth sees age as a greater distance and those wide expanses of time shrink as one gets older.

One reason I went to the reunion was to rekindle my memories of high school itself, because, much to my surprise, the ethic of high school, circa 1963, had, at least in my analysis, become the reigning ethos of the eighties; Most Popular, Most Handsome, Most Likely to Succeed. The success ethic had been eclipsed for a few short years during the much-heralded sixties. It was a lopsided decade: what is usually meant by "the sixties" began in late '63 with the killing of Kennedy and ended ten years later, in 1973, with the start of the Watergate hearings. During the early portion of that period it had been socially desirable not to admire too obviously the rich. But now reverence for the rich has returned, with greater fervor than before. Simply put, it wasn't a disgrace to be poor in the sixties. Those with money didn't flaunt it – even William F. Buckley wasn't overly publicizing his wealth then. Books such as Michael Harrington's *The Other America,* 1962, which described the plight of America's poor, also made the public less enthusiastic for the spectacle of conspicuous consumption. A lot of the children of middle class America were rebelling in the sixties against just such displays of wealth that their parents had gained. Long hair, beat-up clothes, the crash pads, all became icons of a sort in the sixties: badges of belonging, not emblems of failure. That all changed, of course. In 1983, *The Other America* would have made people think of *The Preppy Handbook,* 1980.

One of the least noted casualties of the sixties was bohemia. The rising up of the counterculture eradicated bohemia, which had traditionally existed as an enclave, or refuge, for a self-selected minority, a place free from the disapproving eyes of the majority, the middle class. But the counterculture of the late sixties began to pit the many against the many, not a minority against a majority, and it didn't take long for the counterculture in become the dominant culture: it was relabeled "youth culture" and soon everyone aped it. Advertising swore by it, dads let their own hair grow long, the bourgeoisie accommodated it, and everyone bought a piece of it. What was once considered bohemian in style became mainstream behavior: the lunatic fringe had become the warp and woof. Bohemia, robbed of its *raison d'etre,* in most ways, disbanded. The only bohemia that still flourishes is the criminal side, but that too has taken on the accouterments, the style, that used to be associated with the nouveau riche: gaudy display, trips to tropical countries, resort living.

One reason why the Brink's crimes were so shocking was that they were crimes of the least sophisticated sort: shoot and grab. Even for professional criminals, Wild West methods have been derided for some time now. Only punks stick guns in people's faces and demand the cash. My high school reunion prompted these reflections because a few members of the Brink's gang had begun as idealistic young men and women who desperately wanted to do something, back in the early Sixties, wanted constructive change, a better America. A lot of other young people of their generation shared their desires. And more of them now were likely to go to their 20th reunions than go to jail for the rest of their lives as members of the Brink's gang would do.

I wondered, as I flew, how the Brink's people would be thought of twenty years hence; doubtless they still would be in jail. Ford pardoned Nixon, but no President will pardon them. History is kinder to the violent than contemporaries are wont to be; and, if anything is certain, the Brink's people were already living in the future. Somewhere along the way they heard "history will absolve me" and it stuck. They saw themselves standing proudly alongside others who were condemned for their actions in their own time, but uneasily respected by those who come later: the thugs of the Boston Tea Party, the bomb throwers of the early union movements, the terrorists of the Irgun, the mandarins of the CIA. History usually shows some leniency to those who sacrifice themselves for, or to, an idea, or ideal, however mad, or ill-advised it may seem to those who witness their actions.

One of the Weather Underground's difficulties was that most of the U.S. knew little of contemporary, indigenous terrorism: no forced abductions in the night, no unacknowledged "disappeared." Pockets of that sort of thing can be discovered in American history, but nothing to match the rest of the world's. Our citizens, therefore, do not look understandingly or sympathetically at any retributive violence or terrorism. African Americans in this country, though, might feel they have more than just a nodding acquaintance with that sort of history, that kind of treatment.

And when a few members of my generation decided, with such actions as the Brink's robbery, to "help" create an independent black nation in five Southern states – as bizarre a solution to America's racial problems as any I'd heard – it was from the clear and deep pool of racial injustice that the Brink's people dipped their ladles for a draught of sufficient rage and rationalizations to kill. It is not that odd that, robbed of the anti-war movement, the only cause pure enough to be violent about in the minds of radical white revolutionaries would be America's history of racism, its treatment of black people. And in that history they could even discover the terrorist killing of their own kind in the midnight abductions and murders of the civil rights workers – Schwerner, Goodman, and Chaney – in Mississippi.

It's a long way from Philadelphia, Mississippi to Nyack, N.Y., where the Brink's robbery took place, but, in the minds of the white Weatherpeople involved, it probably was a shorter trip than anyone would imagine. But, of course, there are now a couple of generations of American black men and women who suffer pain and embarrassment from every side: from those who wish to deny them aid and comfort, and from those who wish to provide it.

Obviously, a twentieth high school reunion inspired more reflection than the event itself warrants. My class of '63 had one black student in it. He would have been easy to recognize at the reunion, but he didn't show. Those who did gather were in the same emotional state as those who cross the finish line of some marathon. Twenty-six miles or twenty years, it is the same: exhausted, but exhilarated. We had all accomplished the same thing, survived.

The men were, in most ways, profound strangers to me, but we had all shared four years of our youth, so we spoke with as much intimacy, if not more, than family members use. Since we had all known each other at our most ridiculous, we had nothing really to hide: only candor made sense.

Nothing, though, was made clear to me, except the rush of warm feeling I felt for them all. As boys, we didn't realize how exceptional we were – not in our own virtues or accomplishments, certainly, but in just how good an education we were getting, how privileged we already were because of it. It was an upper-middle-class high school (though a number of us were not) and people took it for granted we would do well. Though I dislike reciting the titles of my books, I needed to do it here, since none of the classmates I talked to at the reunion knew that I had published any, even though my last novel (published two years before) was reviewed widely and prominently (including in the local Kansas City paper – most of those who were at the reunion still lived in town). They might read the Sunday sports section, but not the arts section. My high school classmates, I realized, were not my audience.

The absent at such gatherings are often the quickest recalled. Those who were there spoke of those who were not: two Scholastics, young priests-to-be, who were prominent in our lives and imaginations, had left the Jesuits. One of them had begun my so-called political education by advising me when I was sixteen to read Whittaker Chamber's autobiography *Witness;* and it wasn't until after I graduated from college that I realized he had recommended it to me because he saw Chambers as a hero, not the monster I perceived. The high school's principal also had a role in my political education: by ordering the bookstore – the high school was then located on a college campus – not to sell *The Catcher in the Rye* to any high school student. Like most Americans, I didn't protest or picket this censorship, but just found a way around the problem: I bought a copy at a neighborhood drugstore.

What struck me about the men I went to high school with was the same thought I had back then: if I was in a foxhole under fire they would be good men to have at my side. I realize now that the school was also responsible for that particular figure of speech: other sorts of education wouldn't have made military illustrations spring quite so readily to mind.

One member of the class, now a laborer in the roughest vineyards of law enforcement, and I discussed current trends in penology. He was made distrustful by my telling him I had written a book about seven "radicals" who were accused of conspiring to kidnap Henry Kissinger and blow up heating tunnels in Washington, D.C. "What side was I on?" he demanded to know. My answer ("neither") did not satisfy him. And it wouldn't have satisfied members of the Weather Underground, either.

My classmate thought capital punishment for ordinary burglars would make his job a lot easier. It was then that I recalled being in his basement twenty years, or so, before, reading the men's magazines of the day – not girlie magazines, but adventure rags like *True* – the type that were always full of pictures of "A-rabs" chopping off the hands of petty thieves. My classmate's own experience had just endorsed the lessons we had absorbed from those murky pages.

More quickly than I would have expected, the thirty or so men who were there began to break down into their own former allegiances – affinity groups, the Weather Underground would have called them. And I began to recall all the animosities and rivalries that had been rife in the class twenty years ago. But, for this evening, they were kept at bay, even though slings and arrows not seen for two decades flew over the horizon of memory. Had we been together two nights, they wouldn't have been so contained. There was a dinner dance scheduled for the next evening, but I didn't plan to attend. I just wanted to see the boys I had gone to high school with, turned into men.

Reunions and revolution had been mixing uneasily in my mind, though that solution, I realized, was somewhat strained. Twenty years, twenty years – so much has occurred, so much has changed, and so little. A dozen or so of us hung around until we were locked out of the building. Then we stayed and talked in the parking lot. It was a fragrant fall Midwestern night. And it became clear we all did have one new thing in common. And that is why we had come back to rehash old times. We all had made some sort of peace with our past – something that the members of the Weather Underground would, or could, never allow themselves to do. We had all decided to call a cease fire from every conflict we knew of, and, for one night, be old friends. And that's how the evening ended, as we drifted away to our separate cars, shrouded in the sweet, rueful atmosphere of truce.

TIES

When I was a boy, one thing that served as an emblem for my father's presence in my life was his rack of ties. It was secured to the back of my parent's bedroom closet door. The rack of ties was many things to me: a cynosure, certainly, for it always drew my glance – such a profusion, that excess of ties – three, four dozen, it seemed. Though the largest part of the business my father worked for at the time was a warehouse, he wore a suit and tie everyday; he was the business's young manager. I can't recall him actually wearing a wide selection, but he had many. I would stare at this small waterfall of fabric: wools, cottons, synthetics, somber colors more than bright, a line or two of red and silver cutting through the duller shades, a squiggle of iron through shale.

In the late seventies, a friend of mine, David Black, published a remarkable novel entitled *Like Father*. Besides admiration for it, I also felt envy – a whole novel about fathers! I could never, I felt, write an entire novel about my own. My father was always there – and that, these days, is not the common expectation or experience – but it was the presence of his absence that most accompanied me.

I, like a good number of men of my generation, didn't spend much time with my father as I grew up. My contention is that there wasn't, isn't, anything unusual about that. There are many accounts of men whose fathers died young, divorced their mothers early, leaving sons who, because of one special circumstance or another, were not much in the company of their fathers. And there are, in contrast, the many accounts of the Hemingway-in-our-time sort: fishing with father, hunting with the old man, hitting the ball with pop, etc.

But I experienced my father the way a great many post-war American children did: the few minutes before he would go to work in the morning, and at dinner-time. When I was a kid my father and mother were still in their mid-twenties, still very much young people themselves. My older sister and I, spectators at a bad Broadway comedy, would watch them at the parties they gave on Saturday nights, drinking highballs and conducting cha-cha lessons. My father was still trying to insert our family into the middle class (we were still at its edge) and he took up golfing on Sunday with other businessmen. My parents had things to do and they did them.

I do have a handful of memories of piercing encounters with my father – and they take up a few paragraphs in the novels I have published – but part of their vividness comes from their scarcity. For the most part, I have had the same number of conversations with my father as I have had with the gabby proprietor of the dry cleaner's I used to frequent during the years I lived in New York City. My parents, after a hiatus of seven years, began to have more children (six more, in fact) and that was responsible for some of it – and the times had a lot to do with it, too. Parenting was a long way from becoming a participle, much less a principle, in the 1950s. I like to think of my parents' methods of child-rearing as premature, benign neglect.

As I grew older, my father's rack of ties became a symbol for all that I didn't want to do, didn't want to be. The fifties were becoming the sixties, though I myself identified with the older generation of bohemians – beatniks, who were still receiving some attention back then. I didn't want to wear ties. I didn't want to go off to the office at 7:30 in the morning, come home, fall asleep watching the evening news after mixing martinis, the drink that made you feel you were, for those days, truly upwardly mobile. Gone were the 7&7s of my Chicago relatives, the steelworkers and railroad men my father was attempting to leave behind.

But, nonetheless, I would still stare at his rack of ties, fondle the fabric, study the spectrum the ties represented to me: the world, the public, commerce. I even had a jejune analysis of the ties. They were a gelding mark, a badge of a club, a disarming hank of cloth meant to convey reassurance to other men; demonstrate that you had voluntarily elected to join their company; were, in important ways, one of them.

And, of course, the ties stood for my father, who wasn't there that often, in my company, though his ties were. It didn't enter my young mind then, in the heat of my sociological deconstruction of the ties, that they were also emblematic of other things I didn't want to be: a father who wore one who wasn't able to spend that much time with his son.

Father/son resentments, I realize, are often doubled; I have heard that my father feels I neglected him – didn't, when I was a teenager in high school, ask him to come along with me to basketball games – that sort of thing. Knowing now what I do about his childhood, not much of mine is a mystery, but it is clear to me that those early years, those before puberty, are the times where the real male bonding takes place.

My father was a good father; he was never cruel, except through ignorance. He was responsible; I was looked after. For a son such as myself to have any complaints is slightly perverse.

And so, when I moved into a house in the Midwest similar in kind to the one in which I was raised, I was struck to find in the "master" bedroom, screwed to the back of the closet door, a rack for ties. And, I was surprised to see that I had accumulated, over the years, the same assortment of three-dozen ties: there they were, hanging from the tie rack, though I only wore a handful.

I wear them to work, to class, so the students will realize I am the teacher. Sometimes I consider it a betrayal of my generation, of all the things I felt and lived through during my twenties, and thereafter. The ties are not part of a required uniform – after all, I teach creative writing. But I have come to understand, having stared so long in the past at my father's ties, when I now glance at my own, that I am wearing one of them because of him: all those ties, and every one of them binds.

First appeared in the *Hopewell Review,* vol. 6, 1994.

Dear Dad

I am struck by the fact that this may be the first time in my fifty-two years of life I have written "Dear Dad," addressed only you in a letter, not both you and mom, father and mother, parents. "Dear Folks." I have used that one a lot, not that I have written so many letters all these years.

When you and mom had your fiftieth wedding anniversary, like any good writer/professor, I did some research: I stood at a greeting card display and read many examples of the form most often used on such occasions: expressions of best wishes written by professionals, people being paid for their words – and what words! public endearments, scraps of diary entries, treacly testimonials. My hands were sticky with sap from the experience. But some important themes emerged clearly: the cards for the early years, minor milestones, were always full of encouragement; those for twenty-five years of marriage were thick with celebration; but those for the fiftieth anniversary all glowed with amazement. Fifty years a couple! Who could believe it? I would have offered that fact as my chief excuse for never writing to you directly before.

So: Dear Dad. There is something powerful in the singularity, since I now feel the weight of never having used it before. I have been looking for a photograph of you and me together, just us two, for the last year and haven't turned one up. I expected there to be one at least – just me, a kid in your arms. I noticed, the absence of a picture on my mind, that I have a number of photos of me with my son, Joe, your grandchild. The one I like the best is the snapshot of me holding him in the delivery room, the "birthing" room, some preternatural light beaming out of my eyes, taken by the doctor who delivered him.

Finding no photograph of us alone was troubling, because many memories I revisit are of us together, alone. My mind is filled with those snapshots. Us late at night in a car, you at work delivering a critical part to an anxiously idled factory, me along for the ride, you bringing them salvation, a bearing that would allow everything, those massive buildings, those giant machines, to start up again, to throb and hum.

And our talking alone, the infrequent brief conversations, their brevity and rarity making them indelible. They were often about work; times I let you down; the one time you hit me, so shocked at my impudence, complaining about the adequacy of a favor to me you had arranged. Even then I thought I deserved to be slapped. And the time, at sixteen, I flattened the side of the new car, which provoked no violence at all, but mainly silence and disappointment.

All that alienation we felt those years I wrote off as part of the times. It was the fifties, you were one of the silent generation. I had grown my hair long before the Beatles (my models were the beat generation, not the Brits), and when you saw my high-school graduation picture, you ordered me to the barbershop, and I returned home thoroughly shorn. (Had you not seen me until the picture appeared?) There weren't that many orders actually, which is why I never questioned them.

You were of your times, and I am certainly of mine. But all the clichés came home to roost when I had a son eight years ago, my only child; but everything was different, I told myself, except for that arc between you and me, between him and me.

But, unlike yourself, who had your first child, my sister Marita, the first of eight kids, just when you turned twenty-one, I was forty four. Though I really began to notice the duplications. How, in so many more profound ways, my interactions with Joe remind me of yours with me, especially the dutiful and awkward manner I often assume. When we fall into silence in the car, me behind the wheel, Joe next to me looking out the window, I am reminded so piercingly of you, and me.

Yet I remember when I was around ten and fell atop a small red metal step ladder, while jumping into a half-filled wading pool, and sliced open the back of my leg, leaving a torn, ragged horseshoe of tissue, large blood vessels exposed, but luckily not severed. The wound needed stitches, and later, when it was time to go to bed that night, you carried me up the stairs. You must have done that task before, but this was the only time I recall it happening. I think ahead of carrying my son up a long set of stairs when he becomes ten, and wonder at the strength required, and then I realize you would have been thirty at the time, and when I was thirty I could have carried you up the stairs.

But I do remember being in your arms then. No picture of it, though, except in my mind.

And I have another such mental picture of you with a son in your arms – not me, but the next, Terry, who was some nine years younger. It was in the fifties, and we were in our neighbor Max Sanford's car, a sand-colored Ford coupe. I was in the backseat; the stiff whisker feel of the upholstery on my bare legs is still easy to recapture. Max took a turn a bit fast, and the Ford's large passenger side door sprung graciously open. Terry was in your lap, no more than a year or so old. Out you both went and I stared in amazement. Everything slowed down, and what amazed me was that you never changed position. It was as if the seat had disappeared (which it had), but you remained a mime of repose sailing through the air, finally landing on the street, knees still bent, arms still locked around Terry, as if you had become, many years before they were introduced, his human car safety seat. Bump, bump. Max let out a yell, and pulled the car over, and stopped. We all ran back and found you not really hurt as I feared, your rear end a bit bruised and scratched, but that was all.

But the image of you and your young son flying through the air has always been vivid in my mind. From that day on, before puberty and the onset of battles and conflict, displeasure and disappointment, I thought two things: one was that you were a hero; and two, I knew that you would have done the same if it had been years earlier and me in your lap. You would have never let me go either, flung me out into peril. You behaved, I thought then, like a father: a man who could be trusted, as I always have, even through our years of many silences and nursed complaints. That trust has never been violated, or that clear picture shattered of you, my father, flying through the air, my dear dad.

First appeared as "Us Together, Alone," in Constance Warloe, ed., *From Daughters and Sons to Fathers.* Ashland (OR: Story Line Press, 2001).

Confessions of a Guilty Freelancer

For nearly five years I was a weekly columnist for the *Chicago Sun-Times.* My beat was national politics. For the last three years I appeared in the Sunday paper, the token liberal in the commentary section, there to offer some imperfect balance to a decidedly conservative shipload of pundits. In early September 2005 my column was rather unceremoniously dropped.

In the manner of "all the king's men," I served at the pleasure of the editorial page editor – in the *Sun-Times* case, Steve Huntley. Indeed, in many ways, Steve created me. There is a Dr. Frankenstein element in this sort of relationship. It was Steve who made me a weekly columnist, elevating my occasional status as an irregular contributor to a smoke and mirrors version of a permanent fixture. But any unnaturally spawned creature can readily become a monster. What else can one do at that point but destroy him? Especially when the populace is chasing him around the internet with pitchforks.

There are lessons here. First, how does one become a regular columnist for one of the largest circulation newspapers in the country? By a lot of design and some accident, a lifetime of preparation and chance encounters. My history with journalism has always been glancing, indirect. When I graduated from the Kansas City branch of the

University of Missouri, journalism's reputation was still in the swamp of hackdom, a land of has-beens and wannabes. I was a novelist yet to blossom, off to a graduate writing program Columbia University was just getting underway in 1968.

That period was the golden age of reading. During the 1960s the number of young in institutions of higher learning was tripling, yet the number of "first novelists" was remaining nearly constant, around a hundred a year. The audience for literature was growing, and the number of writers was holding steady, a wonderful situation that only lasted a few years. And novelists were coming to the rescue of journalism. They would transform it in the early stages of its modern ascendancy: Truman Capote in 1965 with *In Cold Blood,* Norman Mailer with "himself" but also *Armies of the Night,* his late sixties book covering the March on the Pentagon.

This was all to become the "New Journalism." Tom Wolfe, a blocked fiction writer – blocked until he became a rich celebrity – became the chief publicist for the "new" form, and helped begin New Journalism's glamour period. But, what really capped the rise was when two young journalists – not latent or blocked fiction writers – Woodward and Bernstein, reclaimed the spotlight from their literary betters, helped topple a president, and returned barely serviceable, but effective, prose to a place of honor in the newspaper world.

Capote and Mailer, and even Tom Wolfe, were always a bit too fancy for regular reporters. But had anyone told me, when I left the Midwest for Columbia in 1968, my first book would be nonfiction, considered by some a high form of journalism, I would have thought them crazy and insulting. Such was the thrall of becoming a novelist was for my generation.

But it came to pass: in 1972 – four years later, two years out of Columbia – I had published *The Harrisburg 7 and the New Catholic Left,* a book nine months in the making – three months of trial in Harrisburg, Pennsylvania, three months of writing, and a bit less than three months being manufactured. I saw an ad for the book in *Publishers Weekly* before I had written a word: a picture of the book's eventual cover.

Unwittingly, I had hitched a ride on the cultural wave, having become involved with a lawyer and her clients, a bunch of Catholic radicals and one Muslim Pakistani, resulting in a book that funded me with a $3,000 advance, enough, I thought, to write it, since I had been living back then on $300 a month – ah, youth.

The book spent six weeks on the *New York Times Book Review*'s New and Recommended list, and was selected as one of the notable books of the year. During the six weeks of my local big city notoriety, I was spending most of it in a street-side garbage bin in the South Bronx, toiling as a manual laborer at Feller's Scenery Studio. My life hadn't groomed me for success, so I didn't know how to leverage my good fortune.

It's a long story, not to be told here, but the connection to my last foray into journalism – five years as a columnist at a major city paper – shares one important similarity. I owed my access to the fashionable world of literary prominence to a single editor: in the NYC case, John Leonard, who was, at the time, editor of the *New York Times Book Review.* The attention the TBR paid to anti-Vietnam War subjects and books was intense during Leonard's reign at the book review, and I certainly profited from it. My first novel, *The Meekness of Isaac,* which followed two years later in 1974, was also prominently reviewed in the TBR, though not with the same degree of enthusiasm. And when Leonard moved from editor of the book review to a daily reviewer, he reviewed my second novel, *Idle Hands,* for the daily *Times* in 1981, a mixed assessment, but nonetheless confirming its worthiness. Subsequent regimes at the *Times* haven't proved as attentive – alas, just the opposite.

In many endeavors, one person can be important, pivotal, indispensable: no John Leonard, no anointing of my work by the *New York Times;* no Steve Huntley, no weekly columns by me in the *Chicago Sun-Times.*

I tend to write short pieces in the fallow times between books, and for a while it appeared that the fallow period was growing longer. It took a while to get my fourth novel, *Notts,* published. It appeared in 1996. It was set in England during the last great strike there, the NUM strike of 1984–85, a capstone victory of the Margaret Thatcher era. Death to unions! Thatcher succeeded.

I thought it strange that I hadn't written another long book of nonfiction, though I had published a collection of short miscellaneous pieces, *Signs of the Literary Times, Essays, Reviews, Profiles 1970–1992,* in 1993, with a university press.

I had a knack for doing different lengths: my first publications were short book reviews for the *Nation* when I was a graduate student at Columbia. I didn't consider my pen for hire, but there were things I could do easily – and book reviews certainly qualified. Then other subjects would interest me, I would do longer pieces, and then hunt for a publisher. The articles accumulated over the years, enough to make a volume.

The job I found to subsidize my writing was teaching, and it seemed to prevent me from doing book-length nonfiction. Most of that writing, given my earlier experience, required one to go somewhere, spend time away researching – or so I thought. I followed Bill Clinton's election in 1992 with some interest and noted that, beyond the hyped odd couple co-authored Mary Matalin and James Carville volume, no literary sort of campaign book had been written. When *Primary*

Colors appeared, it became the campaign book of '92 and its authorship wasn't that hard to guess. Joe Klein hadn't published a nonfiction campaign book, though he had covered the campaign. That negative evidence was sufficient proof for me, before he was unmasked, of authorship.

In any case, Klein intuited the situation: reportage of the Teddy White-sort had become redundant, because the new media now covered so much of the campaign process – making stars of both consultants and reporters, celebrating the rise of hackdom, paid shills and spinners – as well as the candidates themselves.

At the time, I kept telling friends I could have written a campaign book without leaving my house. Cable television, C-Span, and other electronic media were changing news delivery big time. By '96 I decided that things had only changed for the better in that regard, and I decided to put up or shut up. I found a publisher, Marlowe & Co, to do my *Campaign America '96: The View from the Couch,* which appeared in 1997. I was ahead of my time by about a year. The internet in '96 did not play a big role in that campaign, though it was clear it would down the road.

My book was about how the campaigns were consumed, not produced, but covering one reveals a lot of the other. A few months after my book appeared in '97, newspapers began to report with some regularity how the press covers the press. My account was a pre-blog blog, highly literate, everything I thought about the political scene and how it was unfolding, day-by-day.

There was not a lot of public interest, though. No book review editor or publication took it upon themself to make me famous, though I did get a good, prominent review in the *Washington Post*'s Sunday books section, because Washington is a company town and politics is the local business. The *Chicago Tribune,* where I had done a lot of book reviewing over the years, reviewed it quite favorably. But the general media passed.

My connection to the business of journalism was thin, because I have never worked for any journalistic enterprise. I was a *freelancer* – not a position held in high esteem. Since I had a full-time job teaching, I was actually a moonlighter, another off-putting, if hardly used, label. Such a person is about as popular as the rogue male elephant, hanging around outside the tribe, blowing dust in the air, warily waiting to be driven off, no allegiances. I had once, for a few months, worked as a writing "coach" for the *Columbus Dispatch,* part of the duties I had as the first James Thurber Writer at the Thurber House in Columbus, Ohio, but I wasn't paid by the paper.

No, freelance is an odd designation. But, by the start of the new century, it became a synonym for a topical phenomenon, outsourcing. At the *Sun-Times,* I was a version of a guy in Bangalore, solving problems for computer customers in Fargo, North Dakota. I was cheap labor.

But I had the best qualifications for cheap labor: I was dependable. I, in many ways, was a symptom of the sorry decline of newspapers – the shrinking of permanent staffs, the reduction of union labor: those with all the so-called costly benefits and annoying rights. The *Sun-Times,* over the years I wrote weekly, had two rounds of labor negotiations, two possible strike threats. If the writers for the paper had struck, I'd strike, too – or so I told myself. In both cases, I was spared the choice.

Though I could have been in India, South Bend is treated in Chicago as a close suburb of the city because of the presence of Notre Dame, with the attraction of its football team, and the legacy of Catholicism in Chicago. So, my outsider status was somewhat muted. And, as it's said about Cuba in Florida, Chicago is only ninety miles away.

I was born in Chicago and I had always wanted to be thought of as a Chicago writer. My initial contact with the *Sun-Times* was the usual one: toward the end of the nineties I had sent in an op-ed piece on spec. It was about Bill Clinton and his possible impeachment. I was never a fan of Clinton's – I still blame him for everything, including the George W. Bush administration, his actual legacy.

So, though I was a "liberal," in many ways my critique of Clinton was even more progressive, more left, more critical. I reacted to Hillary the same way because of the "all lawyers have to work for banks" side of her. The Clintons and I are more or less contemporaries and they did what a lot of Yale law school graduates do: try to become rich and powerful. Bill Clinton was my president, though; I was surprised someone attached in any way to the anti-Vietnam War movement, who never served in the military, could become president – at least at the age he did. But, he went on to betray my generation as I thought of it, the meritocracy, and hand it all back to the well-born plutocracy.

I presume my critique of Clinton had caught Steve Huntley's eye. I called for Clinton to take the Fifth before the grand jury during the Paula-Jones-suit period. Huntley had left a message at my Notre Dame office, and I called him; he wanted to run the piece, but what was new was his suggestion that I do more for the paper. I said, "sure" and sent in commentary sporadically. He ran everything I sent in, what amounted to a piece or two a month, sometimes after holding them for a week or ten days. When one ran, I'd start thinking of another. When my campaign book was reviewed in the *Washington Post* in the fall of '97, the reviewer, James Ledbetter, had concluded it with the remark that for the 2000 campaign someone should give me a "national weekly column." I don't know if Huntley saw the review, but as we came closer to the 2000 campaign I wrote more columns, and he continued to run them. It was still a surprise when the columns would appear, though, eventually, a pattern emerged.

I wrote enough about the 2000 campaign to get a book out of it, an ebook, a very short sequel to the '96 campaign book. I wanted to see what electronic publishing was like. A Chicago firm specializing in literary authors, PreviewPort, agreed to do it, and I did find out what electronic publishing was about: it was, where I was concerned, about a lot of nothing. Though the publishing house did do a small run of printed books which got around, no one bought an actual e-edition.

But one of the columns I had written immediately after the election had caused a stir. I was incensed by the emergence of red and blue America and wrote about it: "George W.'s America is Yahoo Nation . . . a large, lopsided horseshoe, a twisted W, made up of primarily the deep South and the vast, lowly populated upper-far-west states that are filled with vestiges of gun-loving, Ku Klux Klan-sponsoring, formerly lynching-happy, survivalist-minded, hate-crime-perpetrating, non-blue-blooded, rugged individualists. Yahoo Nation, George W.'s electoral bundle – save contested Florida, the toss-up state – contains not one major city, nor one primary center of creative and intellectual density."

Huntley held on to the column for almost a week before running it on Nov. 14, 2000. The night before it ran, Paul Begala posted some similar remarks on MSNBC's website, so he "scooped" me. But the column, "Yahoo Nation," generated hundreds of e-mails – to me, I don't know what the paper got – and was posted all over the web.

By 2000, the web had come in to its own, and all sorts of journalism ran amok on it. My columns were duplicated on the web and the multiplier effect was large: they were linked and re-posted on many, many sites. And the *Sun-Times* ranks high on lists of popular newspaper websites. The world wide web is word-of-mouth writ large. I should say it was posted by all the folk who hated the column, right-wingers all. You can count on your enemies; they will make you known. If a left site reproduced "Yahoo Nation," I didn't see it, but it went out everywhere on the right-wing drum line.

I had written the '96 campaign book because I was tired of seeing the right wing monopolize savage rhetoric. During the early nineties, there was the switch over, the coup by the right wing, the toppling of the "liberal" media as king-of-the-hill. The right had taken its gloves off; I thought the left should, too.

What the left had going for it in '96 were comedians: Saturday Night Live, Jay Leno, and a bit of David Letterman. Some cable shows, the Comedy Network, the Daily Show sort of thing, were just beginning to have an impact in '96. But, there weren't that many left polemicists who weren't celebrities to begin with. My '96 campaign book didn't make much of a splash. By the start of the Bush campaign at the end of the nineties, left wing authors had caught up big time: there was a flood of progressive books brimming over with heated prose. My "Yahoo Nation" 2000 column made noise, but it was, by that time, rather familiar noise. My e-mail sizzled with denunciations.

Early in my writing life, after the Harrisburg 7 book had appeared, Herbert Mitgang, then a member of the *New York Times* editorial board, who was a fan of the book, had me to lunch at the *Times'* executive dining room. This was 1973. I was a babe in the woods, working intermittently at my scenery construction job in the South Bronx. Ralph Lauren wasn't into the style as yet, but I wore to the lunch what looked like lumberjack chic: an old corduroy jacket, khaki pants, and a plaid flannel shirt – remnants of the beat generation writers I had looked up to while sharing their low-rent lifestyle. Though, at Harrisburg, during the trial, I didn't stand out quite so much, since I constantly wore a foreign correspondent trench coat – it was the winter, after all. That coat was my most costly purchase ever during my lean post-graduate years. But, at the *Times,* I was certainly odd man out. The paper had been long known as "the gray lady," and I found it amusing that we were served our lunch by actual gray ladies: elderly women in gray outfits with mostly gray hair. It was only many years later that it dawned on me that the lunch was a proto-job interview.

But Mitgang asked me to send him an op-ed piece, which I did, and it ran a couple of months later. There wasn't much of a news hook, since I wrote about an incident in Provincetown that had happened a year before: the taking and replacing of benches outside the town hall. The benches were called "the meat rack," and functioned more or less as one; it was a different world in 1973.

So, more than twenty-five years later, I went to Chicago and had lunch with Huntley, and after lunch, he said, "let's do this weekly." The column would run on Tuesday; the paper would get it Friday. Away I went.

The *Sun-Times* is Chicago's blue-collar paper; its politics are, after a number of ownership changes, the usual pro-business Republicanism, but it is marked somewhat by its class interests.

The *Chicago Tribune* had the more fiery conservative past, though since it is aimed at affluent Chicago, it is more "liberal" in its social presentation. It, certainly, is the more powerful corporation, the Tribune Company As a sports columnist said to me at a Christmas party, the *Tribune* is now a fairly good paper. The *Sun-Times* leads the way with its sport pages and Roger Ebert, but its ownership under Conrad Black had become the usual story of corporate malfeasance, and highway robbery. The staff shrunk, took cuts, Black huffed and puffed, but then his whole house fell down, though his company Hollinger, thus far survives, though not with Black at the helm.

I certainly wasn't an insider, so I had to follow the turmoil at the executive level like any reader. One odd thing I discovered was that Huntley's predecessor as editorial page editor had been removed because of his own plagiarism problems, but not fired, and ended up in circulation, where he helped bring about the circulation scandals of 2004, one shared by a number of papers, inflating numbers of copies bought.

Everyone expected the *Sun-Times* to be sold and a shakeup to follow, but it hasn't been as yet. I thought that was one reason I was writing for the paper, since it was in limbo and I was dependable – and cheap, $150 a column, around eight grand a year.

Having a weekly column quickly became an example of look-out-when-you-get-what-you-wish-for. I had always thought a weekly column would be a good outlet for me. I had something to say about most things and could certainly put it into words. Writing short length is a type of miniaturization. There are true oddities in the world, artists painting elaborate scenes on grains of rice, but, if one looks around, short is the leading literary form these days. It was the genesis of *USA Today*, a world without jumps. In the literary world, short short stories came in vogue in the 1980s. Writing columns is the art of putting ships in bottles.

It all starts with the sentence. One of the first writers I ever encountered in the flesh was Edward Dahlberg. At that point Dahlberg was a *belles lettres*-ist, and he took an interest in me because, like him, I had a jejune talent for aphorism. Dahlberg had a book of his own aphorisms published called *Reasons of the Heart*. The first line of my 1972 Harrisburg 7 book, "In the logic of our time, it is better to have a bad experience that turns out well, than to have just a plain good one," was an aphorism of a sort, enough of one that Dahlberg sent a mutual friend to search through his oeuvre to find which book I had stolen it from. If it had any paternity other than my own, it was closer to Camus than Dahlberg, I realized later.

If you can write aphorisms, you can write columns. Form is just content under pressure, and this sort of newspaper writing is unlike the old-fashioned formula news writing, where one just cuts from the end. Column writing requires an end, as well as a beginning, and a middle. You're dealing with wholes, not parts. Sentences are wholes, so are paragraphs. It's prose as fractals; all parts are complete.

In any case, I wrote one each week. I appeared on Tuesdays and I sent the column in on Friday and if something happened over the weekend I sent a change in on Monday morning. This seldom happened, though once, on a weekend, I was able to change an earlier column between editions. It concerned the Elian Gonzalez case. The Janet Reno snatch happened, and I sent in a rewrite that ran after the original column ran in an earlier edition. When I settled in as a weekly columnist, I got fairly good at living four days ahead of the news cycle.

After a couple of years, I was moved to Sunday. I presumed someone noticed that on Tuesday the *Sun-Times* ran a column by Jesse Jackson – I'm not sure who actually writes those – and that made two liberals on Tuesday. So, I was moved to Sunday, where there were no regular liberals. On Tuesdays I was replaced by Bill O'Reilly; they exchanged a real populist for a faux populist, one with slightly fascist tendencies, though self-interest trumps all with O'Reilly. But, he was a celebrity author. It is no longer novelists invading daily journalism, it's TV personalities invading now. O'Reilly rose high enough in the celebrity orbit that even a sex scandal couldn't bring him down.

Steve Huntley made moving to Sunday sound like a promotion, so I asked if a raise accompanied the move. "No." Most everyone had taken cuts following the last round of sour union negotiations.

But, I wasn't doing this for the money. By definition, I was Samuel Johnson's blockhead, and that made me a fool. I still hadn't lost the young writer's need to be read, even though I was far from young.

Basically, there are three sorts of columnists: the first sort is the player, usually someone who has worked for presidential administrations, and insider who becomes an outsider, a semi-journalist. William Safire was the chief example of this sort. The second sort of columnist is a reporter who also writes commentary. Original reporting is done and made use of liberally. The *New York Times* has a number of this sort, currently Friedman and Kristof are examples – they go places and interview people. There is a large spectrum here, from a little reporting to a lot of reporting. Robert Novak can fall into this category. The third is writers with opinions. I was one of them. This last, too, has variations since research is a kind of silent reporting. I. F. Stone, during his newsletter days, was an example of this type, where informed opinion overlaps with reporting. It remains the most vulnerable of the three sorts, since if all you have is opinions, there isn't much underpinning there.

Nonetheless, I had George W. Bush and his administration to write about, and write about them I did. Pre-9/11, Steve Huntley made a suggestion, one of a very few – he was largely hands off throughout my years at the *Sun-Times* – that I might be getting a bit Johnny-one-note about Bush being stupid. I didn't think Bush was stupid, just that by being rich and privileged he only needed to know the minimum about most things, just enough to function. There doubtless is a subject or two (baseball?) that he knows a good bit about, but otherwise, he's used to help. I realize JFK got Arthur Schlesinger to write his books, but Kennedy was certainly intellectually curious in a way that Bush is not.

Then came 9/11, and, as many said, that changed everything.

As a columnist and a novelist I was very conscious of what I wrote as a sequence, one short chapter after another, about the Bush administration. I was telling a long story, I thought, one that could be put together as a book. I did, titling it, *Bring 'Em On: The Problematical Presidency of George W. Bush,* but publishers are, understandably, less interested in what appears to be a collection of columns, which, in the final analysis it was, is – since I still haven't been able to place it.

As the columns went in via e-mail, responses came my way via the same venue. The ratio of compliments to attacks, or favorable to unfavorable, was one to ten. The electronic age is mercilessly exact. As any writer knows, publishers now know exactly how many copies a book sells. In the good old days, numbers could be fudged. Now, exactness rules, and websites keep track of how many "hits" one receives. So, the *Sun-Times* knew how many times my columns were looked at. They didn't share that information with me. I don't know if they had a way to count the number of times it was posted elsewhere.

Novel writing is a bourgeois activity, insofar as it requires some regularity in one's life. So does column writing. I suppose it took about three hours to write a column, an hour to bang out a draft, and an hour each following day to rewrite it. That is one reason why I never really wanted a day job in journalism: not enough time to rewrite. When I was a writing coach at the *Columbus Dispatch,* I was surprised by how much the writers I worked with had to write each day – I had a cross-section, from the most junior hire to their lead editorial writer – and it truly was literature in a hurry. The copy desk was supposed to be able to clean up anything that the editor above didn't catch.

Writers of my sort want to be their own editors, however grateful one can be to copy editors along the way. Time is the craftsman. It took two days to polish a column, maybe a half-hour each sitting, though my subconscious would think about it continuously, just the way it does with anything I write, whatever the length. I wrote on Tuesday, and sent it to them Thursday. It would be printed late Friday, the Sunday edition out on the streets early Saturday morning.

So, I became very intimate with the quotidian. I was up on a lot of things. Cable "news" shows let me know what was on the chattering class's mind. I was always attempting to say what no one else was saying. I had my favorite subjects. One was Social Security, which I wrote about, since I had a family resource, a wife who was a leading expert in the field. I could test my eccentric ideas. I wouldn't have been able to function without access to LexisNexis, which became the check to my memory, the electronic library at my fingertips.

When I started in the seventies, the necessary thing was having a credit card, and I didn't get one of those until after I wrote the Harrisburg book. Famous columnists have their legion of eager, paid researchers. I have an internet connection and the electronic resources of a large university.

I wasn't a complete anomaly at the *Sun-Times*, someone who wasn't syndicated but a regular contributor. Both Jesse Jackson and Father Andrew Greeley, the local Chicago priest and potboiler author, also had similar arrangements, though I would be surprised if the pay scale duplicated exactly. The paper was making use of the resources of the city, giving the commentary section a local flavor.

During the last strike negotiations, Roger Ebert was siding with the underpaid staff writers and criticizing the rapacious Conrad Black for his robber baron ways. Black wrote a letter that the paper published, pointing out that Ebert with lawyerly help had negotiated a contract for a half million a year, and didn't for a moment worry about unequal pay for equal work questions. It's always refreshing to have dirty salary laundry washed in public: pay disparity is always food for thought in the press room. But, Ebert's riches are not singular: throughout the corporate world pay at the top has outraced pay in the middle, much less the bottom. Even in academia, two tier pay systems are in place. "Chairs" are hired at universities at twice or three times the pay of full professors; deans and provosts now command a king's ransom to do the work that used to be done as collegial service in the old days. It's the American way, especially in the Bush era. The widening gap between top executive pay and the ordinary worker is startling, but unimpeded.

Jesse Jackson and Andrew Greeley had their own sort of enduring fame when they began to write commentary for the *Sun-Times*. But the *Sun-Times* had no self-interest in making me famous. Just the opposite, if they made a fuss about me, they would only make me more important, bond me to them in ways they may well have regretted.

Because of that, the paper never nominated me for any journalism prizes, local, state, or national. A freelancer is a necessary evil. The Guild never solicited me in any way, or seemed to take notice of my existence. When the last strike threat bubbled up, I was ready to stop writing.

The state of the freelancer hasn't much improved over the centuries. We have about the same status in the profession as carpetbaggers. There are a variety of reasons for this. One that isn't spoken of as much is the one not complimentary to those who aren't freelance. They get their power from the high capital behind them. Woodward and Bernstein would have been ignored if they hadn't worked for the *Washington Post*. Indeed, Woodward has kept his job at the *Post* for all these years, despite being financially secure, to retain the clout being attached to a powerful corporate entity provides. Imagine how far Judy Miller would have gotten if she was a freelancer and not a reporter for the *New York Times*. We'll see how long she remains unattached, a mere freelancer. The opposite case is Sy Hersh and his My Lai work. He was almost freelance, since the operation he worked for was so small. But it wasn't Hersh's words that moved the My Lai story, it was the picture of the dead women and children and old men in the ditch.

Fashion in this culture is a high-capital operation. If you're going to be fashionable, only the expensive can make you so. I had a little currency in the early seventies, since the *New York Times* found me interesting. When they pulled the plug (personnel changes in the book and editorial sections) I was lost in the wilderness.

Toward the end of the summer 2005, the *Sun-Times* redesigned its Sunday editorial package. It moved the commentary section from inside the tabloid to a new broadsheet insert named "Controversy" and created another pullout section called "Fluff."

"Controversy" incorporated the book section, which had been in the movie/entertainment broadsheet section ("Showcase") for years. (One irony had been that my Harrisburg book had been reviewed on the front page of an earlier incarnation of the book section of the *Sun-Times* in 1972.) To make "Controversy" substantial enough to be a stand alone, a lot of wire copy was added, along with a main cover feature with colorful graphics and design, and a couple of pages of snippets from wire copy and the web.

The perennial newspaper statistics show that the number of readers who actually read the editorials or the book reviews remains at the bottom of the barrel. So, this section was for the hardcore readers: everything, more or less, was a think piece. So, a separate section could either be ignored by the many or devoured by the few. The *Sun-Times* had new presses out in the 'burbs, so it is likely the costs of the change weren't that large.

But the change was unfortunate for me. That was obvious from the first. The old reliables, the usual Sunday commentators, were there in the middle spread, on two pages. But in the old format I was one among equals: Robert Novak, Mark Steyn, George Will, Betsy Hart, and a couple of floaters. Many times, my column would get a large colored news photo, and the photo editor of the Sun-Times was good at picking them. Other times, the paper would have its own illustrator supply a witty drawing or collage.

With the advent of "Controversy," there would be three pages of wire copy by many hands and then the two pages of familiars. In addition, Carol Marin, who had been hired a year earlier to replace the dearly missed Steve Neal, was moved to the section. Though Marin, a former TV reporter, was hired as a city-side political observer, the change put two "liberals" on the page; she and I were now in subtle competition.

My new hole was the upper right hand column, just a straight column of print, a plain, eight foot, two-by-four look, no photo and a hundred words shorter, 550 rather than 650. In the early years of my writing for the paper, I would always write long, trying to push the envelope. Sometimes I would get away with it, but often I would get cut, and they always did a good job, taking out lines from the middle of the piece that were the least important.

I was never censored, though I was shortened. For the last three years or so, I finally decided to hit the mark, and not leave anything to cut. Over that period, I would only lose one sentence, and often not even that.

But now, with the new design, even I had the question, why is that guy there? All the new wire copy gave a variety of voices to the section, bits of this and that, often from the web. It was the more or less free market, wire copy already paid for, or the sort of thing you can take off the web and have for nothing, the author grateful to be put into print.

So, the change deflated my status both visually and literally. The other regulars had their usual length, though fewer news photos. It took a couple of columns for me to get used to the new length.

But this was troubling. The token liberal was less important if a lot of the wire copy could supply bits of liberal rants. My *raison d'être* had vanished. And there was the matter of change for the sake of change.

Part of the problem was the grow-or-die issue. I had thought about getting myself syndicated over the years. I had gone so far as to get the names and addresses of a few companies, but my initiative stopped there. From doing the column on the side, this was moving to doing the column more toward the middle.

And I wondered why no syndicate had solicited me. What? They're not rushing to sign up a fifty-ish white male liberal?! A combination of lassitude and pride kept my ambition at bay. I just let it go.

Live by the sword, die by the sword: my life at the *Sun-Times* was almost entirely an e-mail existence – though I did go to a number of the annual office Christmas parties – and I was handed my hat through an e-mail. Huntley explained they had been "rethinking" the editorial section again and had decided to drop my column. Goodbye.

A number of my anti-fans had been calling for my head for some time. One could do a book on the rhetorical strategies of e-mails (doubtless someone has already), and amid the fumers, and ranters, and insult hurlers, there were always a few directed to the paper that had a judicious tone, more in sorrow than anger, that suggested my "contract" should not be renewed. These folk wanted to sit upon the lofty perches of management, and not sound like they were down in the pit with the rabid throng. But after I disappeared, it appears that most of them don't even know they won, even if by mere coincidence.

About a week before Huntley's e-mail, I had e-mailed a friend, an L.A. TV writer-producer. that Bush was getting too easy to bash. His administration was imploding. Hurricane Katrina had ripped down the veil in front of Bush and Rove's Wizard of Oz machinery. The administration was being exposed for all to see, its glorious incompetence, its collection of inept cronies with their hands on the levers.

Well, from your lips to God's ears. Just when I had a cornucopia of almost unbelievable missteps to chronicle and comment upon, Huntley's e-mail came and snatched my soapbox out from under me.

I presume the decision to dump me was based on a combination of concerns about money, and ideology. Or, if nothing else, the scarcity of space. The question, why are we paying him to attack the president each week? might have entered the top editors heads with some force at last. Or, the roughly eight grand a year I pocketed could look substantial on a balance sheet, when I could be replaced for a small percentage of that by wire copy and cherry-picked local submissions. The expanded section had already allowed them to dip into the pool of left-critical thought.

It was probably more an economic and space decision, I concluded. Newspapers everywhere are still cutting staff and costs, replacing crafted work with modular copy. My nine inches were filled by conservative wire copy or local PR type material, of the more-or-less free variety: nothing like my columns, nothing at all like them.

I might have done this weekly for nearly five years, but it is as if no one noticed. It's a cold world out there, especially in Chicago. Given my freelance status, no Chicago media writers had ever acknowledged my existence when I was writing, so it wasn't surprising they didn't take note of my absence. It is hard to overestimate the low esteem freelancing inspires in the regularly employed. It's a version of: if you're so smart, why hasn't some large corporation hired you?

My experience as a columnist was the same as my experience as a novelist and nonfiction book author. You need an editor who is willing to publish what you write. Without him or her, you're only the guy who points at himself and yells "pay attention, pay attention," the loon in the park dragging around a literal soapbox.

It was a good gig while it lasted and now it's gone. These days I'm trying to avoid being an example of "old columnists never die, they just become bloggers." But the internet siren song is singing to me. And, alas, everywhere newsrooms are losing staff. In my case, though, my disappearance doesn't even count as a statistic.

First appeared as "My Life, and Death, as a Columnist" in *Editor & Publisher,* www.editorandpublisher.com, Shoptalk online column, January 3, 2006.

part two

the personal and the political

Extreme Makeover: TV Home Improvement from Carter to Bush II

I

In the mid-1980s, I was sitting in the living room of the first house I ever owned, watching the television show, *This Old House,* on PBS. Bob Vila was doing a rehab project on Cape Cod. As he would, on occasion, he took a side trip to view other real estate (Vila more often went to factories to see how house products, windows, etc., were made). He went to a home in Hyannis, on the Cape, with a view of the bay. In front of it was one of the last beach-front properties for sale in the town.

Vila pulled up behind the house, because there was no garage, and not much of a front "yard," since the house was built on what was still dune, but a fairly beat-down one, where the land was becoming solid earth, not shifting sand.

There was bright, blinding light all around, the sun glancing off the water of Cape Cod bay and my black and white TV seemed luminous, dream-like, as Vila approached the home's back door, which, more or less, functioned as a front door.

Dream-like, certainly, because it was a door I had approached a good number of times before. I sat straight up, finding it hard to believe Bob Vila was about to walk into my past.

The house and lot once belonged to two of my oldest friends, Robert and Inez Kareka. When I was a college student, I had visited them there a number of times, and spent the entire summer with them the year before I started graduate school in 1968 at Columbia University.

The Karekas owned a craft store in Hyannis that sold handmade enamel trays and jewelry, along with other decorative items. I had known them since 1965 when I dropped out of college for a semester and lived in Hyannis. At that time, they lived above their shop, which was attached to an old house on Main Street. They had bought the house and the lot with a view of the bay a year later as their business boomed.

By the mid eighties a lot of history had come and gone, mine and theirs. Inez had died in January of 1982. Robert was hanging on by his fingertips in Key West, Florida. They had sold their beach-front home, and the lot, a number of years before, and had bought a larger house in Barnstable the year before Inez's battle with cancer began. Their businesses in Hyannis, Nantucket, and Key West were all suffering downturns, and only the Key West business was left as Inez was dying.

By the time Bob Vila walked into their former back/front door (there was no front door, except for sliding glass doors which opened onto a deck across the front of the house), the Key West business was gone, and Robert had moved into a trailer on Stock Island.

But it was my youth, and my friends' golden years, that Bob Vila was about to show to his audience. He walked up a set of short stairs, and his crew's camera panned into the bedroom I occupied that summer, before graduate school, and where I wrote my first novel (unpublished), *The Armless Warrior,* its title redolent of all my adolescent angst during the early years of the Vietnam War.

The room had little in it, and Vila did not linger there; his camera showed the kitchen to the right, still very much as it was, just a room with a small table at the end, regular cabinets and counters and appliances. The great evolution of trophy living, especially with water views, had yet to come to the spec builder who put this house up in the early 1960s. But Vila did linger on the balcony above the house's one great room and its wall of glass that faced the bay. It, too, was an incandescent space; down below, near the wall of glass, were the current owners, blurred by all the reflected light.

Vila, all the while, had been narrating, but I hadn't heard much of it, other than the gist that he was pointing out how few (or no) empty lots were available on the waterfront in this part of the Cape. "Tear downs" had yet not come into the typical vocabulary of the building trades. Here in New England they rehabbed and improved. Tearing down and building anew had yet to become commonplace.

Then Vila and his crew departed. I sat in my living room stunned at what I had just seen, and all that had happened in both my life and the Karekas' since then. A quarter of a century later, more had changed, but what I intend to cover is not my life and Robert's (he, luckily, is still alive), but the changes shown by the distance between Bob Vila's original program, *This Old House* and its newer spawn, *Extreme Makeover: Home Edition.* The evolution between the two is similar to what: the Wright brothers plane and the B2 bomber?

II

Writing about television requires a leap of faith, though, today, writing about books requires the same leap: that one's readers have seen (or read) what one is talking about. In academic environments, it is common, these days, to listen to someone speaking on, say, eighteenth-century literature, refer to a few recent films, rather than recent books. The chance, it is presumed, that even a literate audience might have read the same book, is slim. The chances for shared experience go up when it comes to film.

But television presents even more problems. Television programs tend not to be discrete events, but one long spool: of news, entertainment, story – it doesn't much matter. Whatever the content, it's largely a continuum. If this page was hypertext, and not just text, one could link shows to the actual surface, but then all havoc would descend on the time and space world. A picture may well be worth a thousand words, but it takes thousands and thousands of words to transcribe television and its endless products. As that is impractical, allow me the convenience of theorizing, along with its handmaiden or handyman, brief summarizing.

This Old House began at the dawn of the 1980s, airing first in 1979. WGBH, in Boston, had a hand in its production. One must recall the times, the late 1970s. Back then, globalization was not yet an answer to everything, but what was soon to take hold was a form of nationalization. I taught at Mount Holyoke College from 1978 to 1981 and experienced the transition *in situ*.

My illustration is a pair of duck boots from L.L. Bean. I ordered them from a catalogue a colleague had from the Maine company. Though I had been living on and off in New England (mainly Cape Cod) since I had dropped out of college in 1964, I hadn't ever bought a pair. But, at the college they were practically part of a uniform, especially when winter came. And they appeared *sui generis*. I wouldn't have gotten them during the years I lived in New York City. Some of this was, of course, economics. They weren't cheap, at least not to someone who had just begun to be regularly employed.

But, in 1978, Mount Holyoke was my second full-time academic job. So I bought them, and felt part of the local regional culture.

That culture wasn't to last much longer. By the time I left Mount Holyoke and journeyed out to the Midwest to teach at the University of Notre Dame, L.L. Bean had gone national. Its catalogue and advertising reached everywhere. Then a sub-literate entrepreneur launched his badly punctuated competitor, Lands' End. Then the rubber and leather boots were made in China and became ubiquitous, and cheap. Everything from China was cheap.

Nationalization was the precursor to globalization. Cable television, national marketing, FedEx, all of it was of a piece, and the transformation only took a decade or so to happen. When my wife was a Radcliffe Fellow in Cambridge during the mid-1980s she was amused by a local radio program on WGBH hosted by two Italian guys, Click and Clack.

Soon the nation would be amused. The eighties and nineties became a whirlwind of this sort of economic and cultural homogenization. This, of course, wasn't that strange, given that the nation had just elected the first president who had been both bought and sold by corporate America, the former GE spokesperson, Ronald Reagan. Reagan, with his fake corporate populism, did everything he could to enable the business of America to continue to be business and, further, to allow corporations to have free reign, with freedom from most everything, including taxes. Along the way, he got rid of pesky unions, and the notion of collective bargaining over wages, etc. But, as we all became the same, the nature of what we would share certainly changed. *This Old House,* what it stood for, is far, far from *Extreme Makeover:*

Home Edition. The evolution can be described various ways. In some important aspects, it's the change from literary (*This Old House*) to oral (*EM:HE*), and from liberalism to fascism at its most alarming.

I do mean fascism, not conservatism. It is ironic that Reagan's predecessor, Jimmy Carter, is known in his admired post-presidency for hammering nails, fixing up houses for the poor. Carter, too, was infected by the spirit of *This Old House.* Or, perhaps, it was the other way around – the core values of *This Old House,* those Jimmy Carter values, differ so vastly from the core values of *Extreme Makeover: Home Edition,* which echo some sort of Reaganism on steroids.

The fact is that *This Old House* appealed to its early viewers from a deeply held conservative center: restoration. Bob Vila, the bearded host, crossed a number of cultural boundaries: the professorate, the elfin, a figure of trust and resourcefulness. I didn't know Vila was Cuban American until I began to research this piece. To think of him as my era's Ricky Ricardo is not that far-fetched. *I Love Lucy* was, more than has been acknowledged, about real estate – that one-bedroom apartment set.

In the 1950s, there were a number of apartment set television shows, Jackie Gleason's *Honeymooners* being among the most well known. From that same era, a movie came, *The Apartment.* One can make the point that the 1950s was a period in which the country was urbanized, made sophisticated, since the creators of the shows were urban, sending the message of city life out to the agricultural heartland.

Of course, a reversal started in reaction, and now TV doesn't aim to raise the sights of its viewers. Most of talk TV happens in a Pascalian everywhere and nowhere. *Oprah* is a Chicago show, but its set doesn't echo its location.

This Old House restored the properties it encountered. Complete rebuilding came later, much later. The original show looked to make it new, not make it something different. The homes' owners were the lesser workers of the production. Time spent on them waxed and waned. Their budgets were mentioned, what they could afford. There was a sense they had to pay for what was to happen, though some accommodations were made. As the show gained viewers more was done than could reasonably be paid for. Later, New England barns were turned into mansions. Grandiosity crept in, but often withdrew just as quickly.

What didn't change over time was the relationship of Vila to the workers. He dealt with master craftsmen, union electricians, and plumbers. The lure of the show was this sort of instruction. It was similar to the ads one still sees in newspapers and magazines to take classes with master teachers, listen to them lecture on the history of the world.

They all were being paid. The cameras of *This Old House* would linger lovingly, admiringly, on their work – the intricacies of installation, of cabinetry, of lighting, and heating – how to work, or rework, old materials. Its craftsmanship was a form of populist immortality: how to make something last forever, or to make something a hundred years old look brand new. That was part of its philosophical reach: permanence. Man, the maker, making things endure, the wand of the reborn, the fountain of youth, health restored.

I could go on, but you see its appeal. The first shows seem to take a whole year to redo a house, a home. Then, slightly less time – two would be done in a viewing season. Nonetheless, the time sense would not be violated. The narrative arc was a beginning, a middle, and an end. The work would often begin in the winter and end in the spring. Seasons would matter. It was a form of television realism, which is a far cry from what is now called reality television. And there were no television stars in the show, but all the repeating characters became part of the family;

they all had what TV requires, a certain friendly openness, happy with what they were doing, good at it.

This Old House sampled various tactics that other spin-off and imitative shows would later incorporate. There would be sweat-equity, especially early on, the owners helping to tear down walls, or taking on the more crude manual labor tasks: installing insulation, laying tile, some painting.

Bob Vila would show himself to be a jack of all trades, or would attempt to do something for the first time. He was everyman in this way – willing to learn, an old dog eager for new tricks. That appealed to the audience, for the do-it-yourself movement was beginning to heat up. Those warehouse-sized stores – Lowes, Home Depot – are, in some ways, the result, not the cause, of a grassroots movement to really do-it-yourself.

III

The argument could be made that the two decades between *This Old House* and *Extreme Makeover: Home Edition* chart the stagnation of middle-class incomes. *This Old House*'s methods – hiring master craftsmen, union workers – quickly out-priced the homeowner's ability to hire them. Incomes didn't grow, except on the far end: upper-middle class and the rich. Middle-class homeowners had to do their work on the cheap, mostly by themselves, or by hiring the slightly less expensive nonunion freelancers. Upper-middle-class professionals could afford the rates; their incomes kept pace. *This Old House* began to film renovations around the country, often going to other spots where appreciation values had skyrocketed (Santa Fe, etc.); New England real estate didn't let them down, either.

One of the reasons for my interest in such shows was that I had a history of doing manual labor, mainly carpentry. I kept myself alive by doing these sorts of jobs during my late twenties and early thirties. The "tips" one would learn watching *This Old House* served the purpose of "empowering" a lot of men to attempt the work themselves. The show acted as a master class and gained a lot of apprentices, not all of them overly competent.

One of my brothers rode another economic trend: in the early eighties, he started to buy rental homes, and fix them up, and either resell them or continue to rent them at higher rates. Of course, the fixing up part didn't drive up their value as much as the two decades of rising house prices in various markets, the access to easy credit (credit cards grew rapidly during the same period; everyone became the Federal Reserve, able to print their own money). All of this, by early 2008, is starting to grind to a halt in most markets, and the subprime lending house of cards is beginning to topple.

This Old House, during the eighties, begat a number of spinoffs and competitors. There was a large appetite on cable TV for shows of the sort, including, eventually, entire channels devoted to them. One was *Hometime.* Its website says its founder, Dean Johnson, planned to "produce a series of videotapes for distribution through hardware stores and home centers." The show itself began on PBS in 1986.

The strangest thing about *Hometime* was the sidekick, a short blonde woman who one was to infer (at least I inferred) was the wife of the host Dean Johnson. She wore jeans, had a leather tool belt, and worked alongside on the modest (as the years went on, less modest) do-overs. I would see this show once in a while over the years and was surprised to see the blonde woman kept changing, though the premise didn't: she seemed to be intimately connected to the host, though she was a different woman, but very much always the same physical type. The man stayed the same; the women kept cycling through. That seemed to be its own message in the do-it-yourself world: the guy in charge could change his help as he wished, and there were a lot of those thin, handy blondes in the world to fill the role.

In 1989, at what seemed to be the pinnacle of the popularity of *This Old House,* Bob Vila left the show. It was taken for granted Vila split for the money. Sears wanted to buy him, and his credibility, and make him a shill for the store, and the host of a new program, *Bob Vila's Home Again.*

This Old House hired a younger guy, a good-looking New England sort of prep school fellow, Steve Thomas. Hiring Thomas showed that the show was changing: Vila was no hunk, nor were any of the supporting cast members. Now, television required looks as well as know-how. Thomas filled the bill, but Norm, the master carpenter, was featured more and eventually got his own spinoff show.

All the various fix-it-up shows went on, each altering itself to be different, but the same. A comedy show, *Home Improvement,* began on network TV, making its version of Bob Vila, Tim Allen, a star, with the premise that Allen was the host of a show called *Tool Time.* The actual Vila appeared there a couple of times.

Life went on; real estate prices rose; the rich got richer; the poor got poorer. Then, in 2004, came *Extreme Makeover: Home Edition.*

IV

ABC's *EM:HE* wasn't the first extreme makeover. Its progenitor was the personal improvement movement, which had taken over from the home improvement world. If property could be restored, made better, forever youthful, why not people? These trends were somewhat parallel. I can remember when jogging started, in the early eighties, and physical fitness became an industry, a common cultural movement, not just a Jack LaLane subculture. It was part of the nationalization of subcultures. The avant-garde was dying everywhere in the early eighties; soon, if there were three or four people doing something weird, they would turn up on daytime television, and the whole country would be doing it.

The governor of California is a good case study for this transformation: from a weightlifting sort of freak to governor of the Golden State. Does anyone doubt that if Arnold Schwarzenegger had been born in America he wouldn't be the leading Republican candidate for the 2008 election?

But first came *Extreme Makeover,* the cosmetic surgery show. Plastic surgery for the masses, *Nip/Tuck, Queer Eye for the Straight Guy*: in a world of surfaces, no surface can remain untouched.

Here is a chunk of an abstract of an article in the June 2007 *Feminist Media Studies,* by Sue Tait:

> An exploration of the discursive production of cosmetic surgery on the television shows *Extreme Makeover* and *Nip/Tuck* illustrates that these programmes contribute to and reflect the processes through which cosmetic surgery has become domesticated within increasingly globalized contexts. I demonstrate that across a range of cultural sites, including some feminist scholarship, the press, and surgical television, post-feminist frames have displaced feminist frames for comprehending cosmetic surgery, enabling the culture's surgical turn. Feminist attention to risk, oppressive standards for appearance, and the cultural and discursive location of suffering around the deviant body is displaced by the post-feminist celebration of physical transformation as the route to happiness and personal empowerment.

Ms. Tait is hip to globalization on some level, at least. But the home edition of *Extreme Makeover* makes explicit some of the implicit in domesticating plastic surgery.

V

Success in television is often unplanned: if it wasn't, everything would be a success. Producers have to count on what is thought to be luck, but it actually is, more often, the existence of something they haven't foreseen.

Extreme Makeover: Home Edition isn't a direct descendant of *This Old House*. It shares a mixed paternity, and is something of a TV mongrel. One aspect is its *Millionaire* show tradition: some robber-baron writes you a check for a million and waits to see its effects.

This is where the show is vastly different from *This Old House*. *EM:HE*'s first premise is magic: you are chosen, you win the lottery, your life is about to change forever.

Now, these are powerful fantasies. One thing that it requires is great contrast. The upper-middle class folk wanting their newly acquired homes brought up to speed are already a little too close to their wished-for result. *EM:HE* requires real change. It finds those where the transformation they can render will be stark. In this way, it is sort of the *Beverly Hillbillies* effect. But, how the hillbillies do after being ensconced in their new digs is not the point, and not shown. Indeed, there have been problems associated with those who received the home makeover largesse – more on that later.

The Millionaire was a 1950s television show that lasted until 1960. It was a collective, yet individualistic enterprise: the plot of the drama, that is. John Beresford Tipton would write a check and make someone a millionaire. His functionary would deliver the money; Tipton would remain in the shadows.

Extreme Makeover: Home Edition makes use of this same "transformative" event. One day, you wander around the same old *schlump*, the next you are an instant millionaire. Various game shows dangle this carrot. *The $64,000 Question* seems, these days, not worth answering, but shows like *Who Wants to be a Millionaire?* still have staying power. In each case, the contestant needs to offer him- or herself up for grabs. *EM:HE* hunts for its lucky families in a variety of ways, but all of them end up producing an "audition" video, shown at the start of every show.

One notes immediately the "up-to-dateness" of this method: you need to make a short TV show to be the subject of a TV show. A safe generality to be made about the history of movies, of "film," is to point out that early cinema often resembled the plays they came from. And, often in movies, the "literary" allusions would be to other literary productions. But, by the 1980s, films began to refer to other films; predecessors from the other arts had mostly dropped out over the years. Cinema influenced primarily other cinema. If movies come into novels or plays these days, they come as equals.

So, one requirement to be extremely made-over was television literacy: you had to know the medium. From whatever cultural background the recipients of makeovers were, one thing was central: television had to be in their blood. Since 1973, when the Loud family burst upon the well-educated (*An American Family,* a documentary of their life that began on PBS, viewed first by intellectuals) for twelve hour-long episodes, Americans now know how to behave on TV; some, indeed, act as if the cameras are always on.

The popular culture is just that: it is popular, and is the culture most readily transmitted and reflected. All those hours of television viewing have served as modeling of behavior for generations. Readers of journals are often part of the unpopular culture, as I am.

As any professor of creative writing knows, even college students at elite universities come into a class equipped with an idea of how to tell a story. But, most of them, when asked to write a "story," write some version of a description of a television show.

It is no longer the kitchen table, or the campfire, or the bedside, or at gramp's or grandma's knee that sets the model for narrative. It is the television.

There's a well-known joke told in Hollywood when someone self-identifies as a writer: "half hour, or hour?" is the reply.

So, no matter how beset with woe the families who want their houses redone on *EM:HE,* they find the wherewithal to make an audition video. It is our TV age's tin cup, or cardboard sign asking for alms.

In one case on *EM:HE,* it was clear the audition video was made (or redone) after the fact: one boy of the family is wearing a college sweatshirt he was given at the end of the show in promise of a scholarship at said institution when, and if, he emerged from high school.

So, manipulation of these materials remains suspect. But, many of them look homemade – not always easy to imitate, even by professionals.

Though it has been snowballing, *EM:HE* has turned into this decade's Miss Lonelyhearts. Nathanael West, in his darkest moments, couldn't come up with more appropriate grotesques, more worthy subjects of need. But, with a difference: none could be untelegenic, too repulsive to film. There's some stretching here, and it is amazing to see how the misshapen can be made palatable by context, as long as the context was cheerful, upbeat.

In the beginning, *EM:HE* use to redo actual houses, enlarge them certainly, but keep some of the original structure. But, almost immediately, they took to tearing down whatever was there. In the same way, they took relatively whole people with a few difficulties in the beginning and redid their homes, but soon they were taking basket cases and creating spectacular, new baskets for them.

VI

In 2006, the website "The Smoking Gun" (http://www.thesmokinggun.com/archive/0327062extreme1.html) reprinted an e-mail forwarded by an "ABC employee to network affiliates" detailing the sort of families the program was looking for next season. The first three were: "Extraordinary Mom/Dad Recently diagnosed with ALS; Family who has child w/PROGERIA (aka "little old man disease"); Congenital insensitivity to pain with anhidrosis." The third is a condition referred to as CIPA by the few people who know about it. ("There are 17 known cases in US – let me know if one is in your town!") This is where kids cannot feel any physical pain.

Again, *EM:HE* has fashioned a potent brew of popular culture flash points: money and sickness is just the start, more than icing on the cake of the home improvement genre. Its cast brings in the rest of the world: indeed, their deluxe RV (the bus sort) is the new voyage of the Beagle: Darwin, and his crew, sailing the ocean of America; seeking out islands of the bizarre and wonderful; bringing a special sort of civilization to the natives.

It isn't just what one would think: the urban to the rural, à la *The Honeymooners* or *I Love Lucy*. It's a bi-coastal, New Age, sort of culture, steeped as much in California's brews as in the big city's.

The cast is a bevy of fairies and I don't mean that in an anti-gay, homophobic sense, even though the men are heavy on the, at least, metrosexual side of the gender spectrum. It's *The Tempest* sort of fairies, the magical side of things, where they descend into your life, somewhat secular angels, and make everything wonderful. Who better to do this than interior decorators, carpenters, designers, all good-looking and super friendly and agreeable?

They are a workplace platoon. If you have trouble and are in real danger, you want the SWAT team arriving, or a squad of Navy SEALS. They, like Superman, have come to save the day. You can find bios of the "design team" (and much else) at the show's web site: http://abc.go.com/primetime/xtremehome/index.html. The male designers' backgrounds often include acting, as well as carpentry. The women are, in most cases, from the interior-decorating realm.

Network television shows, as a friend of mine, David Black, likes to point out, follow the same strict forms as Elizabethan sonnets. Though few people do, sit in front of your TV with a stopwatch and view your favorite program. First, you must realize that television programs exist only as blank spaces in between commercials. The purpose of the show is to fill the blank spaces.

My friend was a producer/writer for *Law & Order, Miami Vice,* and other such programs. He once tried to open up a door for me in the television-writing world, but, though I was willing, I seemed to lack the magic words necessary to walk through that particular portal.

Hour shows follow the same form. First there is a teaser that goes on for – in an actual *Law & Order* script – three pages. In the case of *Extreme Makeover: Home Edition,* the teaser happens on a fancy RV/Bus. *Law & Order* has four acts after the teaser. *Extreme Makeover: Home Edition* has the same division: its teaser breaks down into meeting the family, viewing the sad house that will be torn down, sending the family off; the first act is gathering the hordes of volunteers and construction folk, smashing the house, letting the family see that, and the viewers seeing the family at the vacation spot; the next is construction, designing the "special" rooms; the third act is the finishing of the house, the filling it with goodies, with side trips to Sears to buy some; in the fourth act, the family returns, sees the house, tours the house; then there is an epilogue, the outpouring of gratitude by the family to the sponsors. All these pieces take exactly the same amount of time each episode.

But there are different kinds of sonnets. *EM:HE* upends the amount of time of the teaser; instead of being short, it is long: thirteen minutes long. Then come the four acts, each five minutes long, each followed by four minutes of commercials, a ratio of almost one to one. Then there is a three-minute epilogue, where the results are assessed, featuring testimonials of gratitude by the family; they conclude, but as the credits roll by for two minutes, clips of the family are shown, if they are cute enough, along with previews of the next show. Then an hour is gone and so is the show (except for the occasional two-hour special.)

The teaser begins on the bus, where Ty Pennington, the leader of the *EM:HE*'s gang, exhorts his concerned crew after they have watched the audition video, hardly ever a dry-eyed experience. "Can we do this?" Ty bleats. Yes, and they do the athletic sort of mass handshake/push-off demonstrating their fealty and purpose. Its effect, both in the corporate world and this television program is the "Let's put on a show!" gumption à la Mickey Rooney and Judy Garland, a theatrical Americanism of gung-ho, but let's have fun doing it.

Ty Pennington, himself, has become a model for a new leadership figure. He's a shop steward and a supervisor, an independent craftsman and the local primary contact, the seeming general contractor. He talks to the family, but his role is to be a boss without seeming to be a boss.

Ty's everyone's friend, encourager extraordinaire: a leader. Ty came from a home improvement predecessor, *Trading Places,* a show that attempted to combine elements of other successful shows, the kind where one trades wives or husbands for a week, though, in this case, redoing living spaces was the central event.

The group of elves and fairies from *EM:HE* needed a leader who was more like them than unlike them. They all come from planet television and have sophisticated aspects of a lot of familiar places: NYC, LA, the Hamptons. They are the denizens of hip establishments, bars in South Beach, Florida, the sort of establishments twenty-somethings hang out at. Although they are likely to be in their thirties, they all seem younger than they are. One is a Brit; there is a tilt toward transnational fun. They are, in a Shakespearean way, a band of merry players.

It isn't brazen New Yorkers who intrusively are going to show you how to redo your lives; the gang is more primal, stripped of regionalism, bias, clichés of race (except no black designer is in the mix), beyond political correctness, just Americans helping Americans.

The team-building aspect echoes a lot of the country's new industries; those wacky people in software and computers, playing ping pong in the office, which is an old converted industrial loft: the sort of world that produced huge businesses called Apple or Google. That's Ty Pennington's workforce. Ty looks the part of the modern facilitator with his Sting-ish gelled hair; his sincere listening repose; and his very slight, not-quite-a-lisp, speech impairment.

"Hey good buddy," the audience collectively responds. Ty's the guy. He has a bit of both Beaver, and his blond not-quite-without-malevolence friend, Eddie Haskel, from the iconic 1950s show *Leave It to Beaver.* Ty channels both Jerry Mathers, who played Beaver, and Ken Osmond, who played Eddie, with just a touch of James Dean, the doomed movie star of the fifties.

Ty's both sincere and edgy, with the sincere side most in force: likable. In the television-rating, world he must have a very high Q score rating, the measurement of familiarity and appeal.

Bob Vila must have had a high Q score, too. When he left *This Old House,* he had his name in the titles of his shows. He had become a brand. Ty is still far from becoming a brand, though he is now doing commercials.

But, on EM:HE, he's the leader of the pack, almost like the old rock 'n' roll tune of the same name. Ty's crew is a world apart, though, since they are from planet TV and do not resemble their beneficiaries in the slightest. The families they help, even those who aren't the classic lame and halt, aren't from Ty's world. On *This Old House,* everyone looked more or less the same; if anyone stood out, it was the owners of the property. They might look a class, a cut, above; somewhat polished, especially if they weren't wearing work clothes.

What Ty and company are handing out is charity. They have the heart and soul of a Jerry Lewis telethon. Most of the show's families are poor, no matter how hard working, and often could neither pay the mortgage on the old property, nor the higher taxes on the new, reassessed house.

This Old House had some of that, the IRS or local tax collectors gumming up the transformational fun. But *Extreme Makeover: Home Edition,* due to criticisms of this paradoxical condition (living in houses they couldn't afford), now has the builders pay off the old mortgage, and various fund raisers are held during the week it takes to build the house for a minor endowment to stave off the bill collectors from the front door. Mean tax people, why can't they get with the program?

This Old House made use of sweat equity and showed the owners taking on a second job (working on one's property), creating more wealth literarily under one's feet, and paying taxes, in the beginning, was rarely an issue. The owners weren't, for the most part, jumping class.

EM:HE is about luck, hitting the jackpot, charity. The show sends the family away for a week, usually to some all-American family vacation spot, something garish and corporate, a fun spot associated with cartoon characters. They appear, via videotape once or twice during the show, to reward whatever location is hosting them, and to participate in one fixed feature: they watch while their house is demolished.

In the beginning, houses were enlarged, so demolition was minor, but quickly the show's creators realized the power and effect of starting fresh. The homes weren't being improved, they were replaced: the family watches as Ty leads the way to a new life. He holds the video camera in front of his face, and films, supposedly, what the family sees on a computer while they vacation.

After a few shows, they began to vary how the homes were torn down. Attempts were made to personalize the destruction, something different than the old bulldozers and backhoes. One used monster trucks, those with huge tires. Regardless, this moment in the show is the one filled with the most ambivalence, one of the few that actually slides off the surface, and, for a fleeting second, goes beneath it.

It's illuminating to watch the faces of the family as they see their old home destroyed. They know they are supposed to look happy, and cheer the process on, but occasionally you can see true alarm in their eyes, something, at times, that even approaches horror at the spectacle, even regret. It just flickers there for a second, and we are back to Ty's enthusiasm for the rack and ruin that is taking place. No one reacts with the shock one would display at watching a loved one hit by a car, but some family members, especially the children, do show a twinge of non-joyous emotion as their pasts are being obliterated.

The telethon aspect is re-enforced by the weeklong deadline imposed. Day and night, twenty-four/seven, is the new, and preferred, workweek of twenty-first century American business. This is one reason Ty and company don't dwell on the craftsmanship aspect of building the house. They don't even comment on how they force the concrete to dry so quickly. (A short-lived spin off – let no videotape go unused – of how they did what they did ran during the 2004–05 season; I did not see any of those.) The house is literarily thrown up, debouched on the site: magic. What craftsmanship we are treated to comes from the design team, what bric-a-brac one or another of them is doing for one of the kids' bedrooms.

These are usually done in stereotypical boy/girl themes. Boys get beds made out of cars, or sports paraphernalia everywhere, including athletes themselves showing up to sign jerseys or equipment; Girls get themes of acting, or dancing, or tropical island retreats: fantasy lands. We see the cast cutting out the stars, making the palm trees, doing the applique.

Ty has a "secret room" project, most often the master bedroom, because Ty has a special place with the progenitors of the family. Again, he deals with them.

VII

Here's part of a February 5, 2007, AP story, originating from Brandon, Mississippi:

> *Extreme Makeover: Home Edition* surprised a Brandon family with its new home Monday afternoon. The show's host, Ty Pennington, surprised Sabrena Jones and her children last Monday with the news that their home had been selected for a makeover. Demolition started last week on the Jones' home, which was scheduled to be rebuilt as a four-bedroom, 3 ½ bathroom home. Jones and her three children, Marjon, 18, Mardaireus, 17, and Marjiya, 9, have lived in their West Jasper home for the past 15 years. Marjon plays football at Mississippi College, and the two younger ones attend University Christian School. Mississippi College is giving scholarships worth a total of $150,000 to all three children. . . .
>
> Hundreds of fans of the show, volunteers and others caught shuttle buses from Shiloh Park in Brandon to be on hand for the celebration Monday. Jones is a nurse at the Scott Regional Hospital in Forest, but wasn't able to afford to make the necessary repairs to her aging home. . . .

I watched that show on April 8th, 2007. In many ways it was a typical outing, in other ways, a one-of-a-kind spectacle.

EM:HE often visits poverty, but it is usually disguised, shown as a working-class lifestyle, people down on their luck. But, here was poverty on the level of the Mississippi Delta, circa 1967. Well, the home, one step above a windowless shack, was in Mississippi.

And Ty Pennington, forty years later, in 2007, gets to fill the role of Bobby Kennedy, wandering among the children with distended bellies. Of course, there were no distended bellies, just a home where the family defecated in plastic bags, since the bathroom plumbing had gone bad.

Ty did his best not to look shocked; his face is usually a study in calm, neutral empathy, right up there with Bill Clinton and other great feelers of others' pain. But this was a bit much even for Ty. His empathy expression drifted toward the appalled. The owner of the house, Sabrena Jones, identified as a nurse in the AP article above, has a retail shop in the house's front room, selling used and new nurses uniforms. It appeared that was her main source of income.

Ty sends them off on their fun vacation for a week, to a resort with better plumbing.

It is odd that large American audiences are exposed to the poverty of the working poor on this show more than any other, expect perhaps for documentaries of the sort usually shown on PBS. Here you will see people missing teeth, not often a usual sight on prime-time television.

One other oddity did happen. The neighborhood of the house appeared to be rural, though it sat close to a substantial street, perhaps a state highway. A shot of the back of the house showed it to be on a fairly large piece of land, but the home was held up by stilts in the back and the failed plumbing, a maze of pipes, was visible.

They went through the usual videotaping on the structure's destruction, but none of the vacationing family looked distraught at its obliteration. The big bad wolf could have blown this place down.

After the debris was cleared came the one-of-a-kind event. It turned out that the soil was too unstable to build the kind of replacement *EM:HE* had in mind. They had to truck many loads of clay and other soil to the site in order to make it suitable for modern construction. Once that was done, the house rose rapidly in its usual time-lapse fashion.

The design crew plays the role of social workers and pop psychologists as they discuss how the children's rooms are to be decorated. They dress the set. There is something too momentary about the results, as if the snapshot in time they are preserving will live on forever. So, if the boy is a NASCAR fan, that motif is carried through in spades, as if the boy will remain the same age forever, with the same interests. The room, with its bolted-on appurtenances, will be hard to change. How long will one sleep in a bed built out of a race car?

But the world of TV is the world of the here and now, not the then and gone. And when the kids reach eighteen, they will not be living there anymore. In fact, children reaching their majority has been one of the scandals of *EM:HE*. A house full of foster children, part of the feel good lure for the show, were kicked out when they became legal adults (the Higgins family).

In the case of the Jones family, the hope is the two older boys go off, or continue, in college, since everyone was saddled with scholarships to Mississippi College, where the older brother was currently enrolled.

Mississippi College bills itself as "A Christian University," and its web site has a lot of white kids, and one black kid toting a backpack, pictured on its first page.

Back from their week vacation the Jones family returns, the bus is rolled away, and their new domicile is revealed. The matriarch does the usual screaming in joy routine, falling to the ground, being rendered speechless, the obligatory I-can't-believe-it dance of ecstasy, even though it resembles women keening at funerals around the world.

Ty and crew have fashioned one other exception to the norm. A retail shop has been constructed, attached to the house in the front, and they tour it, along with the house. Her used and new clothing shop now resembles a Coach store at an outlet mall, all display: recessed shelving and theatrical lighting. Before, it looked like a downscale Goodwill store, stuffed with sad, discarded work clothing.

Sabrena Jones does utter a metaphysical remark to Ty upon viewing all the splendor that is now hers: "I couldn't've dreamed it, but it is a dream come true."

There is often a clash as cultures collide when class is jumped. If a family is used to living in a shack without plumbing, what will the "McMansion" look like six months later? In the world of *This Old House,* people fulfilled their class dreams with their upgrading, their restoration, remodeling. But, with most of the families of *EM:HE,* they view the new home as if it is a strange place, never imagined. We don't get to see how they actually live in their new digs.

VIII

The economic structure of *EM:HE* may be simple charity, but when it comes to the world of philanthropy, there are all sorts of ways of giving.

Most of the heads of households of *EM:HE* are women. Even when a man is in evidence, he is either infirm, or in some other way compromised, and the woman of the family is the leader, the mover, of the enterprise. She, in most every case, deals with Ty.

Though it was not shown as clearly with Sabrena Jones, since there was no adult male in evidence, Ty's principal role is that of "Lord of the Manor." Or, given Ty's demeanor, perhaps the Lord of the Manor's representative, and ABC is the "Lord of the Manor."

In the universe of *EM:HE,* most men helped are marginalized, rendered ineffectual. The construction companies are, almost universally, headed by men, and often two companies are enlisted to build the house. The guys of the design team, no matter how touchy-feely they appear, are get-it-done, go-to guys. And they all will get testy if pushed too far. But the household males of the sad stories are relegated to bit players, there only to be grateful and full of praise of the "Lady of the House."

On 4/22/07, a show aired about a paraplegic Iraq war veteran. This was a show that featured, at greater length, the male of the family. But it was not enough to be a wounded veteran. The twist here was that his van was in a car wreck, the circumstances of which remained opaque. The accident caused the son to be paralyzed. So now we have two generations of men in wheelchairs. The emotional tone, as usual, is kept upbeat: love, love, love, the chosen emotional state of this segment of TV, the talk show sort where psychologists and marriage counselors are involved.

The injured boy has the same gapped teeth of his mother, who is the mover of the project. The immobile vet is provided with a chair that will allow him to stand up. No journalism, of course, is done in any of these shows, though the program ends with shots of soldiers in Iraq, buddies, or at least fellow soldiers from the same unit, are wearing blue *EM:HE* T-shirts. One of the magic acts of TV is that it can go anywhere in the world for a bit of videotape.

When the man isn't a symbol of war and patriotism Ty's connection to the female head of household is pronounced. The relationship is feudal, or worse. When the male is ineffectual and/or absent, Ty steps into his "Lord of the Manor" surrogate routine. The man, if on the premises, is a hopeless serf.

Ty's virile elf persona, his slight lisp, mutes the overseer's role a bit, but you can see in a variety of episodes of how the women offer themselves to him. We're in the age of chivalry, primogeniture, squires and knights, *droit du seigneur*: the Lord's right.

Corporations are medieval structures. They can dispense favor and often life itself. (The recent court troubles of any number of CEOs and their wives exposed once again the noblesse oblige of the corporate lifestyle.) If Ty didn't have an ambiguous sexuality – if he looked like, for television, the typical leading man – this aspect of the woman falling for him, offering herself to him, would look too obvious, too blatant. It's not the right of the first night in question here, it's the right of any night Ty might chose. He gets kissed a lot. Luckily, most of the women look a little too medieval themselves for Ty to want to cash in on his position. Though, there was one show (season four, episode twenty-two) that Ty asked the divorced single mom to hug him, since, she, a dancer, was the most attractive needy mom he had encountered. At the show's end, she didn't utter the usual formula of gratitude; she said, "Thank you for taking care of me."

IX

The harshest critique of *Extreme Makeover: Home Edition* is that it is, at its heart, fascist. *This Old House,* in this formulation, would be liberal. In *This Old House,* workers are paid; their dignity, and the craft of their labor, are emphasized. In *EM:HE* the workers are volunteers. The mob literally descends every week upon the site to tear, and rend, and then construct, and vanish. They pillage, but they also sow and reap. If you are a friend of this ideology, like the Bush family, you would see a thousand points of light here, not the Albert Speer-designed spectacles taking place in the outdoor stadiums of the Third Reich. In *EM:HE*, crowds are manipulated with periodic hortatory speeches. Ty is no *Führer*, of course, though he has the same pint-sized frenetic enthusiasm (more of the Charlie Chaplin sort), but he's there as the center of attention, yelling through his megaphone, working up the crowd. They are doing it for Ty, and for what Ty stands for.

Ty does do commercials for Bayer aspirin, which is made by Bayer AG, progenitor and heir of the infamous German firm I.G. Farben, maker of the concentration camp gases, but Ty is there for his popularity with the demographic group that takes aspirin. *EM:HE* appeals to the old and the sedentary.

EM:HE is a kind of fascism that completely embraces capitalism, and its message of how to deal with poverty. The plight of Sabrena Jones, her family defecating in bags, not dreaming ("I couldn't dream it, but . . . "), yet striving, with her nurse uniform business, was not caused by capitalism, a job, or jobs that don't pay her enough (or Wal-Mart that eats the dreams of small business owners for lunch), or the rich, or the maldistribution of income and opportunity, but just, what, circumstances? The Jones's aren't the result of unbridled capitalism, and the free-market coup of the last two decades; they're just what they are, and the rich are going to save them.

The model of the many helping the few – one at a time! – is the preferred solution, not the many, via the tax base, helping the many.

Just as the rich are unique in their ability to be rich, since they work for it, deserve it, have the special talents that created it (see Louis Uchitelle, "The Richest of the Rich, Proud of a New Gilded Age," *New York Times*, July 15, 2007), the Jones family, and others, have the rare good fortune to have *EM:HE* pick them for their transformation. Somehow that video beseechment they sent in showed they understood how to succeed on TV – voilà: each according not to their needs, but their abilities.

x

But, ultimately, *EM:HE* is in many ways beyond satire, beyond analysis – at least in the sense that they know what they are, and don't care what anyone says. In a recent movie, *Wild Hogs,* starring John Travolta, Martin Lawrence, William Macy and Tim Allen (who, recall, was the TV series version of Bob Vila in a show which debuted on ABC in 1991) play a bunch of professionals who act as motorcycle afficionados on weekends; they take a cross-country trip with the usual cultural clashes, amateurs meeting up disastrously with professionals. *EM:HE,* in the form of Ty, makes an appearance at the end, during the credits. In the movie, the suburban types have caused the destruction of the real bikers headquarters/bar. As the credits roll, Ty appears in his *EM:HE* role, having rebuilt the bar with the program's usual embellishments, bigger and better, with motorcycles attached to the roof. The actors-beneficiaries react with the same mixture of pathos and glee.

All of this is, after all, the Walt Disney Corporation, which owns both the studio, Touchstone, and the distributor of the movie, Buena Vista, as well as ABC. This interconnection is way beyond product placement.

Yes, they are making fun of themselves, or, at least, Ty was making fun of himself and them, and the Walt Disney Corporation is making fun of itself – or, at least, having the last laugh. There is one branch of intellectual endeavor that aims to correct or change things, make improvements all around. This sort of critique, the dominant one in academia for decades, has proven to be as ineffectual as most of the males who receive the largesse of Ty's crew. Nothing will change EM:HE except the lessening of its audience, the usual capitalist bottom line.

We've come a long way since *This Old House,* which may be as anachronistic as "This Old House on the Prairie." Corporations mirror their world on television. As John Kerry might say, "who among us would expect any different?"

One episode of *Law & Order,* long ago, dealt with laetrile and alternate medical treatments. Ripped from the headlines the story lines may be – this one had cancer as a theme, and trips to iffy clinics south of the border. In the end, the laetrile people were shown to be frauds and worse. During the show, which ran on NBC in its original presentations, a GE commercial appeared, for its medical unit, and its machines that detect diseases, especially those that detect cancer. It was one of GE's feel good ads – not that many viewers were out to buy a MRI machine. "Look what we do for you," was the message. And the episode of *Law & Order* was reassuring the folk, the audience, that just such treatments were the thing to do.

I'm pretty sure none of the writers of that episode were told to make alternate medicine bad, corporate medicine good. But, somewhere along the chain, there was a link that knew what it was doing, since that is why they ran the ad. GE, of course, owns NBC.

It's not just a free press as long as you own one, it's only free entertainment as long as you own the circus.

David Chase, the "creator" of *The Sopranos* – after *Law & Order,* the most beloved television crime show among the overeducated – is opposed to corporate America, too. In an article about the end of *The Sopranos* in the *New York Review of Books* on August 16, 2007 (where else, given the devotion of the show's academic fans?) Chase is quoted, saying, "I loathe and despise almost every second of [network television]. . . . I consider network TV to be propaganda for the corporate state." Chase, in the article, is identified as a fellow who has worked in the "medium all his adult life," and has written for such shows as *The Night Stalker, The Rockford Files,* and *Northern Exposure,* which, Chase holds, rammed "home every week the message that 'life is nothing but great', 'Americans are great', and 'heartfelt emotion and sharing conquers everything'." (The Chase quotes, a NYRB footnote tells us, come from a 2000 book by Allen Rucker and David Chase, *The Sopranos: A Family History.*)

Whatever one thinks of *The Sopranos* (and I think it is an educated liberal's wishful thinking of what New Jersey gangsters are really like, not the actuality, which could be seen on parade in the recent trial of the "Outfit" gangsters that took place during August, 2007 in Chicago), we have come to a bad pass when a chief practitioner and beneficiary of corporate TV (Chase), including HBO's *Sopranos,* is its most successful (financially, at least) critic. This is yet another example that network TV is beyond the reach of meaningful, or effective, criticism.

At the end of nearly every episode of *Extreme Makeover: Home Edition,* the newly housed family, dressed in brand new clothes, yells collectively and singingly, "Thank you ABC, Thank You ABC," and they mean it.

And what can I say, too, given the subject of this piece, but the same, "Thank You, ABC. Thank you, ABC. Thank You."

First appeared as "This Old House on the Prairie: Extreme Makeover" in *Third Coast,* Fall 2008.

Five Male Chroniclers of Bill Clinton and His World: Christopher Hitchens, Michael Isikoff, Andrew Morton, George Stephanopoulos, Bob Woodward

There are blow jobs, and then there are blow jobs. The volumes at hand deal with both figurative, and literal, examples of the genre. And they manage to range over, as well as map, the landscape of what is loosely called print journalism in book form. They reveal not just hidden agendas, but the transformation journalism has undergone at the end of the twentieth century.

One might first note the obvious: they are all written by men. There are books written by women inspired by Bill Clinton's life and loves (Gennifer Flowers, Dolly Kyle Browning), but these are, in the main, reminiscences. Ann Coulter, the author of *High Crimes and Misdemeanors: The Case Against Bill Clinton* (Regnery Publishing, 1998), who can be called a journalist (if not being called something else: lawyer, elf, part of the right wing conspiracy, etc.), would doubtless be the best seller of the small journalistic sorority mining the Clinton lode, her contribution being in the attack biography genre, with Elizabeth Drew standing in as the more respectable, though stodgier, contender, her Clinton books lagging behind in sales. The skewed proportions of male versus female authors writing about Bill Clinton at book length would not matter much, except that one can readily detect the very mano-a-mano tone the male authors share. Bill Clinton is the representative generational male figure; he is the norm from which their standard deviations are measured.

But it is journalistic practice that is chiefly under consideration and on display here: we have Bob (and that Bob is the only informal thing about him) Woodward's *sui generis* sort, in the sense that he (along with Carl Bernstein) is credited with inventing it. During the heady days of the mid-seventies, when there was a "new journalist" lurking behind every mailbox, there came to be the hugely successful hybrid example of Bob Woodward and Carl Bernstein's 1974 book, *All the President's Men,* which was taken as a subset of the form by most commentators of its time. Of course, the most substantial difference went unmentioned: "new journalists" were almost all freelance writers. Thumb through Tom Wolfe's 1973 anthology, *The New Journalism,* and look at the names. Almost none were staff writers of well-established publications (of the twenty-three listed, only Rex Reed, Richard Goldstein, and "Adam Smith" would be the exceptions – Gay Talese had worked for the *New York Times,* but freelancing, by and large, went with the territory).

As the years have gone by, Woodward's name alone has graced the cover of his successive books, co-authors having been long discarded, though the reader is usually treated to a fulsome thanks for a remarkable underling (from the example *Shadow: Five Presidents and the Legacy of Watergate* provides), one (Jeff Glasser) who serves as Woodward's "assistant and collaborator for the last three years," one who "tirelessly and resourcefully" labors in his behalf.

A reader can be forgiven if he or she is reminded of the acknowledgments prefacing a politician's ghosted recollections when encountering such gratitude for able staff assistance, because Woodward over the years has become a senator of the Fourth Estate, and as the voice of official Washington, he is now more politician than journalist. And who would deny him the luxury of a staff?

By never letting go of a position at the *Washington Post*, Woodward has fashioned himself into a pillar of the establishment. In the old days, his and Bernstein's information collecting technique was, by necessity (with the large exception of "Deep Throat"), bottom up. For a number of books now (*Veil, The Commanders, The Agenda, The Choice*) his interviewing has been top down. The ditch, the rough patch in the road, that brought about the permanent change was Woodward's one non-Washington book, *Wired,* his 1984 excursion into the life of the actor John Belushi, Woodward's first book without a co-author in tow. That scary experience (bad reviews, fewer sales, being tagged as an outsider) appears to have taught him a number of lessons.

One might have been to listen more carefully to his long-time editor, Alice Mayhew, who suggested the topic that turned into *Shadow.* Woodward writes that Mayhew "rekindled" his interest in the subject of the presidents he had written about. Mayhew was interested in book making and, taking away the pomp from Woodward's description of the process, showed him how to put together a book from the parts he left out of the other books. Woodward, though, doesn't make clear what he already knew and what he has newly learned, but one can assume he missed a number of things in his original investigations of the same ground. To do so would have required Woodward to critique himself, which he is loath to do. Nonetheless, we are treated to a reprise of the Nixon years, the brief Ford tenure, Carter's single term, then Reagan and Bush, all accomplished in 223 pages, less than half the length taken by Part Five, the Bill Clinton years. But the premise of *Shadow*'s subtitle created one problem, a real stretch for Woodward.

If there is a "legacy" of Watergate, how does one discuss it, especially if one is a large part of that legacy? Woodward did not go away; he has become an institution himself.

Beyond the trademark you-are-there transcript recreations that have been his narrative style and device (producing results which always sound like high school actors badly reciting sententious historical drama), he would finally have to step out from behind the curtain and analyze, or, at least, draw some conclusions from his amassed gab fests, tell us just what the legacy, the lesson, of Watergate is. So he tries mightily. Here it is, Woodward's summation, his lessons hard learned that future presidents need heed: "First, if there is questionable activity, release the facts, whatever they are, as early and completely as possible. Second, do not allow outside inquiries, whether conducted by prosecutors, congressman or reporters, to harden into a permanent state of suspicion and warfare."

It may be hard to see the forest from the trees if one is a tree oneself, but Woodward does seem to miss the point. His books nourished leaks into more than plants; he left the emperor without any clothes, and then complained that the ruler was naked. In sixties-speak, one doesn't have a solution if one is part of the problem, and Woodward doesn't see himself as part of the problem.

It is not so much Woodward's use of anonymous sources that is bothersome, as it is his wooden use of the "omniscient" point of view. Such a literary device begs for sophisticated abilities, abilities that Woodward lacks almost totally. In that regard, he appears amateurish. But it is not just Woodward's use of "fictional" techniques that is the problem, it's the unreality of the world his style produces. If he wrote fiction, he might be judged the equivalent of the romance writer Danielle Steel; she doesn't improve either, no matter how many books she publishes. The impact of the "new journalism," at least for the fiction writers who produced it, was substantial, because they were very good writers of fiction to begin with. In an age of recorded speech (from the Watergate tapes to Linda Tripp's), Woodward's age, there is endless proof that no one ever talks like Bob Woodward has people talk.

Be that as it may, in "Woodward World," the style is not the point. It is the information, or the attribution, which is important. He has long become the establishment's Linda Tripp, recreating, over the years, so much "conversation" thought once upon a time to be private. "He said that? She said that?" official Washington wants to know.

It was clear in the seventies that, even though a number of so-called progressive journalists could have explained Watergate and its players to the country with remarkable precision, it required a powerful corporate entity to "uncover" it: ". . . of the *Washington Post*" was the Siamese twin label attached to both Woodward and Bernstein's names, and it was that "Inc.", not printer's ink, that was opening doors.

It is the point that Michael Isikoff, a self-described child of Watergate, makes – well, he doesn't actually make it, he lets it be made – in his contribution to Clinton studies, *Uncovering Clinton*.

Isikoff relegates it to a footnote: "Tripp also claimed I'd told her that, while I doubted she'd find a publisher 'in the present climate', she should work with me to 'allow some of this to get out into the mainstream media' in order to create a more favorable environment. This, too, is ridiculous." What is ridiculous, Isikoff argues, is that he would have settled for part of the story, not the bit about the power of the "mainstream media."

The lesson learned, by the nineties, had become subliminal: if some important publication doesn't run with your news, it will have no legs. Goldberg and Tripp had absorbed the truth of that, which is why they left so much room on their dance card for "Spikey" (their affectionate name for Isikoff). Given the example of Matt Drudge (the other reporter, other than Isikoff, who made a national name for himself on the back of Lewinsky), some have concluded that there is now an openness of information, a healthy flow from high to low. But one has to consider if Drudge himself would have made such a noise if his website headline had been "National Enquirer spikes story of Clinton Oval Office affair. . . ."

One of the many things that all the books under discussion here have in common is their open obeisance to caste and status. Woodward, in *Shadow,* describing the Clinton White House trying to decide where to leak documents, writes, "Fabiani didn't want to give the material to some pro-Clinton reporter or someone who covered politics. Instead, he selected Michael Isikoff, a hard-nosed junkyard-dog investigator who worked for a publication, *Newsweek,* with wide national circulation." There are a number of interesting things to point out in that second uninteresting sentence. One is that if Woodward did write it, he might have felt obliged to mention that Isikoff was his former colleague at the *Washington Post.* And, at the *Post,* Isikoff was the "investigator" who worked the Clinton scandal beat, not so much for the delectation of the public, but for the personal gossip-hungry knowledge of the *Post*'s editors. They wanted to be in the know, even if they didn't intend to pass on the information to the paper's readers.

But, Woodward, at least, is being forthcoming with his depiction of Isikoff as an "investigator." Nowhere in Isikoff's book do you learn from Isikoff what the writing process is at *Newsweek*. He and other field reporters file reports, reams of material, much like the FBI field agents' 302s, full of raw data and sporadic narrative. Editors, or writers, at *Newsweek*'s New York office, turn the material into stories. The only time Isikoff refers to that process is in his acknowledgments: "Assistant managing editor Evan Thomas lent his considerable writing talents to all that appeared in the magazine and gave wise counsel at every stage."

So, Woodward labels Isikoff correctly, an investigator, while at the same time disowning any human connection to him. Such admissions don't come easily to Woodward, and one of the strangest excursions is his description of his and Ben Bradlee's meeting with Jimmy Carter: "Carter had lied about his meeting with us." The sentence before that declaration is: "I called Powell to complain and told him that we felt sandbagged, summoned to an off-the-record meeting, led to believe one story and now confronted with a well-publicized version – Carter's own interpretation apparently – that conveyed a rather different impression."

Yes, I might not admit that I know and work with the people I write about, but I am pissed when the President puts his own spin on a meeting that was supposed to be off the record, one to which we were "summoned!" The idea that the President would waste our time, have the nerve to summon us.

Well, you see the pecking order Woodward swears by. They needed to be summoned to a meeting; not that they would bother to talk to "the Prez" privately, unless they had nothing more important to do. This meeting was about whether or not CIA payments to King Hussein had stopped under Carter's watch.

Woodward is still having trouble with the analysis thing; with the exception of, say, his deathbed conversation with the old CIA Director William J. Casey, he doesn't like to be out on the paper stage himself.

Given the history of Woodward's methods, he is something of an "investigator" himself, more of the Isikoff school and tradition, than, say, the one-man-bands of I. F. Stone, or Murray Kempton, or A. J. Liebling, or for that matter, David Halberstam, or J. Anthony Lukas (after they left the *New York Times*). Yet, Woodward is more powerful than any of those brethren. He might be a naïf when it comes to using the first person, but he isn't as naive as George Stephanopoulos appears to be.

Now, I'm not saying Stephanopoulos is naive: he's made his way in the world by being very savvy indeed. But, he is naive when it comes to employing a literary form. *All Too Human* is just that, a bildungsroman, a growing up book that has yet to reach the grownup stage. But it is not without its savvy-ness. From its "Note on sourcing": "I did not keep a diary while I worked in the White House, but on about a dozen weekend afternoons at that time, I had a series of conversations with my friend Eric Alterman. Eric, who was working on his dissertation in American history at Stanford University, taped and stored these talks to create a historical record. After I left the White House he allowed me to use this material for my book." Stephanopoulos is being Clintonian in the extreme. That this taping does not fall under the legal definition of a "diary" would be convincing only to a lawyer. But, hey, he's the altar boy, the keeper of Clinton's secrets.

And he was certainly blown away by Bob Woodward. Stephanopoulos was so taken with Woodward he gave *carte blanche* to him for Woodward's book, *The Agenda*. Here are his first thoughts about Woodward: "In the summer of 1993, several months into his project

[*The Agenda*], Woodward's first call to me had sparked two simultaneous thoughts: Oh, no! And I have arrived."

Seduced by Woodward's "stature," Stephanopoulos "encouraged friends and allies . . . to cooperate with Woodward." But Stephanopoulos shares more with Monica Lewinsky than the willingness to be seduced (and their books' similar glossy, white, innocent covers, graced with flattering photographs). Any number of times in *All Too Human* is this sort of depiction of his relationship with the president: "But, at that point, doing the president's bidding was my reason for being; his favor was my fuel."

There has been a major shift in the career paths of most reporters during my lifetime. During the early sixties, when I was in college, journalism schools were the educational capstone for young reporters-to-be. The idea of a Neiman Fellowship was as close to a post-doc as anyone could hope for. But, around that time, there was talk, as the post-World War II "professionalization" of the profession became complete, of having lawyer-reporters covering courts, economists covering the economy. But, like the maps one sees of how a virus can quickly spread, what was once the exception soon became the rule.

Now, reporting is largely conducted by what I term "creatures of the event." Especially in video land. Just as Eisenhower, long ago, pointed to the revolving door of the military-industrial complex, there has long been a government-journalism complex at work. First, one worked for someone on the hill, or for some failed campaign, or as a speech-writer for brain-dead politicians, and then one became a journalist. Watching cable news today is like visiting a hiring hall full of former campaign consultants.

The smaller world of campaign books also provides an apt illustration. There was Teddy White for many years, then Joe McGinnis, then Hunter Thompson, then James Carville and Mary Matalin. In 1994 their jointly-written book became the new model: creatures of the event who give their own self-censoring versions of history. And their book, *All's Fair,* because of their celebrity status, became the most prominent one on the '92 campaign. (Joe Klein, an actual journalist, felt it necessary to retreat into fiction [in *Primary Colors*] to tell the "truth" of the campaign as he saw it. Anonymity became a stand-in for objectivity because one couldn't immediately tell the bias at work, the agenda that was being worked out. And, who knew? the author could be someone famous!)

The O. J. Simpson trial became the final straw in the complete transformation of late-twentieth-century American journalism, at least in television. The one profession that has grown disproportionately since the early seventies has been the number of lawyers let loose in the land. That has something to do with it. But journalists were shunted aside when lawyers were ordained as the priests of cable news commentary.

Creatures of the event rule now, especially in political reporting. Take, for instance, Dick Morris, Clinton's buddy and *bête noire* (and the only person he immediately told the "truth" to about Monica Lewinsky), whose disgraceful fall only added to his notoriety, hence his fame. It's as if Bedlam has produced the talent pool. Morris has the most painful smile ever seen on television. He knows he must smile, but it hurts so much – much more than a wince.

Television news departments, especially at the cable outlets, are now staffed by former campaign consultants and lawyers. At the heart of both professions is the need to mask the truth from outside observers. Or, more bluntly, both groups are paid to lie. This is what journalism has come to: the messengers, at the most, are converts to the straight and narrow, repentant sinners asking for our trust.

(And print journalism is only marginally better, as these books all attest. Isikoff, in a more tawdry way than Woodward, has become part of the story [his subtitle: *A Reporter's Story*], which is why we are reading his story. Isikoff understands the difference between print and television all too well. Given the opportunity to listen to the Tripp tapes, he, at first, declines. Among the reasons he offers is this: "And I was in a bit of a hurry to make it to *Hardball.*" Why, I've only been working this Clinton sex beat for years now, but I am booked on TV and I have my priorities straight!)

Stephanopoulos follows in the tried and true "iron-triangle" tradition (lobbyist, government worker, journalist): boot camp in politics, and on to the television set thereafter. It is much like former, badly paid, prosecutors who become far richer defense attorneys: first they must get to know a lot of criminals personally. Stephanopoulos quotes Clinton complaining, ". . . I never should have brought anyone under forty into the White House." And, after reading *All Too Human,* one tends to agree, noting that would have left Monica Lewinsky out in the cold, too.

Which brings me to the two Brits, both tilling different forms of celebrity journalism. These books are all subsets of celebrity journalism. Forget old or new journalism, in fiction there are two forms: one sort about people who will never read about themselves, the other about people who will read about themselves, who are readers. In journalism, there are also two sorts today: about the famous and the unknown, and written by the famous or the unknown.

Andrew Morton and Christopher Hitchens are the purest writers under consideration. One writes about celebrities, the other has attempted to become one. But, what both men can do, first and foremost, is write, whereas writing comes unnaturally to George Stephanopoulos, Bob Woodward, and Michael Isikoff. What that group does best is investigate, interview, fawn, serve or berate, but when actual writing is the subject, they huff and puff.

But not the Brits: doubtless it has to do with education and tradition. I was surprised by only one book in this batch and it was Morton's. His control of the material was impressive. All that time spent with Princess Di did not go to waste; he knows how to package and he knows what real people (such as himself) might raise as objections to his subject. Like Stephanopoulos talking to Eric Alterman's tape recorder, Lewinsky avoided various gag orders (of the legal sort) by having Morton pen her tale. The weakest aspect is his flight to decorum when it comes to the physical aspects of Lewinsky's trysts with the boy from Arkansas. Morton doesn't even ascend to the heights of Barbara Cartland romanticism in the little recounting he does do. Ah, more's the pity. Perhaps Lewinsky wished to save something for her memoir, other than the depictions in the Starr Report.

Choosing an English author was not necessarily a stroke of genius, but it was certainly smart. Any American author would have had a difficult time keeping a straight face. But it did not keep me from speculating on what, let's say, Joyce Carol Oates could have done with the material; or Robert Stone; or, for that matter, Bret Easton Ellis; or the hearse-chasing Lawrence Schiller, once Norman Mailer's collaborator. In fact, it could have been Mailer's swan song: first Jesus's story, then Monica Lewinsky's! One can only imagine.

Morton does presume (as I do, also) that most readers of his book will have already looked to the Starr Report for the gamey details; he steers any reader not familiar with them to that amazing document, in any case. (The Starr Report must be the apotheosis of what has been taught in law schools for the last decade and a half, a low bow to Stanley Fish, and the narratology he has inspired in the legal profession, though one of the Report's principal assemblers had the additional benefit of fiction writing workshops, another influential stream in the academic culture of the last twenty years.)

Morton has Lewinsky muse about her years in the White House as effectively as George Stephanopoulos, certainly as insightfully:

> In the taxi on the way to the airport to return to Washington, she burst into tears. It truly hit home that her dream of working at the White House was over. She had lived with the idea for so long, had had her hopes of a return raised and then dashed. . . . Now, seeing another office in another city, and being considered for a post involving a wholly new line of work, that hope had finally been extinguished. "I realized then that no office atmosphere would ever compare to the White House," she says. "It was very painful to come to terms with that bitter disappointment."

Here is Stephanopoulos on the same subject, visiting for the first time after he left the White House, a visit that does not include seeing the president:

> . . . a uniformed agent reached into the room to close the four-inch-thick door facing the Oval's formal entrance. The president was in. My heart beat more rapidly. My stomach floated with butterflies. . . . I didn't know what to do. Walking in on the president during one of his rare moments alone seemed presumptuous. Walking by without saying hello seemed rude. I was suddenly shy, and slightly afraid. This was not my place anymore. Clinton was still president, but I could no longer maintain the illusion that he was somehow my president in some special way. Not knowing what to do at that moment was the surest sign that I didn't belong.

All these authors have something to hide, and reading them all is one way to see what that might be for each individual case. Woodward hides his all too often personal involvement, his hope to be above the fray, though by now he is his own Heisenberg principle. As I wrote in my book on the '96 presidential campaign, Woodward has always been the oddest kind of "investigative" reporter: an ardent supporter of the status quo.

Isikoff hides, though none too well, his function as a sewer system that only channels information, rather than his preferred image of the guy with his hands on the shut-off valves. Stephanopoulos hides what he knows, self-censors, in the tradition of Matalin and Carville, and tries to find a way to be the supposed conveyor of "inside" information, usually couched in the same circumlocutions of his explanation about his non-diary, not-under-personal-control tape recordings. Morton may have the least to hide, though he scurries behind decorum whenever it suits him, though most of his role is to burnish his image, to gild the lily that is Monica Lewinsky.

What Christopher Hitchens has to hide is, perhaps, more than he has put into his small book. Though his distaste for the Clintons appears so fundamental it seems to be a case of old-fashioned visceral prejudice, the sort I usually hear from educated Brits about, say, the Irish, after enough liquor has been poured.

As an expert on all Clinton sins, it is unfortunate that, at the start of his book, Hitchens gets something wrong in his description of the Willey affair. On page sixteen, he writes, "Willey had been a volunteer worker at the White House, had suddenly become a widow, had gone in distress to the Oval Office for comfort and for a discussion about the possibility of a paying job, and had been rewarded with a crushing embrace, some cliched words of bar-room courtship, and the guiding by the presidential mitt of her own hand onto his distended penis."

He gets the sequence wrong. Willey did not know she was a widow when she went to the White House that day, did not know until later, after Clinton's embrace, that her husband had killed himself. No one contests that timeline. I know even Homer nods, but given his need for authority, Hitchens should avoid nodding off at all.

And, at the book's end, in his brief discussion of his eleventh hour involvement in the Senate trial, when he disclosed Sidney Blumenthal's fraudulent flacking on behalf of the president, he complains, "It was instantly said of me that I did what I did in order to promote this very book – still then uncompleted," as if the fact that it was unfinished made such a charge superfluous, even though his publisher had been advertising the book, and it had been announced some time before – as if the manuscript's incompleteness absolves him of any thoughts to the book's future notice.

Hitchens is in line with a number of expatriate British intellectuals who have taken up outposts here in the States for decades. It's part of the brain drain. And being bright as he is, Hitchens has been doing as much as he can to be, if not in the public eye, in the private high-society scene, securely on the D.C. journalist A-list. Once someone has been part of the *McLaughlin Group* it's hard to claim too much remove from that madding crowd. In fact, he is maddeningly up front about all that, in the same manner his fellow countryman, Alexander Cockburn, has been often in the past, telling of being happy to find more wealth and power so conspicuously available to suck up to. Now sucking-up-to may not be the same thing as blowing-out-to, though the phrase itself, blow job, has always been a curious one. It isn't quite right, isn't really descriptive, though it does capture something more metaphoric than literal.

So, in all these books, we observe the wonderful daisy chain of different sorts of sucking up and blowing out: Bob Woodward and his charmed or complaisant interviewees; Michael Isikoff and his talkative cache of ladies, including the boundary-ignoring Kathleen Willey (Isikoff writes: "We walked to my car. 'All I want to do is hear your story,' I said again. She understood. She said good-bye. As she did, she was standing just a tad closer than I was accustomed to standing to a source."); Stephanopoulos and the President that caused so many butterflies, who drove him to counseling and anti-depressant drugs, the same sad cycle to which Lewinsky had been driven by the President; Lewinsky herself, the only one who got to be real, not virtual, or figurative, with the president; Andrew Morton's courtship and knee-bending service to her (and good service it was!); and Hitchens, more self-lovingly, perhaps, more onanistic (if that can be), than the others, being, as he is, the most postmodern of them all, the one most likely to be aware of all the theories of writing as forms of masturbation.

Given the sorry state journalism has come to, one might ask what any reader might learn about Clinton that is new from these books, news that a cable news watcher wouldn't have picked up by now. Well, not much. But one does learn that the presidency is not what it once might have been. It is now middle management and that, as a friend said, is why we don't get the best people these days applying for the job.

Now that the world is dominated by international corporations and global financial firms, the president's role is little more than that of the attractive account executive, the good looking fellow who handles rich people's money. When Robert Rubin was Treasury Secretary his nickname was President Rubin. Clinton was merely the crown prince, the smooth underling sent out to speak at fund-raising dinners and ceremonial occasions.

When, long ago, John Dean testified in the first go-round of televised hearings leading to the possible impeachment of Richard Nixon, Dean reported he said to Nixon that "there was a cancer – within – close to the Presidency." Well, Dean was guilty of understatement, since there was much more wrong with Nixon's presidency than that. But Dean could have been speaking about Bill Clinton. Since it is the presidency, itself, that has been diminished and more readily exposed since Watergate (its real, continuing legacy). It is a much more superficial office; the surface now counts for everything. And that is why Clinton's personal failing, his taste for women on their knees, has had such a large consequence. If Clinton was a man of parts, not a hollow shell, one of singular vision, of true confidence and fixed goals, such conduct as these books outline could have been seen as minor, an aberration rather than a trait. But, since all Clinton's many virtues are so much on the surface, such a cancer on that surface was truly unsightly.

Given the old sort of triangulation, reading these books together is healthy and helpful, since each of them checks the other, gives a reader a true multiple point of view; not fake omniscience, but something that feels like the actual story.

If Watergate was, as its perpetrators like to call it, "a third-rate burglary," Bill Clinton's impeachment was brought about by a third-rate conspiracy. As was true with Watergate, Clinton's sex scandal – its revelations, the momentum of disclosures – could have been stopped at any number of points. But Clinton, like Nixon, did receive bad medical care for the cancer on his presidency. It was small, but it was persistent, and no one who had noticed it wanted to remove it before it was too late.

Clinton's often-cited recklessness, though, wasn't reckless as he saw it: Lewinsky wouldn't have been a problem if it hadn't been for the linkage, however forged, of her, Linda Tripp, Lucianne Goldberg, and the right-wing legal elves looking to bring Clinton, if not down, to heel. Because of that linkage, unknown to Lewinsky and the president, the country got to see all that these volumes recount. It wasn't the film-version Deep Throat's advice to young Bob Woodward, "Follow the money," coming back again to haunt the nation, it was just an accommodating Deep Throat and all that then inexorably followed.

First appeared as "Exposed: on the beat of the Clinton Beat," in *Electronic Book Review*, ebr10, Winter 99/00, www.altx.com/ebr/. Review-Essay of Christopher Hitchens, *No One Left to Lie to: The Triangulations of William Jefferson Clinton* (New York: Verso, 1999); Michael Isikoff, *Uncovering Clinton: A Reporter's Story* New York: Crown Publishers, 1999); Andrew Morton, *Monica's Story* (New York: St. Martin's Press, 1999); George Stephanopoulos, *All Too Human: A Political Education* (Boston: Little, Brown, 1999); Bob Woodward, *Shadow: Five Presidents and the Legacy of Watergate* (New York: Simon & Schuster, 1999).

9/11: What We Saw

Since writing my first television-laden campaign book (*Campaign America '96: The View From the Couch*) I have avoided the vice of early morning TV. I listen to the radio, which has become, by default, the generally preferred intellectual medium, providing more information per minute more densely, stripped as it is of the crutch of visual images. But, unfortunately, some visual images are the story.

On September 11th, shortly after eight AM in the Midwest, a sonorous male voice during NPR's Morning Edition said, rather hesitantly, "It's been reported a plane has struck the World Trade Center." I pictured many things at once, but I put down my razor and walked into the living room and turned on the television. I had imagined a small plane, like the model that came to a stop at the White House's outer wall early in Bill Clinton's presidency, flown by a disenchanted man (Frank Corder), who quickly, like the event, dropped out of history.

There it was, tower number one burning like a cheap candle, smoke billowing upwards. It had been no small plane.

I stood watching and then saw a large jet curving toward the second tower and heard – not really hearing, since the sight was so stunning – a FOX News male voice say something like, Here comes another one!

From the camera's point of view, the plane disappeared from sight, and a plume of flame and debris exploded out the opposite side of the tower. It was now more than clear this was no accident.

The tape of the second plane coming at the tower was run again and again. Old thoughts masquerading as new ones began to fill my mind. A friend (who still wants anonymity) had written a television movie based on the first bombing of the World Trade Center in 1993. It was titled *Path to Paradise* and he used an Irish pseudonym for the screenwriter's credits when it aired, not wanting to be easily identifiable to the network of Middle Eastern terrorists who had done the deed.

And, to me at least, it was obvious that the jet I had just seen was a new path to paradise for whoever was piloting it. I had always thought it strange that, when the Oklahoma City Federal Building went down, everyone assumed it was Middle Eastern terrorists who had blown it up, though, after quickly discovering otherwise, that notion (that Middle Eastern terrorists had the motive and the wherewithal to do it) was promptly forgotten and, seemingly, forever put aside as a potential threat to fear.

Both towers were now aflame, and, living as close to Chicago as I do, I said to myself that those towers would be coming down soon. I had seen too much film of high-rise low income housing being destroyed not to pick up the physics involved. It was unthinkable that the towers' structural supports of a floor or two wouldn't have been cut or damaged beyond their tolerances.

I presumed everyone would be evacuating them. Then it was reported that there was some sort of fire or explosion in Washington. Cameras showed more billowing black smoke coming from the direction of the Pentagon. There was no film of what had occurred, just the smoky aftermath. We saw uniformed personnel running across a bridge. That sight was more than galvanizing, because, in their uniforms, the event, at least, looked military.

It took a while for that story to straighten itself out, and it straightened out only when cameras got close enough to show what happened. Pictures here first told the tale: "You are there."

President Bush appeared, obviously shaken, standing on a school's stage, the backdrop's childish decorations adding to the unease. He was in Florida, at one of his many, many visits to a primary school, confirming what viewers knew, "Two airplanes have crashed into the World Trade Center in an apparent terrorist attack on our country."

Then we saw the White House itself being evacuated – the expensively dressed rushing out of their offices, across the green lawns, out, away. Some of the women removed their high heels to run more quickly.

I, like most Americans, had something I needed to do, so I finished getting dressed and returned to the world of radio. The FAA had grounded all the planes in the country. Those in the air were to land at the nearest airport. There were reports of more hijackings, and of a plane crashing in Pennsylvania.

Passengers, using their cell phones aboard the doomed airliners, had been providing most of the news to the country. Amateurs and professionals are often equal in this new age of media. Then I heard the report that a tower had collapsed. Shortly thereafter, I came upon a black and white TV turned on in a campus coffee shop. It wasn't hooked up to cable, so the image was fuzzy, but I saw the second tower fall, pancake, just like Cabrini-Green: a dark flower blooming in reverse, sinking back into the earth.

Walking to class, I discovered that the president of Notre Dame had canceled all of them. A memorial mass was hastily scheduled for later in the afternoon. Everything was, in the way our media amplifies, speeding up. The mourning had begun, even before events had sorted themselves out.

Television is a passive medium, and it often points its cameras as single-mindedly as Andy Warhol did decades ago, letting his audience stare mindlessly at the Empire State Building.

Recently, we had been staring mindlessly at the front door of Gary Condit's building and, in the not so distant past, O.J. Simpson's white Bronco, Monica Lewinsky's black beret.

Television doesn't invent anything; it is the great scavenger, evolutionarily equipped to absorb whatever passes by. When it went to a twenty-four/seven existence (not, strange as it seems, that many years ago), it just needed to stare longer.

News is now a nationwide cram session, all-nighters for the general public. What changes is what we are currently studying. The inclination of the nation as a whole is to take gut courses, the arts and entertainment curriculum, with heavy doses of sex and death preferably. But, for the last few weeks, the country has learned where the "stans" are on the map of the world, and more about Islam and its subsets than ninety-nine percent of us ever knew.

Images, except for traumatic ones, are water off a duck's back. But the planes hitting the towers (of course, more film was eventually found, more views provided) are embedded in our collective memories. And other sights of the last four weeks are burned there, too.

But, the precedent for the press coverage is not the Gulf War, or even Oklahoma City. It is older, more resonant, than that. It is the assassination of John F. Kennedy. The kamikaze hijackers have been called many things, but what they were foremost were assassins.

And it was an assassination on a scale never before seen. But the nation and media's response has all the earmarks of post-assassination behavior. What was murdered was the self-image of America that we cherished – safe, strong, inviolate.

The attacks were over quickly and accomplished by mysterious forces, faceless men, without clear rhyme or reason. Like Lee Harvey Oswald, apocalyptic motives may be discerned, full of hatred and grandiosity. But, it is no longer the lone gunman, it is a gang. Following that trail, we have been left to investigate murky underworlds, caves in Afghanistan. That has been the media's underlying narrative.

The Bush administration is calling it war and has begun to fight it that way, but it is not so much war as it is a search for killers and what created them. The two towers being struck, along with the Pentagon, had the emotional force of Kennedy being killed with three bullets. The towers falling were Jack Ruby shooting Lee Harvey Oswald (which is when the Kennedy assassination became live television), a coda so final, and devastating, that it elevated the event even further into the realm of the fantastic and the mythical. The parallels are everywhere. The networks and cable news went commercial-free for four days, just as television broadcasting did when JFK was killed, at a cost of nearly 300 million dollars.

Kennedy's assassination created a deep psychological shift in America. The World Trade Center/Pentagon attack is creating one even larger, but the media's response remains the same. Will John-John's salute standing next to his mother be replaced by George W. Bush's arm around the retired fireman atop a pile of WTC rubble? Never, but it is the same.

Two weeks later, on September 26th, the satirical paper *The Onion* produced this headline: "U.S. Vows to Defeat Whoever It Is We're At War With." We have been in a period of national mourning, not one of war fever. The ubiquitous flags are more the bunting of grief, than military banners. Such sights are somewhat garish, reminiscent of a mob funeral.

The media coverage, these past weeks, has been not necessarily cathartic, but absolutely necessary. In its headlong pursuit of images, it primitively exposes, giving us unforgettable mental pictures. And some of them have been raw and uncensored: Jerry Falwell and Pat Robertson sharing Christian confidences, Falwell blaming gays, abortionists, pagans and the ACLU for 9/11 on the 700 Club, Vice President Cheney admitting on *Meet the Press* he was telling the president what to do.

And George W. Bush, just as Rudy Giuliani accomplished in New York, finally recast himself as a national leader, delivering a well-crafted speech to Congress during the week after the attack, declaring a new war on terrorism unlike any other. It is clear, regardless of whatever intellectual failings President Bush may demonstrate, he has learned how to read a teleprompter. But, given the somberness of the moment, what was disturbingly eerie was the look of satisfaction and enjoyment that so suffused Bush's face during the speech.

Now that military strikes in Afghanistan have begun, the flow of information will be severely checked. There is no reason that Bush II won't do as well as Bush I did during the Gulf War in hobbling the press. The paradox of our oral/visual age is as more is visible to a wide audience, what is kept from view becomes all the more controlled.

But television has performed a service during the first dreadful days. It has had a story as large as its appetites. Television did what it does best – it shows. And though what it merely tells trails fitfully behind, there will be more of that to come, in time.

First appeared in *Commonweal,* vol. CXXVIII, no. 18, October 26, 2001;

Blue & Red America Post September 11th

Shortly after the November 7th, 2000 election, I wrote a commentary for the *Chicago Sun-Times* that began:

> The cliffhanger 2000 election reveals not only a divided government, but a nation divided in a specific way. Looking at the various colored maps of the United States showing states won and lost, it is clear that George W.'s America is Yahoo Nation (not the dot com Yahoo, but Swift's *Gulliver's Travels* sort).
>
> It is a large, lopsided horseshoe, a twisted W, made up of primarily the deep south and the vast, lowly populated upper-far-west states that are filled with vestiges of gun-loving, Ku Klux Klan-sponsoring, formerly lynching-happy, survivalist-minded, hate-crime-perpetrating, non-blue-blooded, rugged individualists. Yahoo Nation, George W.'s electoral bundle – save contested Florida, the toss-up state – contains not one major city, nor one primary center of creative and intellectual density.

That column generated a lot of protest; I received over 500 e-mails of denunciation. My piece was a bit intemperate; but, nonetheless, I wrote an e-mail reply that I sent to the unhappy 500. Below is a portion of what it contained:

> Obviously, all the other states of the union have their own vestiges of gun-loving, etc. What they don't have are the great cities I

> mentioned in the piece. The city/country conflict has been a subject of discussion for centuries. Don't you think it is peculiar that George W. did not win one of those cities? When Bush's father, and Ronald Reagan, captured the presidency, they won a number of them. (And, even in the states young Bush won, he lost many of their large, metropolitan centers.) Don't you think that circumstance is worth pointing out forcefully? It is, as I wrote, unprecedented in modern America history.
>
> The elder Bush's administration (and the Bushes are no Yahoos) let the more Yahoo-inclined Republicans in congress do their best to end federal support of the arts and humanities. When government attempts to end certain programs, it is not getting off the backs of the people, but just setting its own kind of preferred social policy. There is a cultural divide in this country, exacerbated not by me, but by conservative groups that choose to demonize whatever they decide they don't like. It would be nice to bring the country together, but young Bush, unfortunately, owes the right wing of the Republican Party big time. The cultural differences involved are found in the classic city/country conflict. They are significant and they were hardly discussed in the campaign – unless abortion (barely spoken of by both candidates) is to be made a proxy for all cultural conflicts.

Of course, I don't think Americans living in states Bush won are Yahoos – only a self-chosen selected few. But George W.'s campaign certainly made profitable use of them.

What my many e-mailers vehemently objected to was the idea of big cities themselves. "Big cities" functioned as code words (though some e-mails were quite explicit) in their complaints for minority populations, especially blacks and Jews.

And then, not a year into George W. Bush's presidency, came September 11th, and the world changed. Red and Blue America, for the short term, at least, became Red, White, and Blue America. New York

City, the place so many of my e-mailers hated, became beloved by all. Across the country, money was collected, to be sent to the bereaved of the City, especially the relatives of the police and fire department personnel who were killed.

It has been pointed out by many that Americans, as a group, have short memories and attention spans. But this national quality is not all bad. The war against terrorism has forced a national amnesia in a lot of areas, an erasing of historic memory.

In fact, because we can forget, Americans can move on in any number of areas. It's the remembering which often divides us. The sort of memory that drove the Middle Eastern terrorists to attack us, and continues to divide eastern Europe, the former Yugoslavia, Ireland, Israel, and other sites of continuing religious and national conflict.

We forget: it's our country's blessing, and curse. Very few voters going to the polls last November remembered anything (or much) about the cultural conflicts of the Bush I administration, those that raged from 1988–92, which resulted in the crippling and the shrinking of the National Endowment for the Arts and the National Endowment for the Humanities.

In the elder George Bush's presidential campaign of 1988, he called for more "social controls" to stem the slide into moral decadence. What followed during his administration was the NEA becoming the scapegoat for all right-wing discontents. Here is the short chronology of those times: Serrano/Mapplethorpe/Corcoran Gallery/Helms amendment/"loyalty oath"/Karen Finley.

I hope some of that sounds familiar. If not, here is the nutshell version. Jesse Helms protested the NEA giving a grant to the artist Andres Serrano. One of Serrano's photographs is an image of a crucifix submerged in a vat of urine (Serrano's urine, as I recall). Helms also objected to Robert Mapplethorpe's homoerotic photographs, which were on display at Washington's Corcoran Gallery of Art, which had somewhere along the way received some NEA funds. The so-called Helms amendment was passed, which forbade the NEA from awarding funds to any art that lacked artistic merit, which seemed to be some sort of self-defeating tautology, since the NEA conferred the judgment of artistic merit by awarding an artist a grant.

The Helms amendment (though, finally, so crafted by Congress into such meaningless verbiage that Jesse Helms himself voted against it) prompted the NEA to require any artist awarded a grant to sign a document saying that he or she would comply with that "restriction," though the restriction placed upon the NEA was patently gobbledygook. Lower courts struck it down, but, in 1998, the U.S. Supreme Court issued its own convoluted ruling, holding that if decency was used to punish "dangerous ideas" it would be unconstitutional, though the Court wouldn't strike down the statute as unconstitutional, since it was so unlikely the decency standard would be applied. (This tongue-twisting ruling, clearly a political one, presaged the election-stopping ruling Bush v. Gore in 2000.)

But, at the time, the restriction got labeled a "loyalty oath" (who first used the term, I was never able to track down, though one of its first usages showed up in early April, 1990 in the *New Republic*), which set parts of the art world against one another, thereby doing more public relations damage to the NEA than Helms was able to do on his own.

I found the absence of writing (no one could find any offensive prose or poetry to complain about, only photos, film and performances) in all that somewhat painful, but our culture is not so much about writing as it is about seeing. (I was on a panel discussing censorship in early 1991 when an Indiana state legislator complained about *Playboy* magazine and "boys' reading habits." "Seeing habits," I corrected.)

Previous to September 11th, the election map colors of blue and red acted as stand-ins for liberal and conservative, intellectual and business cultures, the sacred and the profane, rock vs. folk, practically any two opposing ideologies one wished to concoct.

That division was most clearly seen in the "Presidential Vote" map the *New York Times* published on November 9, 2000; it showed the popular vote county-by-county, and was a much more subtle version of the state results shown so often on the television news, the red states for Bush, the blue for Gore.

In Indiana, Blue America was found in its northern-most western counties (which include South Bend). Three other small counties, two near the state's southern border and one on its mid-western edge were also Blue America. Otherwise, Indiana was Red America, from deep crimson shades of more than seventy percent of the vote going to Bush (counties surrounding Indianapolis), to blushing pink shades where a bare plurality prevailed (Indianapolis itself and Bloomington).

The county-by-county voting map was a pointillist image of the United States that spawned endless reflection and odd revelations. For instance, though California voted overwhelmingly for Gore, the bulk of the state was actually Red America, Bush country. Blue California ran narrowly along the coastline, but that is where the state's large cities are.

All of this would not have been significant if it hadn't been so stark and nation-wide, and because the election was the closest in the nation's history. That's why it became so representational and symbolic: the nation divided, at odds.

But, the Bush administration, as well as the country at large, has had its own turnabout post-September 11th. Bush no longer bashes big government so freely, no longer plans to go it alone in foreign affairs, and the disappearance of the huge projected budget surpluses has made the president take notice of the down-and-out, both here at home, and abroad.

Whether any of Bush's ideological backtracking will trickle down to the rest of his administration remains to be seen. John Ashcroft's rights-curbing Justice Department and the rapacious House Republicans still seem immune to the changed world they inhabit. For all appearances, they think September 11th happened only for their benefit – to be more conservative, more restrictive, more ideological.

The Bush II administration is, as many have noted, the restoration of Bush I (though Bush I got thirty-seven percent of the big city [population over 500,000] vote, Bush II only earned twenty-six percent). But, what has not been noted is that it is Bush "Plus." "Plus" in Bush II is actually "Minus:" it is minus the eastern elite aspects George W.'s father was never able to shed. What is "Plus" is George W.'s "ordinariness," his pickup-truck-loving, dare I say, Yahoo side. His father mangled a high-brow English; George W. still has trouble with a low-brow version of the American colloquial.

Even his marriage reflected this transformation. Unlike his father, who married an east-coast heiress, George W. married a local Midland, Texas, girl, a librarian, which, to me, is an archetypal, almost Hollywood, choice. Think of *High Noon:* the laconic Westerner (Gary Cooper) marries a woman with more education (Grace Kelly). But that's as high as Bush chooses to go. Unlike Bill Clinton, Bush would have never married a lawyer.

Cliff Becker, when director of the literature program, pointed out that the NEA received a seven million dollar increase last fiscal year, the first increase in some time. That increase, of course, though long in coming during the Clinton Administration, was less than the eight million dollars Hillary Clinton received as a book advance.

Becker went on to say, "We don't know what the Bush administration's priorities are, but Texas state arts budgets increased under Bush." Becker hoped that Laura Bush, who he described as "committed to books, authors, and reading" would counter any predictions of "gloom and doom."

It is not strange that the Texas state arts budgets increased under Bush, since they, like the reading scores that went up, and were often referred to during the campaign, were low to begin with. And, back in the early nineties, the compromise most moderate Republicans wanted was more money to go to the states, less to be given to the NEA itself.

On November 5, 2001, President Bush signed the Interior Appropriations bill, which included 115 million dollars for the NEA for 2002, a ten million dollar increase.

And Bush has picked Michael Hammond, the dean of The Shepard School of Music at Rice University, to be his choice as the next chairman of the NEA. Hammond, upon hearing of his selection, said, among other things, "The arts can help heal our country and be a source of pride and comfort."

Given the present state of affairs, the arts, like many other things, will be far back in the line of groups vying for attention, given the shrinking budgets and growing deficits, both in the states and in the federal government. My guess, given the precedents, is that Bush will do what his father did, though with more common-touch savvy. The NEA will continue to shrink its mission, more money will go to the states, and less will be dispensed to individuals, always the source of the most trouble during his father's presidency.

But, though Red and Blue America still exists, if there will be any permanent changes in the collective psyche of the nation because of

September 11th, one can only hope they are for the better, if not for the best. I presume big cities will not be quite as hated as they were, even if they remain partial to the Democratic Party.

When the capital of Blue America was attacked, Rudy Giuliani, its mayor, became a national hero. And Giuliani, subsequently, stopped attacking the arts (which he was doing, pre-September 11th) and found a voice that was truly inclusive, afraid of nothing, certainly not of the perceived blasphemies he had been seeing in city-supported museums before then. All the flag waving of the last few months may turn out to be a sign that signals a permanent mutual surrender in the war between Red and Blue America. If that turns out to be the case, as the new NEA chair-to-be hopes, our country could then certainly begin to heal.

First appeared in *Arts Indiana Online*,
www.artsindiana.org, Fall–Winter 2002.

Virginia Tech

Like so many writers of my generation, I have spent a lot of time in classrooms, teaching creative writing – in my case, over thirty years. I don't have many rules, being a child of the sixties, but I do have one, at least for undergraduates. In my fiction writing classes, the first day, I tell them my one and only rule: I don't want them to write about anyone they wouldn't spend five minutes alone with in a room.

That would spare me from chainsaw-wielding stories, tales starring psychotics of the popular culture sort. Hearing Professor Lucinda Roy talk about Cho Seung Hui, her creative writing student who carried out the Virginia Tech massacre, those of us in the academic creative writing community, I'm sure, were particularly and personally affected. I certainly was.

Cho was an English major, a student of creative writing, one of ours. Roy, the co-director of Virginia Tech's creative writing program, and her colleagues, have appeared to have, at least, taken some appropriate measures. Unfortunately, for her and them, those steps are likely to become the stuff of lawsuits, dissected and detailed.

One of Cho's classmates from a playwriting class has posted Cho's work in that class online and recalled speculation amongst his fellow students that one day Cho could turn into a "school shooter." In one play, a chainsaw makes an appearance.

There are very few teachers, over the last two decades, who have not joked about students showing up with Uzis and taking revenge over some imagined, or real, grievance. "Going postal" has become a too familiar cliché. Unlike Columbine, school shootings at the college level seemed to be workplace incidents. In California, Arkansas, Virginia, graduate students, in 1996, 2000, and 2002, killed professors who supervised them.

Such incidents launched cynical comments over the years, protective humor. But undergraduates weren't, until now, lethal: suicides, yes, killers, no.

Semi-automatics have been weapons of choice for most of these workplace shootings. Universities are workplaces. Disgruntled employees shoot their coworkers or bosses across the country. But Cho's number of victims has never been reached before. Classrooms are the barrels you can shoot the fish in. "Locking down" a campus as large as Virginia Tech may be futile, but nothing is easier than canceling classes. That kind of news travels fast, since it pleases both the teachers, as well as the students.

Cho is America's version of a suicide bomber. Americans remain individuals to the end – even our killers like to kill one at a time – but the result is the same.

The suicide bombers of the Middle East we hear about so often these days take similar numbers with them, but it is collective, impersonal. Cho looked at everyone he killed.

Creative writing is unlike other courses universities offer. It isn't just the writing, but the writer, who is judged. What I also tell my undergraduates on the first day of class is that, counter to what they are often told, most people write badly on purpose, because writing is revealing of who they are. I ask for a writing sample that they have already written to read, because as soon as I read it, I will know something about them, in fact, quite a bit. Out in the world, away from the island culture of a university, a lot of people decide they don't want to reveal themselves that way, and bad writing is often the mask they choose.

Others, like Cho, want to reveal who they are. But it is difficult for a teacher to think a young person is a monster. It wasn't so much Cho's writing that has been exposed that showed that, but his lack of contact, his absence of speech, his signing his name as a question mark, his aloneness.

It would have been difficult for Cho to make himself any clearer to one and all, but it is the nature of an institution of higher learning to think that the job of a university is to educate the young, make them better, improved. Why Cho hadn't failed the creative writing classes he took that have been described remains a mystery. But any explanation of that, too, will be saved for another time. The thirty-two individuals who died will haunt the consciences of all university teachers, perhaps, most of all, creative writing professors. It is a hard blow to be taught this terrible way just how serious what we do is.

First appeared "Creative Writing and the Virginia Tech Massacre," in *Chronicle of Higher Education,* vol. LIII, no. 36, May 11, 2007;

Imus

Back in the day, Don Imus's radio show was local flavor on the New York City-area radio dial. Its appeal was an acquired taste, one of those programs where you could eavesdrop on what seems like personal conversation. It was that you're-one-of-the-bunch, a part of the in-crowd, atmosphere: listen to the I-Man talk to his friends, and you became one of the friends.

There's a great appetite in the culture to make the private public, and it was, and continues to be, a market niche in the media: see, that's what they really think, and really say and do to each other. Of course, what happened to Imus recently, the proper battering he has been taking for his racist remarks about the players on the Rutgers University women's basketball team, shows that the private made public isn't always a winning strategy. What one would say in the locker room, or the local saloon, won't necessarily play well on the national stage.

Globalization gets all the press, but there has been a similar nationalization over the last three decades. Local brands have become national ones, and not just coffee and clothes; nativist media figures, products of regional cultures, have gone coast to coast. Because of the web, every local paper is a national one today. Imus on MSNBC is a far cry from the naughty frat-boy addicts who made up his early audiences.

The promise of cable TV is that every particular audience will be supplied with whatever weird subculture fodder they require.

Imus made a similar news splash in 1996, but it wasn't racist, just irreverent. At the Radio and Television Correspondents Dinner that presidential campaign year, he delivered biting commentary on the Clintons, to the amusement of all present except for the First Lady and the President. That served as the whole nation's introduction to Don Imus.

On the Tuesday before Imus's denigrating comments about the Rutgers players, I happened to be on the New Jersey Turnpike, driving with my son on a spring break college tour. The electronic boards suspended over the turnpike used for traffic messages had only one: GO RUTGERS!! It was cute. Rutgers is the state university; the championship game was that night.

Imus's offensive remarks followed the next day. Of course, if one wants to discuss racism, it was Imus's Irish-American sidekick, Bernard McGuirk, who introduced the subject, first calling the women "hos." White boys using that term is cringe-making all by itself. How the Irish immigrants became white in this country was by name-calling and worse bigotry, and McGuirk carried on the tradition. Stereotypes abound, and a lot of folk fall into such sinkholes daily, including me.

But, Imus's offensive comments illustrate an aspect of Americans' long struggle with free speech and expression. One of the last Supreme Court cases on the subject, *Barnes v. Glen Theatre,* had similar elements. The offensive behavior in that case was not racist, denigrating remarks, but nudity, or nude dancing. The Rehnquist court, in 1991, did not grant nude dancing First Amendment protection as "speech." Why? Well, in the briefest of shorthand, the nude dancing at hand didn't contain enough "ideas" to protect it as expression, and the five-to-four Rehnquist court decision also denounced nude dancing's ancillary effects, along with the need to protect societal order and morality.

Had Imus, after making his purported "fun" of the Rutgers team, actually said something about the exploitative nature of big-time college sports, how athletes are brought into universities for their skills on hardwood and football fields, the abysmally low graduation rates for so many highly-ranked sports teams at elite institutions, where black athletes are used to win games for largely white schools, he wouldn't be abjectly apologizing and off the air.

But Imus didn't discuss anything. What he said was just mean, demeaning, devoid of ideas and bigoted, even though so much of his audience doubtless had, or would say, the same thing, except they wouldn't say it to the world on MSNBC.

First appeared as "Acquired Tastelessness: Don Imus' Fall" in *NUVO*, vol. 18, no. 8, April 18–25, 2007;

Susan Braudy: Family Circle

We can't pick our parents, but it is even more perilous to pick your biographer. Susan Braudy was an unlucky choice, though Jean and Leonard Boudin did not pick her: she volunteered. Leonard Boudin had died by then, and Jean Boudin was, as usual, more generous than leery. Since I once was part of the Boudins' "Circle," I am not inclined to be so generous.

Braudy and Kathy Boudin were classmates at Bryn Mawr College in the early 1960s. And even though there are a number of precedents for biographers who hate their subjects (the Robert Frost biography by Lawrance Thompson comes to mind), none make it quite as clear as Susan Braudy does. In her preface, she admits that in her college days envy for Kathy drove her to "the edge of tears," that in her presence she "wilted"; "To someone like me," Braudy writes, "a scholarship student from Philadelphia, Kathy was far scarier than preppies like Das Oughton."

Braudy, despite her lower-class pretensions, does not divulge any of her alleged childhood deprivations – her brother was a student at Swarthmore, Bryn Mawr's male counterpart. Nonetheless, she and Kathy were a clash of cultures, a clash that played itself out during the seventies and eighties – the counterculture vs. the acquiring culture, Abbie Hoffman vs. Andy Warhol.

Braudy's list of previously published books reads like a found poem of her life and times. *Between Marriage and Divorce* (1975), *Who Killed Sal Mineo?* (1982), *What the Movies Made Me Do* (1985), *This Crazy Thing Called Love* (1992): that about sums up Braudy's universe. But, to that list is added *Family Circle,* about another world altogether.

For this book, Braudy turns herself into the Kitty Kelley of left politics. What Kelley did for the Royals, Braudy does for the Boudins.

And theirs is quite a story: the stuff of potboiler novels. In outline, a famous radical lawyer, a seducer of juries and judges (along with any number of women), battles the government and courts on behalf of both well-heeled progressives and the down-and-out, winning famous cases – Judith Coplon, Paul Robeson, Ben Spock, the Harrisburg 7, Daniel Ellsberg – either in the courtroom or on appeal. His two children both rebel: one becoming a George H. W. Bush-appointed federal judge, a potential candidate for the Supreme Court, and the other an imprisoned accomplice to murder. A noble and long-suffering wife holds home and hearth together throughout the tempestuous times.

Braudy's version of this made-for-TV tale is largely a cut-and-paste job from a number of earlier books. Her original contribution is confined to both Leonard and Jean Boudin's early years. Once the public events of the sixties, seventies and eighties begin, Braudy has very little new to offer.

Her central thesis, that Kathy Boudin's self-destructive behavior is largely the fault of her narcissistic father, an attempt to gain his attention and regard, even more than his love, is a reworking of Ellen Frankfort's central theme in her 1983 book, *Kathy Boudin and the Dance of Death.* Though Frankfort's book is listed in *Family Circle*'s bibliography, it is not referred to at all in the text. Braudy wipes out a past that does not serve her interests.

Ellen Frankfort's version of the father/daughter dynamic is somewhat crude, whereas Braudy's is much more polished. Frankfort was a blunt personality, but often brilliant, nonetheless. Susan Braudy is the opposite, refined, but not much given to brilliance. Braudy's general aspect certainly allowed her to jump class, if that is what she did, by attending an expensive Seven Sisters school. She always looked like she went to Bryn Mawr. No one would have mistaken Ellen Frankfort for a Bryn Mawr graduate. But in 2003, unlike 1983, Braudy's intellectual shoplifting (however cheap the goods) is highly rewarded and praised. The American left is hardly fashionable these days, and certainly not glamorous. The Hollywood celebrities who may claim some connection to left politics only have their fame slightly diminished by the association.

Jean Boudin gave Braudy access to papers, as did Leonard's law partner, Victor Rabinowitz. Both were interviewed, as were a few dozen acquaintances of the Boudins. The cooperation that Braudy enjoyed wasn't so much a case of bait and switch, as it might appear; it was an honest interest to have Jean and Leonard's life recorded.

When this book was first announced a few years ago, it was said to be about the social and intellectual life of the Boudins, their milieu and lifestyles, the salon culture they had maintained. The publication of the book was sped up when, unexpectedly, Kathy Boudin was paroled, after 22 years, in the fall of 2003.

Well, there isn't much about their intellectual life, but there is quite a lot about the Boudins' personal life. In 1996, Braudy visited Kathy Boudin at Bedford Hills prison, and Kathy asked "what the point was of this book." Braudy says she "wanted to tell her the truth. 'I blame your father.' Kathy reacted as if I hit her."

Kathy could have replied we already have had a book like that, since the notion couldn't have been a new notion to her, given the existence of Frankfort's book. But nothing like that is recorded. Often real-life accounts become fiction, not because of what is put in, but because of what is left out. And Braudy leaves a lot out in *Family Circle*, but she does manage to exact revenge on the fellow college student who drove her to "tears."

Braudy knows how publishing works, and there is a market for this dyspeptic tale – at least in critical circles – coming as it does after the decades-long triumph of the acquisitive culture, the restoration of the Bush dynasty, and all that it stands for.

The book's respectful, and largely positive, reception reflects this climate. Right-wing organs like *The Weekly Standard* find much to praise, and only fault Braudy for a few less-than-accurate facts recounting the American Communist Party and its offenses. The *New Republic*'s Alan Wolfe gets to huff and puff over the sordidness of it all, finally calling the Boudins an "awful family." Doubtless, his own is one of probity and forbearance. (He can pray no one sics Susan Braudy on the case.) The *New York Times Book Review* lets Thomas Powers review the book, lauding it mightily, but neglecting to mention that he and his book on "Das" Oughton (*Diana: The Making of a Terrorist,* 1971) is warmly praised in its pages. The so-called liberal media's bastion, NPR, conducts chummy, gracious interviews with Braudy, giving her book its stamp of approval. Michael Kazin, in the *Los Angeles Times,* offers a rare sagacious demurral.

Braudy reverses the usual formula: it is no longer the sins of the father being visited on his children, but the sins of the child being visited on the father.

The book has more substance (but less interest) when Braudy is glossing Leonard Boudin's career, rather than Kathy's. Those encounters with the law had more complexities than the Weatherman's. Kathy went underground after the eleventh street townhouse explosion, and remained there nearly a decade, until she resurfaced in 1981 in a U-Haul truck, after the bloody Brink's robbery at the Nanuet mall. Men were killed.

When the Symbionese Liberation Army made news after it kidnaped Patty Hearst, I thought of, and wrote of, the SLA as a cartoon version of the Weatherman. But, as time went on, the Weatherman, Kathy Boudin's surviving tiny faction, turned itself into a cartoon version of the Symbionese Liberation Army.

Many radical groups of the sixties, foes of the Vietnam War, came out of the civil rights movement. America's slave history is enough to warrant almost any extreme reaction by those who feel it deeply, and it did act as an excuse to wage war against the authority that condoned it, and profited by it. Certainly Kathy Boudin thought so. So much so, it drove her and a few others mad.

Violent bank robberies have always been an America tradition, but not as an act of anti-government protest. It's Bonnie and Clyde at best, folk heroes known for bravado and fearlessness.

What motivated many of Kathy Boudin's generation, as I have written elsewhere, was the fear of being cowards. Those who protested the Vietnam War were often accused, by the government and its supporters, of only wanting to save their own skins. So, a number of radicals wanted to prove they, too, would risk their lives, just like any grunt in the rice paddies of Vietnam.

They were jihadists of the American way. Our culture values such self-sacrifice on the part of others. Government officials spend a lot of time honoring the war dead. Boudin and her compatriots wanted to do no less – but without the official "pig" approbation.

Braudy could have had an interesting subject if she would have explored that part of the Vietnam-era protests, or even had delved into what does seem like her central concern, what class and privilege do to a society that claims egalitarian roots.

She profits from a class bias herself: her book is published by Alfred A. Knopf, once (and still?) the toniest American publisher, though now it does more than its share of celebrity books by celebrity authors (see the incipient fictionist Rick Bragg's book on Jessica Lynch, private extraordinaire).

But Braudy lacks a novelist's ability to tell overlapping stories, which results in a lot of chronological confusion, especially around the years of 1970–73, when Leonard Boudin was handling a number of cases. Unless you know more about that period than Braudy, you won't be able to keep it straight.

Those were heady days, and there was a lot going on, but don't look to Braudy's book to sort it out. If historical coherence and accuracy occasionally elude her, she isn't overly bothered by their absence. In another context, when she is trying to paint the Boudins as master manipulators, she writes: "Manhattan District Attorney Robert Morgenthau and his wife, Lucinda Franks, were invited to brunch. Morgenthau was the person who could dismiss the old legal charges against Kathy in New York stemming from the town house explosion. Lucinda, with Tom Powers, had written the Pulitzer Prize-winning articles on Diana Oughton. No one remembers that the Morgenthaus ever came to brunch."

That's the trouble with writing history: it's full of no ones. It wasn't a brunch, it was a dinner and there was one other guest besides the Morgenthaus – me. Braudy's point would not be buttressed by my account of the evening.

But, Braudy's book, however flawed, is, finally, a mixed pleasure. She does capture Jean Boudin. Everything she quotes Jean saying sparkles. Braudy had almost no personal contact with Leonard (God knows he would have flirted with her and she would have remembered that!), so she doesn't understand or portray him very well. But she spent time with Jean after Leonard's death in 1989 and Jean is there on the page. Braudy claims no obituary was done of Jean (there was a public memorial service a few months after her death in 1994, but Braudy seems to have missed it), but this book offers one.

But, what Susan Braudy ends up doing is what J. Edgar Hoover and E. Howard Hunt, among others, could never accomplish, though they certainly tried and tried: besmirch the Boudins' reputations forever, leaving behind to mark their graves the sourest of tombstones – this book, this poor, damning book.

First appeared in *American Book Review*, vol. 25, no. 5, July–August 2004; Review of Susan Braudy, *Family Circle: The Boudins and the Aristocracy of the Left* (New York: Knopf, 2003).

Joe Conason: Big Lies

It is now a truism that there is no liberal equivalent of Rush Limbaugh broadcasting progressive commentary across the radio airwaves; at least, no liberal with Limbaugh's vast, national audience. Likewise, in the world of books, there is no liberal Limbaugh, or, for that matter, Ann Coulter, Sean Hannity, Michael Savage, or the half-dozen other right-wing polemical authors of the last decade whose anti-Clinton, anti-liberal rants have hit bestseller lists. Indeed, one of the rare "liberal" writers to reach those sales figures is David Block, whose 2003 book *Blinded by the Right* is an apology for once having been a right-wing, best-selling author.

These conservative writers are not the muckrakers of the early 1900s, so many Ida Tarbells going after the oil trusts. No, they are mudslingers, chiefly partisan ideologues who do a type of reverse PR: instead of puffing up individuals (the Clintons), or groups (liberals), they try to incinerate their targets. Such books are talk radio and cable TV yell-fests brought to the page.

Without the amplification of a populist television or radio network to champion them, few left-leaning authors have captured similarly large readerships. Two lefty authors who have produced best sellers, Michael Moore and Al Franken, were already celebrities, though in other fields.

But Joe Conason is straight out of the liberal muckraker tradition, a journalist (not a radio personality, a filmmaker, an actor, etc.) who sets out to expose corruption in big business and government. And, unlike Moore and Franken, Conason doesn't heap on humor and exaggeration to make his points. He deplores the "spiteful, malignant discourse that became so common during the Clinton era. . . ."

Nonetheless, *Big Lies* is being marketed as a corrective to all the successful right-wing attack books of the last few years. It is that, but it also is a rigorous and devastating portrait of the last three Republican administrations, and the "crony capitalism" they have supported and encouraged.

Conason writes for the *New York Observer* and *Salon.com* and is the co-author of *The Hunting of the President* (with Gene Lyons, 2001), an account of the hounding of the Clintons by a cadre of radical Republicans who considered Bill Clinton an illegitimate president. In *Big Lies,* Conason takes on the reigning conventional wisdom preached by the right-wing media publicists.

Conason's counter-claims are not the sort that can be shouted out as sound bites on a TV talk show. They need the quiet patience of print, and his book comes armored with eighteen pages of notes and sources. Even those familiar with the history Conason recounts will be freshly appalled seeing it all put down in one place. For liberals who do want to shout on TV, *Big Lies* will be an indispensable reference.

Conason begins by comparing "Limousine Liberals and Corporate Jet Conservatives." Conason writes, "Bush is a modern master of pseudopopulist style. What that style blurs is the profound Republican cynicism toward the same people he embraces and cajoles." Though Conason thoroughly rakes over Enron and the Bushes dealings with Ken Lay, he also describes earlier, relevant examples. Conason quotes David Stockman, Ronald Reagan's budget director, describing Reagan's broad tax cuts as a "Trojan Horse" to reduce the top income tax rate paid by the wealthiest families. "Working families saw their tax burden continue to rise, while the rich enjoyed tax breaks on capital gains, personal investments, estates, depreciation, and profits. Under Reagan's plan, a family earning $30,000 a year would suffer a slight increase in taxes, while a family with an annual income of $200,000 would enjoy a cut of ten percent. There were even some special tax breaks for the owners of oil leases." Sound familiar?

The chapter on the Republicans' "family values" reads as if it was torn from the pages of the fifties-era exposé of sin and sinners in the nation's capital, *Washington Confidential.* Conason replays the Clinton-era scandals, and the sorry record of Clinton's chief antagonists in the Congress, but he also fills in various sideshows, like the GOP homosexual-baiting campaign against the Democratic Speaker of the House (1989–95), Tom Foley, launched by Newt Gingrich's lieutenants. Conason reports, "When openly gay Representative Barney Frank of Massachusetts warned that he would begin outing gay Republicans if the attacks on Foley continued, they ended overnight." By chapter's end, the amount of Republican hypocrisy exposed would choke an elephant (and Conason's book stops before William Bennett's immoderate gambling habit was in the news.)

Likewise, Conason's chapter on race matters is an ignominious parade of Republican racial demagoguery and continuing opposition to, among other things, the Voting Rights Act: "To anyone familiar with this shabby history, the inescapable question is not why more minorities don't flock to conservatism and vote Republican. The wonder is why any would at all." Conason demonstrates that Senator Trent Lott's disgrace was no exception, but more or less the rule.

Two important, and damning, chapters are those on "crony capitalism" and the canard that "Conservatives are tough on terrorism, while liberal Democrats are soft." Conason points out that the term crony capitalism "originated under the kleptocratic regime of Philippine dictator Ferdinand Marcos," and "was once reserved for corrupt economic systems in developing or formerly Communist countries." He shows where the worlds of crony capitalism and terrorism cross and, for the Bush family, they come together most vividly in Saudi Arabia, via Iran-Contra. And Conason debunks the myth that Bill Clinton was more concerned with Monica Lewinsky than he was with Osama bin Laden. Don't take my word for it, look to Conason's book.

Whether *Big Lies* ascends to the bestseller list is another question all together. Conason is not preaching to the choir; he hopes to reach the unconverted. The teeming audience out there for the right-wing attack books may simply ignore this volume, not wanting to know. One difference between liberals and conservatives will likely show itself – besides the fact that liberals are to thank for promoting freedom of speech laws that allow books by Coulter, et al., to be published. Conservatives often want to silence those they oppose. Liberals do read books that contain ideas and analysis they disagree with; readers of right-wing attack books rarely do. Here's a case where I'd be happy to be proved wrong.

First appeared in the *Chicago Sun-Times,* August 17, 2003.
Review of Joe Conason, *Big Lies: The Right-Wing Propaganda Machine and How It Distorts the Truth* (New York: Thomas Dunne Books/St. Martin's Press, 2003).

Daniel Ellsberg: *Secrets*

The history of the Vietnam-era anti-war movement has been written in layers, often through autobiography. In *Secrets,* Daniel Ellsberg adds an important, compelling contribution. Its focus, not unsurprisingly, is on what Ellsberg saw and did during the sixties and early seventies, though bits and pieces of what others were doing can be glimpsed throughout. After nearly thirty years, the whole story is finally getting out.

Apart from that history, Ellsberg's valuable book offers a portrait rarely sketched, especially by a critic, of the defense-policy, think-tank insider. Indeed, Ellsberg had been such an insider that he never questions the breed, or how he became one. He went to Harvard, got a Ph.D. (game theory), lectured to Professor Kissinger's class on "The Political Benefits of Madness" (a tact Kissinger endorsed), and voilà, the insider was born.

Ellsberg joined the economics department of the RAND Corporation, a California defense-consulting firm that harbored one of the few extant copies of the McNamara-ordered study of the Vietnam War that came to be known as the Pentagon Papers. A copy went to RAND because of Ellsberg's urging, and the well-founded fear that the study might be destroyed, or left inaccessible forever from the prying eyes of historians.

Ellsberg paints this male culture of secrecy and exclusivity vividly. He was forsaking many things when he gave the Pentagon Papers (he authored a section on President Kennedy's decision making of 1961) to the press. Most of all, he was giving up, forever, his membership in the elite world of insiders, those who run the government, especially its foreign policy.

Unfortunately, this book is almost too pertinent today, given the Bush administration's penchant for secrecy in all things. It is difficult to imagine Donald Rumsfeld ordering a comprehensive study of America's involvement in the Middle East generally and various countries specifically. One can only fear that the blunders made and lies told will be kept from public view, because they won't be recorded, and no one in the Bush orbit will grow too sick at what is being done to defect and tell all.

Ellsberg did become sick of what he had been seeing, and doing, in Vietnam. Sick enough that he describes what can be only considered a breakdown at an anti-war conference he attended, sobbing for over an hour in a bathroom, deciding then to cast his "whole vote" to stop what he concluded was an "immoral" war.

His establishment credentials were hard to ignore, or belittle: a former officer in the Marines, a defense department specialist on nuclear weapons first, and then the Vietnam conflict second, one of the few men in the room who had actually been in Vietnam during the early stages of American involvement, a respected analyst, someone praised by Henry Kissinger after Kissinger began working for Richard Nixon. Kissinger eventually called Ellsberg the "most dangerous" man in America.

Ellsberg's conversion to the anti-war movement was assisted by a woman, Patricia Marx, the toy heiress, who eventually became his second wife. She led him from the elite inner circles of government to elite inner circles of the anti-war movement. Ellsberg does not play-down, or play-up, her influence. Indeed, this memoir is decidedly more an intellectual exercise than an emotional one. Go to Tom Wells's aptly titled biography of Ellsberg, *Wild Man,* published in 2001, for that side. Ellsberg, in *Secrets,* wants to be taken seriously again.

He can be maddeningly self-centered in his depictions, but this is somewhat forgivable in a memoir. The publication of the Pentagon Papers did help to bring about the end of the war, but it also brought about other beneficial changes Ellsberg doesn't mention. For one, it changed journalism for a decade or more, leading newspapers to become true papers of record by printing lengthy documents themselves, rather than summaries. The Pentagon Papers were followed by trial transcripts, congressional hearings, and the Watergate tapes.

Robert McNamara provided us with historical analysis in the form of the Pentagon Papers, but Richard Nixon gave us history in the making in the form of his taping system. The Pentagon Papers hastened the war's end, but Nixon's own taping did him in and, subsequently, the war. Though Ellsberg, too, credits overmuch our withdrawal from the war, rather than the Vietnamese winning it.

Ellsberg himself, in a most touching way, believes deeply that the truth will set you free. He wanted the true history of the war to come, out and felt then Congress and the public would do the right thing. Evidently, he still believes that lessons learned from history will make our leaders act correctly, and behave accordingly – in the case of the Vietnam War, to see its folly. That, if nothing else, makes him a patriot. Though, the reason the folly continued was not because it was right or wrong, but because both Johnson and Nixon wanted to demonstrate Cold War determination, rather than good sense. It wasn't micro reasons; it was macro reasons. And they would sacrifice young Americans to do so.

Ellsberg's trial in 1973 was stopped because of the egregious conduct of the White House, which burglarized his psychiatrist's office, wiretapped Ellsberg, offered the trial judge a job, etc. And the issue his attorney Leonard Boudin (the Boston 5 and Harrisburg 7 lawyer) – that what Ellsberg did was not against the law – was never adjudicated. He was tried under the Espionage Act, but he hadn't given the papers to a foreign government; he gave them to Congress and the American people.

Given the Bush administration's adoption of a preemptive war doctrine, Ellsberg's truth-telling book is a must read for anyone who cares about peace and justice.

First appeared in *National Catholic Reporter,* vol. 39, no. 5, November 22, 2002;
Review of Daniel Ellsberg, *Secrets: A Memoir or Vietnam and the Pentagon Papers* (New York: Viking, 2002).

John Frohnmayer: Leaving Town Alive

John Frohnmayer, George Bush's pick, in 1989, for head of the National Endowment for the Arts, a job Frohnmayer kept for the most turbulent two and a half years in the endowment's near 30-year history, hadn't voted for the man who selected him. Frohnmayer, a lifelong Republican, couldn't vote for "a ticket that included Dan Quayle," he writes in *Leaving Town Alive,* his memoir of his brief period of public service.

Frohnmayer, who was fired during the early part of the 1992 presidential campaign, when George Bush was handing his party over to its far-right wing, should have known what was coming when he left Oregon, one son of a prominent legal and political family, for Washington, but he wanted the NEA job badly.

He unsuccessfully had lobbied for it when Ronald Reagan had fist been elected president. This time around he got it and, if for no other reason, Frohnmayer's memoir should be read as a valuable primer for how political jobs are obtained and what working for an administration is really like. One of the tales involves a political appointee to the NEA, whom Frohnmayer was obliged to keep on salary for $50,000 a year, whose only duty, as far as Frohnmayer could make out, was to be the mistress of a highly-placed government official.

Frohnmayer's book certainly confirms everyone's worst fears about Congress, the Bush administration, the arts "community," Frohnmayer himself, and the religious right-wing fundraisers who rode the hobbyhorse of the NEA controversies (Andres Serrano's photograph, "Piss Christ," Robert Mapplethorpe's photos, Karen Finley's body) to a stampede of successful fund raising. Had Robert Mapplethorpe not existed, the religious right-wing fundraisers would have had to invent him; it is clear, from Frohnmayer's account of all these sorry battles, that homophobia fueled the cry for censorship more than run-of-the-mill "obscenity" (Karen Finley would have easily slipped by.)

The budget for the NEA was seven million dollars when it began in 1965, and had only grown to 169 million dollars by 1988, less than the cost, as Frohnmayer points out, "of a single low-tech military aircraft," less than the cost of our military bands, less than the cost of a cup of coffee in Washington, D.C. for each American.

The agency became a thorn in the side of the Bush administration. For decades, the NEA had gone about its work outside of much public notice (while creating a lot of public good). But Jesse Helms, and a handful of other politicians and public preachers (Jerry Falwell, Donald Wildmon), desperate to gain notoriety and funds and wishing to resurrect the Christian right wing from the political grave that Jimmy Swaggart and Jim and Tammy Bakker had dug for it a few years before, seized upon the NEA and a handful of controversial grants and shook them, like tambourines, for all they were worth.

Frohnmayer's book describes his role in the various controversies, his motives for vetoing and rescinding a number of grants, and for placing the paragraph that came to be erroneously known as "the loyalty oath" prominently in the acceptance letters which grant recipients were to sign. He hoped to prompt a lawsuit that would eventually cause the language to be declared unconstitutional. Because he is a lawyer, Frohnmayer's first choice for a solution is litigation.

The so-called restriction was no restriction at all, though it was quickly advertised as one by a segment of the arts community, and the time for legal action was not at the grant-receiving stage, but at the point the art was produced. My view, therefore, was, let them prosecute the artists. See how far that would get them.

As Frohnmayer writes, "Obscenity had come to mean whatever the complainant didn't like, because no court in any jurisdiction in the United States had ever found any Endowment-supported endeavor obscene."

But Frohnmayer hoped that someone would sue immediately: "Congress had put the law there and Congress could take it away, but only a court, by declaring it constitutionally infirm could get it out of our hair permanently."

Some suits were eventually started, but this was another case of Frohnmayer showing bad judgment: Congress did remove the so-called content restriction the next year, but added a "decency" clause that was then struck down by a California court (and is being appealed by the Reno Department of Justice). Frohnmayer wanted a legal solution, not a political one, since the political world he was dealing with was so much of an anti-intellectual swamp.

There has now been a political solution, the election of Bill Clinton, but it is not clear, at all, what will become of the NEA (not much, I suppose; the damage it sustained is more or less permanent; it will limp on – an invalid). But what is clear is that the NEA is of no more importance to Clinton than it was to Bush; perhaps even less.

Of this writing, Clinton still hasn't named a new head of the NEA. Frohnmayer may have set out to write an exposé of the NEA, but he ended up casting a much wider net, thanks to his unextinguished naiveté. He's an educated, self-described "bumpkin," but a bumpkin nonetheless, and that ends up being good for us all, since he wouldn't put down half the things he's saying on paper if he knew what was being said. It is startling, given Frohnmayer's advertised "master's degree in Christian ethics," how many times he describes lying to someone in this volume.

Looking back, Frohnmayer may well have been the best person for the job (though George Bush might differ). There were many worse waiting in the wings. Trying to save the NEA, Frohnmayer came perilously close to destroying it. He seems to be a Dr. Jekyll who isn't aware he could also be a Mr. Hyde, but his better self, eventually, prevailed. Toward the end of this highly readable, eye-opening memoir, he writes:

> Members of Congress who received hate mail about the NEA were seldom willing to write back saying, "You are misinformed" and explaining that the Endowment either didn't fund what it was accused of funding or that the story the critics had been told was at best partial and at worst probably false – much less than hearing (and even supporting with tax dollars) opinions with which we disagree is a reward, not a burden, of democracy. The rules of honorable engagement in political warfare – that is, truthful claims, reliance on facts and a recognition that ultimately, regardless of political affiliation, the common good is our goal – have vanished and will not return until enough of the populace demands them (or a daring politician gets some publicity for reinventing them). Congress, I fear, reflects the disengagement of the ordinary citizen. While Congress has earned the low regard in which it is held, those very citizens (ourselves) who allow its members to preen and bluster instead of honestly addressing problems are to blame.

Luckily, *Leaving Town Alive* provides a detailed, long list of individuals to blame, in addition to the faceless citizenry.

First appeared in the *South Bend Tribune,* May 23, 1993; © 1993 The South Bend Tribune Corp. Review of John Frohnmayer, *Leaving Town Alive* (Boston: Houghton Mifflin, 1993).

Dick Morris: *Off With Their Heads*

Once again, Dick Morris is attempting to rain on Bill and Hillary Clinton's parade. The tabloid revelations about Morris's dalliance with a forty-something prostitute helped dampen the mood of the 1996 Democratic convention and, since Clinton left office and Hillary joined the Senate, Morris has been giving them raspberries, under the guise of doing commentary, at FOX News.

Now, he has rushed in to print a cantankerous volume to coincide with the publication of Hillary Clinton's memoir, so they could share the same stage, or at least be in the news during the same month, hawking their wares.

Morris's book is made for the burgeoning market of readers developed over the last two decades, and harvested by authors of many anti-Clinton and anti-"liberal media" books, such as those by Ann Coulter, Bill Gertz, and Bernard Goldberg, among others. Rush Limbaugh was one of this expanding readership's early cultivators, and now Dick Morris hopes to reap its rewards.

The phrase, "off with their heads," of course, comes from Lewis Carroll's *Alice's Adventures in Wonderland,* spoken often by the Queen of Hearts; Morris's volume is "Dick's Adventures in Washingtonland," and he is, and always will be, like the Queen of Hearts, something of a comic figure himself.

Morris has the good, or bad, luck to begin his book with an attack upon the *New York Times*. The public might be a bit sated, given all the print that has been spilled recently about the Jayson Blair imbroglio. None of that is in the book, but Morris does take after the "liberal" Howell Raines, the *Times*'s executive editor, who recently resigned. But most of Morris's critique involves something he does know a lot about, the polling practices of the *New York Times* and CBS. His argument is that the polls are rigged to support the *Times*'s liberal view of the world. These pages read like an article one might find in the *Columbia Journalism Review,* and I'm sure Morris's contentions will be argued over for some time to come, since they turn on rarefied technical points.

But the fair-and-balanced debate at the heart of Morris's charges, similar to other conservative press critics, is the straw-man argument that newspapers are "objective." In England, no one keeps up the charade that newspapers don't reflect the politics of their owners. Liberal or conservative bias is not hidden there: it is proclaimed. Yet, the history of American journalism is littered with instances of news being twisted to reflect the views of the owners. *Time* magazine, under Henry Luce, is one case study. But Morris keeps acting shocked, shocked, that the *Times* favors a liberal point-of-view. Outright fakery, ignoring verifiable facts, still leads, we see, to resignations. The book's next section, an attack on Bill Clinton's presidency, and Clinton's lack of response to the threat of terrorism throughout the nineties, is more compelling, since Morris was an insider toward the end of Clinton's first term, coming back on board after the Democrats lost the House in the disastrous '94 midterm elections.

Bill Clinton did span the culture like no other president. He had one foot in a trailer park and another in Oxford yard. But, the only place Clinton found no comfort was with the military, and Morris correctly points out this defect. "Bill Clinton could have confronted al

Qaeda more forcefully," Morris writes. "He could have thrown down the gauntlet at North Korea.... But all these actions would have compromised his grip on the presidency.... Each might possibly have led to war and casualties, which terrified him in view of his absence of military service."

Clinton took more risks in his private life than in his public life, and the nation paid a price for that.

Morris then lights out for other easy-pickin' targets, those whom he calls "The Hollywood Apologists." It isn't strange that Hollywood stars have become spokespersons for left-ish views in the country. Morris doesn't seem to understand that "celebrity" alone gives their comments authority. He complains, "And who are these actors and actresses that we should listen to them? On stage, they are human parrots, regurgitating what others have written for them. Off stage, why would we think that they had any wisdom?" The left doesn't have many celebrity intellectuals, because it doesn't have the same system of manufacturing that the right has employed. Many have pointed out there is no left version of Rush Limbaugh. In the vacuum that exists, Hollywood stars, or other entertainment figures, substitute. And they remain rather fat targets.

Unlike the right, which promotes its writers, public figures, former political consultants turned journalists, the left does not. The few that exist have come through the same star-making machinery as Dick Morris has, proximity to power, often the presidency itself. George Stephanopoulos, who comes in for a few knocks from Morris in *Off With Their Heads,* made that trip. And now, at ABC, Stephanopoulos has been trying to fashion some centrist credentials while his show trails in the ratings.

Progressives are partly responsible for this lack of stars in their own ranks; left intellectuals do not like to praise any but themselves.

There is too much battling for the few prominent positions that exist. They do have a presence in academia, but not much in the mass media. Other than universities, no large institutions actively showcase them. The right has had a couple of decades of think-tank promotion of a young cadre, helped along by new publications and television networks and shows, to make their names and faces known.

After Hollywood, Morris takes on France, the latest right-wing whipping post. He knows what anyone who didn't sleep through a high school world history course knows, though he makes good use of numbers here, especially casualty figures in World Wars I and II. Morris is a numbers maven. He saves the best for last. The final four chapters are worth the price of the book. His depiction of the scandal of the permanent Congress, and the malfeasance it perpetrated preparing the way for the corporate scandals of the Bush years, is a valuable contribution. Here Morris, the insider, rises from Morris, the mud-hurler. He knows how elections work, given his years as a highly paid political consultant who has worked both sides of the street.

Morris follows his sobering assessment of Congress with attacks on the use of the tobacco settlement, where states now have made a devil's bargain with the tobacco companies, basing their economic health on the health of the tobacco companies, since the states are dependent on the huge tobacco settlement they "won." Morris then goes after the nursing home industry. Throughout the book, there are scattered criticisms of President Bush, and these last two sections contain the most. Bush will need to mount a "leave no old person behind" campaign to counter this bad press.

Morris's book, ultimately, becomes a difficult one to pigeonhole, insofar as Morris believes a number of contradictory things. He – like his most famous client, Bill Clinton – seems to be able to compartmentalize. Morris's book contains a number of compartments, some at odds, and some with little connection to one another. But all of them are lively, and a few pertinent and important. For a man who has worked for all sorts of people, perhaps it isn't strange that Morris has produced a book that will offend many and please many. The surprise is that they are likely to be the same people.

First appeared in the *Chicago Sun-Times,* June 22, 2003.
Review of Dick Morris, *Off With Their Heads: Duplicity, Obstruction, and Deception in American Politics, Media, Business, and Life* (New York: Regan Books/HarperCollins, 2003).

Kevin Phillips: American Dynasty (1)

Well, it's officially the presidential campaign year, and Kevin Phillips has set a high water mark for any other Bush books appearing in 2004 with the publication of *American Dynasty*. Given its relevance and revelations, no other work is likely to surpass it.

Kevin Phillips is no bomb-thrower, no hot-headed upstart out to make a reputation by means of an inflammatory exposé, but a seasoned, wise man, with deep roots in the Republican Party. Nonetheless, in many ways, *American Dynasty* is more incendiary than the Bill-Clinton-murdered-Vince-Foster books so popular during the nineties. Unlike those productions, Phillips' book is not sensationalistic, and its claims are historically verifiable.

Kevin Phillips' career is instructional: his first book, *The Emerging Republican Majority* (1969), was accepted as a bible for the party faithful, predicting, as it did, the successful Sun Belt-dominated rise of the GOP. But, since 1990, with the publication of *The Politics of Rich and Poor,* Phillips has become more and more alarmed over the divergence of wealth and social position in this country. His last book, *Wealth and Democracy* (2002), is a clarion call, warning readers that democracy and such polarization can't coexist.

American Dynasty extends that analysis, centering on one family, which he calls "the House of Bush." His book tells the story of four generations of Bushes, covering over a century, from World War I, up to the ongoing Iraq conflict.

Phillips examines, at length, the current president's grandfather Prescott Bush (and his father-in-law, George Herbert Walker), and Prescott Bush's attempts to duck his family's "aura of wealth" when he ran for the Senate: "The original, mild version of the family's public ethos began with Prescott Bush, whose representation of midcentury Connecticut required much less artifice than did catering to the family's later southern electoral base. . . . he had tried to minimize the connotations of his rich-family, Wall Street resume by seeming less stuffy and emphasizing his involvement in charitable, educational, and civil rights causes."

What Phillips makes clear is how similar successive generations of the political Bushes are: each masquerade as the common man. For those who have paid keen attention to the career of George W. Bush, a lot of the facts in *American Dynasty* are not news, however startling. But it is Phillips' training as a historian, and the context he provides, that make his book so fresh and damning.

Indeed, having spent so much time considering the Bush family, Phillips admits to being somewhat aghast at what he discovered:

> In examining two Bush presidencies and a four-generation pursuit of national prominence and power through an unusual lens – one that highlighted elite associations, recurring political practices, and dynastic ambitions – I learned much more, and I admit to being shocked at some of what I found. The result is an unusual and unflattering portrait of a great family (in power, not morality) that has built a base over the course of the twentieth century in the back corridors of the new military-industrial complex and in close

association with the growing national security establishment. In doing so, the family has threaded its way through damning political and armaments scandals and, since the 1980s, faint hints, never more, of acts that in another climate might have led to presidential impeachment.

If the writing of poetry is thought of as "emotion recollected in tranquility," histories, usually, share the pose of tranquility. Phillips' book maintains that tone, though the experience of reading it is disconcerting, similar to reading histories of the Vietnam War while that long war was being waged.

Phillips seems most exercised by two verities at the heart of the Bush family: the first being that their wealth and power comes principally from the investment communities, oil being just a paper holding to them, not a tangible thing that produces something (other than profit), and that this interest has been forever entwined with government intelligence work. The Bushes, son and father, might live in Texas, but their family oil and business interests are in the Middle East and the Caribbean.

The intelligence-global-corporation combination produced amounted to a government within a government, which, at this point, is now becoming one and the same thing. Phillips writes: "No previous presidential family has been so wholeheartedly involved with a single economic sector over two generations, yet with so little scrutiny of the resulting narrowness of its public policy views. If representing Texas for ten or twenty years stamped a senator's or congressman's view of the national agenda, what would have been imprinted on a presidential family by a century of working to increase the wealth of a small slice of Upper America?"

Senator Prescott Bush and his father-in-law's involvements with Nazi-era German holding companies became useful resources for the post-World War II CIA, especially when the Cold War pitted two former allies against one another, our country and the USSR.

The interlocking directorships, and contacts with the Yale graduates who made up a good part of the east coast investment and political establishment, became, over time, a permanent power base. Phillips shows how "crony capitalism" is not a new phenomenon, but has been the basis for business in the Bush family for nearly 100 years.

When George H. W. Bush was elected president in 1988, many Americans were aware that he had been head of the CIA. Fewer understood that method of ascendancy to the oval office was unheard of in American history. Most didn't give it much thought. Phillips' recounting of the Bush family history, and the history of the OSS and CIA, is thorough and troubling. It's a small world, and Phillips's examination of the personnel of the second Bush White House is proof of that.

American Dynasty revisits many national traumas through the direct involvement of the Bushes: the Kennedy assassination, Cuba, Nicaragua, Arms for Hostages, the Iran-Iraq War, up to, and including, the current Iraq conflict.

This steady march of history, and Phillips' marshaling of evidence, has cumulative power. None of the other recent critical, liberal books about George W. Bush has this sort of sweep or impact.

Phillips doesn't neglect the simple fact that Bill Clinton impeded the rise of the House of Bush and the 2000 election almost thwarted its restoration: ". . . Bill Clinton's moral shortcomings and impeachment may have been a precondition for Bush's accession in 2000. Even so, the speed and seriousness of the family's efforts to make George W. Bush governor of Texas in 1994 and to likewise for his brother in Florida more than hinted at its higher goals."

In the same way that the Bush White House calls a spade a plow, Phillips points out how the anger that drove the impeachment of Bill

Clinton may have worn the public face of the most yokel-like members of Congress, the loony right of the talk radio circuit, but actually was fueled by the grievances of the Bush family and its circle of highly-placed establishment figures. The Clinton destruction crew (the vast right wing conspiracy) was a very successful version of deceptive branding, letting the parochial members of Congress take the heat for the excesses of the Clinton haters.

This deep-seated anger carried over to the contested 2000 election. The Republicans fought a no-holds-barred battle, feeding off eight years of rage at the Clinton usurpation; Al Gore did much less, feeling equivocal, at best, because of Clinton's failings, plus Gore's old-fashioned and un-Bush-like worries about the legitimacy of the presidency being weakened if he protested too much: "Gore, the first Tennessee presidential candidate ever to have been a member of the Harvard Board of Overseers, declined to fight. . . ." Phillips points out how both Bushes came to high office through manipulated elections: the October surprise of the 1980 election, and the Supreme Court decision that ended the 2000 contest.

But, these issues are relative sideshows to the main event, the depiction of the rise of the Bush dynasty, and how dynasties are antithetical to democratic systems.

American Dynasty is so sober and steeped in learning, even critics of the president will find themselves wondering how President Bush, or any man's family, could stand this depth of exposure. Most likely, Kevin Phillips will be attacked by the same machinery that so effectively pummeled Bill Clinton.

All in all, *American Dynasty* is as depressing as it is brilliant and important. Doubtless, it will become one of the most talked about books of the year.

First appeared in the *Chicago Sun-Times,* January 18, 2004. Review of Kevin Phillips, *American Dynasty: Aristocracy, Fortune, and the Politics of Deceit in the House of Bush* (New York: Viking, 2004).

Kevin Phillips: American Theocracy (2)

Kevin Phillips tells us he has been "studying and writing about the emerging Republican presidential coalition for half a century." He calls his last three books – *Wealth and Democracy* (2002), which concentrated on how democracies are stressed when income gaps widen, *American Dynasty* (2004), his dissection and exploration of the Bush family, and the one under present consideration, *American Theocracy* – "indictments," adding that such an outcome was something he never would have "imagined" when he started writing his first book, "*The Emerging Republican Majority* back in 1966." Phillips has evolved from a staunch Republican who served in Republican administrations to a recovering Republican critic.

American Theocracy is an indictment – though the defendants are legion, or, as Walt Kelly's old Pogo cartoon would have it, "they are us." Of course, there are some specific bad actors, but all the rest of us appear as enablers: "Reckless dependency on shrinking oil supplies, a milieu of radicalized (and much too influential) religion, and a reliance on borrowed money – debt, in its ballooning size and multiple domestic and international deficits – now constitute the three major perils to the United States of the twenty-first century."

Much has been said, and written, during recent years about the ascendancy of fundamentalist religions across the world, about the dominance of oil politics, and the growth of both debt and the growing gap between the income of the rich and everyone else. What hasn't been done hitherto is to take those subjects and show how they are interconnected, making clear not just the "what," but also the "why," and the "how," and the "who."

Phillips's book serves as an invaluable resource, given its marshaling of facts and figures, as well as its breadth and depth of historical analysis. He employs a historian's measured perspective and clarity of expression, though it is likely that he will be accused of rank partisanship by those most stung by his analysis, those he labels "The Erring Republican Majority." He moves easily from both academic scholarship, and the popular press, for information that supports his theme, which is that no explanation for the current state of affairs "can ignore the Republican party and its electoral coalition's" encouragement of "U.S. oil vulnerability, excessive indebtedness, and indulgence of radical religion."

The Bush administration claims the Iraq war is not about oil, but Phillips makes the case that of course Iraq is about oil – since quite a bit of the world's history is about oil, or its larger category, energy. Phillips explains – perhaps more than some readers may want to know – how the Spanish and Dutch and English lost their preeminence among, and domination of, nations: "Over generations, the world's energy leaderships – seventeenth-century Dutch ingenuity with water, wind, and wood, British aptitude with coal, and the U.S. cleverness with oil – have invariably developed related infrastructures of corporate, government, and cultural commitment. One generation's innovations become another's entrenchments."

As Phillips does with energy, he provides an exacting examination of religion in America, its precedents, factions and movements. Indeed, given the three-panel aspect of this book – oil, religion, debt – Phillips is able to make use of his own scholarship of the last five decades. He takes, from his earlier books, the pertinent parts, and elaborates upon them to reinforce his new arguments. *American Theocracy* is, in this way, a capstone to his life's work.

Phillips has been able to see, over the passage of time, which of his insights and predictions have taken hold in the world. And he appears truly alarmed by those that have. What was barely mentioned in his first book, *The Emerging Republican Majority,* forty years ago, becomes, in this one, an entire section: "The Southernization of America." He admits that hitherto he had written "little about southern fundamentalists and evangelicals," and, by way of correction, they appear front and center in this volume. Phillips painstakingly shows how the Civil War may also have been a religious war, as well as a war of emancipation, and how our current electoral map of Red and Blue America is just as accurately a depiction of America's church-going habits as it is of its political allegiances. They are, in Phillips view, one and the same: even the "battleground or 'new border' states can also be located by a religious calculus."

There is plenty of calculus in *American Theocracy.* Phillips loves numbers, and he supplies a lot of them – as well as graphs and charts, each startling in its own way. Though he makes use of grand terms," Southernization," "Financialization," "Disenlightment," he takes pains – and pages – to explain how each works. Phillips has braided his three unwieldy subjects into a forceful and provocative rhetorical whip. And he does lash out: "Never before has a U.S. political coalition been so dominated by an array of outsider religious denominations caught up in biblical morality, distrust of science, and a global imperative of political and religious evangelicalism."

Democrats are not spared: "The inadequacy of the Democrats – every four years they seem to resemble the Not Ready for Prime Time Players who made Saturday Night Live a byword three decades ago – complicates things but hardly excuses what the Republican party has become." But, overall, Phillips's book is thoughtful and somber jeremiad, one written throughout with a graceful wryness. Its brilliance is so abundant that even its asides are insightful: Phillips points out, speaking of evangelical, fundamentalist, and Pentacostal churches, "Broadcast, publishing, and direct-mail empires have grown up around these fellowships and communities, creating umbrellas against the effects of secular communications. The viewpoints of so-called sophisticates have little access to the minds of the faithful." Our "age of information" has become a new "tower of Babel:" individuals can pick and chose what they want to believe, and still find many adherents to agree with them.

It will be a shame if Phillips's important and timely book is restricted to "so-called sophisticates." Everyone should have access to what *American Theocracy* so powerfully tells us about our country at this critical time.

First appeared in the *Chicago Sun-Times,* March 12, 2006.
Review of Kevin Phillips, *American Theocracy: The Peril and Politics of Radical Religion, Oil, and Borrowed Money in the 21st Century* (New York: Viking, 2006).

Molly Ivins and Lou Dubose: *Bushwacked*

Molly Ivins, depending on how you look at it, has had the good luck to be in the right place at the right time – in Texas, that is. She, and her sidekick, Lou Dubose, have been able to chronicle the life and career of the forty-third president from the ground up. But, had Al Gore been the favorite candidate of Supreme Court Justice Antonin Scalia, this book wouldn't exist.

Not that the two authors didn't try to make that happen back then. Their first book, *Shrub: The Short but Happy Political Life of George W. Bush,* laid out in 2000 most of the reasons not to vote for then Texas governor Bush. And the voters did reject him. But, that book's title was way too hopeful. President Bush's political life isn't short, though. Despite the long odds, if it is brought to an end in '04, *Bushwacked* will have helped.

To say that Ivins and Dubose have written a devastating portrait (and indictment) of "GeeDubya" and his administration is an understatement.

Bushwacked, despite its snappy title, isn't just another example of the current legion of political attack books. That's what I expected, given the fact that Ivins is a syndicated columnist, one of the most perceptive and biting of the liberal persuasion. When she writes in short length, she's a master at cracking a rhetorical bullwhip. But what I found was more along the lines of an I. F. Stone investigation, western style. Stone was a maverick Washington journalist famous for reading what other reporters overlooked, long government reports and endless congressional records, and finding nuggets therein. Ivins and Dubose follow that lead. Their book delves deeply below the surface of weekly pontificating. As they point out, "Keeping an eye on the Corps of Engineers alone is enough to occupy a citizen full-time." But they manage to follow down the stories of the Bush administration's "malfeeance" (as they print George W.'s pronunciation of malfeasance). Ivins and Dubose accomplish this through both printed sources, and interviews with the subjects involved: "This book is about the connections between what happens in people's lives and the decisions made by often obscure parts of the federal government." Then they add their typical self-deprecating stylistic flourish: "Some concept, eh? Policy matters; stop the presses."

Most of people they deal with are the folk who are on the short end of the policies President Bush has set down – though one of the best chapters details the effect on one Texas millionaire, who considers Bush's largesse to the rich scandalous. Here's what the tax cuts have wrought, what the environmental roll-backs have done, why hamburgers occasionally kill people, portraits of the children who are left behind, how the Bush-Cheney energy handouts to their corporate friends, while championing government deregulation and competition over cooperation, result in the August blackout, and other debacles yet to come.

But, what the book ultimately offers is a cure to the national historical amnesia the country has suffered since 9/11. Ivins and Dubose aren't taken in by the image most Americans have been sold of George W. Bush. They watched him develop as a public figure up close and personal in Texas. One of the myths they debunk is that George W. "speaks" Spanish: a couple of sentences come out and "then they cue the mariachis."

But, as they acknowledge, Americans want to think our president is fluent in the language of Cervantes. Cynicism and optimism are at war in the American character. Missouri might call itself the "show me" state, but we all live in the "land of opportunity." They point out that, after 9/11, "The whole country was dying to help – ready to donate blood, money, sign up for the Marines, ride bikes, anything we could think of. Instead our president told us to shop."

Here's an example of the authors' regular history-rich method. When discussing Bush's fight in '02 over extending (or, rather, not extending) unemployment insurance, we learn: "Unemployment insurance was a New Deal program, created in 1935. Even then everyone understood that it served two purposes. Soft-hearted liberals celebrate the first: it provides income support for jobless workers and their families. Clear-eyed business people celebrate the second: it props up the economy by keeping consumer spending alive during economic slowdowns. Those dollars flow right through the hands of the unemployed working class and into the bank accounts of the owning class. The dirty secret of the New Deal is what a giveaway it was to businesses big and small." That sort of clarity leaps from every page. If there is a populist style, Ivins and Dubose have mastered it.

Writing about the Iraq adventure, they report that "the war itself brought an almost surreal disjuncture between what Americans saw of the war and what the rest of the world saw. A pop-eyed young reporter for FOX News, assigned to watch Arab television, announced indignantly, 'They are reporting about a completely different war. They say this is a war of unprovoked aggression in order to get the Iraqi oil fields and control the whole region.' As they say in Sweetwater, no shit?"

It is just that sort of earthiness that causes the authors to comment so sharply on the media's general timid superficiality when it comes to covering the Bush presidency. In the final chapter, they write, "No fair, we think, to sit around taking potshots at the people trying to govern the joint, unless you can present better ideas." The better ideas follow – ending "the legalized bribery that has rotted the democratic political system" by installing campaign finance reform with teeth and getting more people to vote, along with putting a stop to the "polarized system of redistricting," which leads to endless congressional job security and the lack of incentive to compromise. Though these ideas, and other ones the authors put forth, are good ones that would bring about better government, given the evidence of their book, the chance of implementing such ideas seems slim to none. Be that as it may, *Bushwacked,* without a doubt, is one of the most important books of the political year.

First appeared in the *Chicago Sun-Times,* September 21, 2003. Review of Molly Ivins and Lou Dubose, *Bushwacked: Life in George W. Bush's America* (New York: Random House, 2003).

Robert B. Reich: Reason

A presidential campaign year has become, for political books, what Christmas is for toys: a time to sell, when everyone is prepared to buy more than usual. This extended campaign season has been good for the Democrats's side, producing a number of best sellers: Kevin Phillips's *American Dynasty,* Molly Ivins & Lou Dubose's *Bushwacked,* as well as insider-fueled books such as Richard Clarke's *Against All Enemies,* Ron Suskind's *The Price of Loyalty,* and Bob Woodward's *Plan of Attack.*

Robert B. Reich now weighs in with his own book. Reich, Bill Clinton's first-term secretary of labor, wrote a critical insider book on the Clinton White House, called *Locked in the Cabinet* (1997), which came out during Clinton's embattled second term. But it is President Bush who may have set the record for insider books appearing during a first term. Reich's main target in *Reason* is not Bush, but the ideological force Reich calls "radical conservatism" and its shock troops: "Radcons," for short.

Reich is not trying to write the typical attack book, but a positive one, a call for a rebirth of a liberal ascendancy, instead of the conservative one we've all seen lately. The first third of Reich's book could have been titled "Liberalism for Dummies," for he is more or less introducing readers to liberalism, its present and past incarnations. America, Reich points out, was founded on liberal principles. Tolerance is its bulwark. Why have we come so far from that understanding? Reich offers: "We live in an era when 'liberalism,' a great and essential tradition, is mocked, and its meaning grossly distorted. Radical conservatives have made a point of doing so, akin to demonizing an enemy during a war. They have depicted liberalism as a caricature of the sixties left."

Reich lists and refutes the "liberal" sins often cited by Radcons: "moral laxity and sexual permissiveness," "taxes on the middle class in order to spend money on the undeserving poor," "the creed of 'blame America first' pacifists," and so on.

As befits a former secretary of labor, Reich spends a great deal of time on the effects of liberal economics: "American liberalism has also functioned like a balance wheel, saving capitalism from its worst excesses. It moved reformers at the turn of the last century to stand firm against monopolies and political corruption. It inspired progressives to battle for safety, health, and food and drug regulations. In the wake of the Great Crash of 1929, it led New Dealers to regulate banking and clean up Wall Street."

Though Reich is a booster for liberalism, his book does make clear how it has been undermined during the last two decades: "In the twenty-four years between 1980 and 2004, the Democrats controlled the executive branch for exactly eight. Now Republicans have taken it all over, including most governorships."

Who is to blame? Reich is not completely clear about that: it is not so much liberals' failure, he contends, but the Radcons' superior organizing and thirst for power: "Radcons began organizing two decades ago around a set of common values, with an eye on the long term. They recruited people who share their beliefs and who would run for local, state, or federal office. They supported the campaigns of these people and held them accountable once in office.... They recruited broadcast pundits and writers, and supported them and spread the word. They created long-term alliances and coalitions with the religious right, small businesses, trade associations, and key lobbyists in Washington."

Whereas, Reich points out, liberals have fragmented themselves, and, given the nature of liberalism, have resisted putting aside intellectual and doctrinaire differences to come together into one cohesive group: "The only time there's even a semblance of a national Democratic Party is when Democrats come up with a presidential candidate."

For die-hard liberals, Reich's information is not often news, though his own synthesis is valuable. But it isn't likely that this book will be read by many who wouldn't want to be called "liberal." In the heyday of the liberal ascendancy, pre-1980s, liberals were derided by the left as middle-of-the-road copouts. Reich is all that – middle-of-the-road – but these days, middle-of-the-road looks pretty radical.

Throughout *Reason,* Reich offers insights based not just on his knowledge of liberal thought, but those generated by his own personal experience. He's particularly sharp and fresh in his critique of Newt Gingrich, one of the leaders of the Radcon ascendancy: "[Gingrich] liked to describe himself as a revolutionary force, but he often behaved more like a naughty boy – grinning uncontrollably.... His office was adorned with figurines of dinosaurs, as you might find in the bedrooms of little boys who dream of one day being huge and powerful."

Reich often quotes William Bennett, Robert Bork, and Michael Savage as Radcon foils – Bork, especially, who taught both Reich and the Clintons at Yale law school. "Negative patriotism," Reich writes, "is just about all we hear from Radcons. Talk show host Michael Savage's harangues are typical: '[O]ur future as a nation depends on reawakening to the American identity that made us the greatest nation on the Earth,'" and Reich continues, quoting Bork, "'... the United States

[was] more or less culturally unified in the 1950s, but now we are reversing direction and becoming a chaos of cultures that cannot, or more accurately will not, be unified.'"

Reich comments: "Savage and Bork long for a cultural purity America never had." But, what Reich's book illustrates is what the Radcons long for is not so much cultural purity as the continued purity of just who runs things in this country, which is pretty much the same folk who ran the show in the 1950s.

Reason is a number of books at once: part memoir, part explication of the contending and contentious ruling ideologies of Red and Blue America – radical conservatism and liberalism at odds – and part call-to-arms. It is not a Bush-bashing book, but it does admirably dissect the political world Bush represents and the high stakes involved. And it will introduce and reacquaint readers with America's long-established liberal underpinnings. *Reason* most succeeds in that mission. Whether it succeeds as a call-to-arms, only November 2 will make clear.

First appeared in the *Chicago Sun-Times,* May 9, 2004.
Review of Robert B. Reich, *Reason: Why Liberals Will Win the Battle for America* (New York: Knopf, 2004).

David McCullough: John Adams

Of American historians, David McCullough is the most gifted and accomplished storyteller. Throughout his long and distinguished career, he has written books about great achievements of engineering: the Brooklyn Bridge, the Panama Canal, monumental endeavors which take learning, courage, and the labor of many hands. In his latest book, *John Adams,* he writes about the making of America, an abstraction that became real, took on shape, produced a government with enduring structures, which, at its beginning, was very much a work in progress, and one that remains so today.

McCullough is present at the creation through the long life (1735–1826) of Massachusetts born and bred John Adams, our second president, "the 'voice' of independence," as Adams was known to his contemporaries.

The entire Adams family is a gift to historians. As McCullough writes in his acknowledgments, "There is no comparable written record of a prominent American family." During an age of limited literacy, John Adams was hyper-literate. Among the many astounding feats McCullough's majestic account describes – amazing ocean crossings, startling encounters, momentous events – the constant movement of Adams's quill pen upon the page is perhaps the most dumbfounding.

Any writer would be impressed by such productive labor, and McCullough is no exception. His 1993 Pulitzer-Prize-winning volume, *Truman,* was criticized by some for the author's evident fondness for its subject: Harry Truman. Happily, McCullough likes John Adams, too, and, given his vivid portrait of Adams, it is difficult for a reader not to share his admiration and regard.

Every generation should have its own accounts of historic figures, even those who have been well-examined previously. The life and times of these personages need to be passed through the contemporary filters of our own age. McCullough does this splendidly. His depiction of eighteenth century America is stereoscopic. It blends into one image, two pictures: the historic facts of the 1700s and early 1800s seen through the point of view of the late twentieth century. It allows us to view it afresh in three dimensions. It's better than the movies.

And what scenes! The Continental Congress gathering, the signing of the Declaration of Independence, the American Revolution, the tumult and the tedium accompanying the birth of a nation. As John Adams asserted, he lived "in serious times."

McCullough uses the towering Thomas Jefferson and Adams as contrasting figures throughout. In a letter to Adams, by his old friend Benjamin Rush, Rush wrote, speaking of Adams and Jefferson, "I consider you and him as the North and South Poles of the American Revolution. Some talked, some wrote, and some fought to promote and establish it, but you and Mr. Jefferson thought for us all."

Indeed, they were North and South Poles. Here is McCullough on that difference: "By 1776, with the addition of the land inherited from his father-in-law, Jefferson reckoned himself a wealthy man and lived like one. With the inheritance also came substantial debts and still more slaves, but then in Virginia this was seen as a matter of course. The whole economy and way of life was built on slaves and debt, with tobacco planters in particular dependent on slave labor and money borrowed from English creditors against future crops. John Adams, by contrast, had neither debts nor slaves and abhorred the idea of either." Adams did inherit the farm he was born on, some forty acres, after his father, Deacon John, died; owning the land made Adams a "freeholder, and thus the equal of anyone."

McCullough walks us through the steamy streets of Philadelphia in summer, sits us at the tables, and lets us eat the fare served in Adams' home ("a pudding of corn meal, molasses, and butter"), has us attend a mastectomy (yes, a mastectomy) performed on Adams's forty-six year old daughter, Nabby, puts us bedside at many an affecting death scene, places us in cities beset by pestilence. He also guides us through the intricacies of the political factions and arguments that followed the nation's founding, the Federalists (pro-British, favoring strong central government), the Anti-Federalists (pro-French, championing states' rights), the Republicans, and their subsets.

In a long book about one of America's founding fathers, some readers will be surprised to spend such a large part of it in France, England and Holland. Adams was our country's most significant ambassador, and there are more details of diplomacy within McCullough's pages than descriptions of the military encounters of the Revolution, more time spent in the salons of the powerful than on the sacrificial battlefields of the common soldier.

McCullough, without calling attention to them, describes many contemporary parallels, some profound, some amusing. Adams complains about the need for eighteenth century "spinmeisters," the fact a politician "must get his picture drawn, his statue made, and must hire all the artists in his turn to set about works to spread his name, make the mob stare and gape, and perpetuate his fame." Adams's wife Abigail, herself "an avid reader," the Hillary Clinton of her day, disliked the press no less than our recent First Lady did, charging that some editors had the "malice and falsehood of Satan." And, given the present occupant of the White House, it is both timely and important to have the full story of our second president and his son who became the sixth.

McCullough never lets us forget the physical actuality of John Adams's world – and not just through his adept descriptions of the street-life and domestic habitats. McCullough writes: "In truth, black slavery had long since become an accepted part of life in all the thirteen colonies. Of a total population in the colonies of nearly 2,500,000 people in 1776, approximately one in five were slaves, some 500,000 men, women and children."

And, later: "The great majority of Americans lived and worked on farms, and fully two-thirds of the population was concentrated in a narrow band along the eastern seaboard from Maine to Spanish Florida. . . . Approximately half the territory of the United States in 1789 was still occupied by American Indians, most of whom lived west of the Appalachians, and though no one knew how many there were, they probably numbered 100,000."

McCullough not only makes Adams's time live, he prepares the ground for the history yet to come. One can feel the Civil War looming. He quotes Adams writing Jefferson in 1819, predicting that a struggle between the states over slavery "might rend this mighty fabric in twain."

Adams owned no slaves: almost a unique condition among the prominent founding fathers. McCullough, nonetheless, does not overlook Adams's faults or missteps. His account of Adams's role in the perfidious Alien and Sedition Acts of 1798, directed at the anti-Federalists, is forthright and complete, as well as his depiction of Adams's eccentricities, such as his wanting a fancy title ("His Majesty the President") for our first president, George Washington.

Both Jefferson and Adams were contradictory figures, though, as even the opposition press of the time admitted, "Adams is an aristocrat only in theory," whereas Jefferson was one in practice.

McCullough's teeming and compelling volume captures all the contradictions of the age, as well as shedding light on our own. "'Who shall write the history of the American Revolution? Who can write it?'" Adams asked Jefferson toward the end of his life. "'Nobody,' Jefferson answered, 'except perhaps in its external facts.'"

Thomas Jefferson was right about many things, but wrong about that. David McCullough has done the job magnificently. And, for that, we are all in his debt.

First appeared in the *Chicago Sun-Times,* June 3, 2001. Review of David McCullough, *John Adams* (New York: Simon & Schuster, 2001).

Edmund Morris: *Theodore Rex*

Throughout the 555 riveting pages of action-packed narrative of *Theodore Rex,* Edmund Morris's long awaited sequel to his Pulitzer-Prize-winning volume, *The Rise of Theodore Roosevelt*(1979), one can feel the sense of relief and zest Morris had returning to Teddy Roosevelt as a subject after the morass of conflicting emotions and literary hesitations he displayed in *Dutch,* his 1999 "memoir" of Ronald Reagan.

Morris's new book picks up Roosevelt's story at full gallop, with the vice president "bouncing in a buckboard down the rainswept slopes of Mount Marcy," after Roosevelt had received telegrams at his vacation cabin in the Adirondacks documenting "the spread of gangrene through his bullet-ridden Chief."

William McKinley's assassination in 1901, at the start of his second term, by the anarchist Leon Czolgosz, elevated Roosevelt to the presidency, and exposed him to charges of illegitimacy, not so much from the public, which accepted him readily, but from within his own party. McKinley was hardly cold in his grave when Mark Hanna, the Republican power broker, told Roosevelt, "Do not think anything about a second term." This dynamic – acceptance by the public at large and opposition within his own party – was a hallmark of Roosevelt's seven years in office, and kept his natural skepticism fresh.

At forty-two, Roosevelt was the youngest man to serve as president, and America was the youngest of world powers. He inherited the job at the dawn of a new century. Modern America was being invented then: its institutions, its language, its landscape. And Roosevelt put his stamp on all of it; he is even responsible for the "teddy bear."

That Roosevelt became president because of a murder was, indeed, "Rex"-like, king-like. The novelist Henry James dubbed him "Theodore Rex," though that was because Roosevelt enhanced the powers of the executive branch of government. But, Roosevelt was haunted by his method of ascendancy. His crashing through life (he was the T. Rex of presidents), his abundant energies and exaggerated appetites, were life-long defenses against the charges of usurpation, and fear of chaos he saw lurking at the edges of democracy. Morris makes Roosevelt's stance clear: "Youth, size, and strength: these things, surely, would render America proof against the anarchic strain."

Morris's *The Rise of Theodore Roosevelt* was published in 1979. He interrupted work on the second volume for the contentious Reagan memoir, but that experience certainly aided the book at hand: since Morris was Reagan's authorized biographer, he had free access to the White House during a long presidency, and *Theodore Rex* is the beneficiary.

Morris can, and does, re-imagine Roosevelt's daily life as president, in all its permutations. (The current president will envy Roosevelt's long summer vacations.) Morris's familiarity with the territory enhances his narrative. He knows, firsthand, how power is distributed throughout the government, and what the force of personality can bestow on the office.

Morris's portrait intertwines a number of narrative threads. One is Roosevelt the quixotic imperialist, spreading American hegemony around the globe; another is Roosevelt the visionary, who alters the landscape, ours and the hemisphere's, with the creation of the Panama Canal and the federalizing of so many of our natural wonders.

And there is the domestic Roosevelt, the trust-buster, the rich boy with a yen for a "square deal" for everyone, the man of privilege who, nonetheless, was sympathetic to issues of class and race. As Roosevelt said himself, "I find I can work best with those people in whom the money sense is not too highly developed."

Morris follows these parallel stories, scene after scene. It is not so much a cinematic depiction, but more like modern television drama, where storylines alternate throughout the hour.

Surveying the world, Roosevelt saw, Morris writes, "A gulf, not merely of years but of ideology, separated him from these heroes of the past. They had fought to preserve the Union; he had fought to create a world power. The old soldiers had cheered when the young soldiers liberated Cuba, but they fell silent when similar 'freedoms' were imposed on Puerto Rico, Guam, and the Philippines."

Following McKinley's footsteps, Roosevelt was a proponent of expansion (and his weight increased in size as did American territories). It wasn't quite the racist "white man's burden," but Roosevelt did see it as, at least, a burden, a responsibility. Morris, doubtless because of the earlier volume, and its Pulitzer Prize, is such a fan of Roosevelt he cannot brook any criticism of him. *Theodore Rex* is Roosevelt as Roosevelt might have wished to have seen himself.

Luckily, such an impassioned and opinionated point of view by an historian is warranted by its subject. Roosevelt deserves this sort of allegiance (perhaps more than Ronald Reagan did, who tested Morris's loyalty and caused his torturous, shape-shifting strategies in *Dutch*).

The undercurrent of class war at the end of the Gilded Age, the savage against the elite, as sketched by Morris, is stark. He describes the view from a train: "for a few seconds Roosevelt and his fellow passengers could exchange stares with four hundred filthy coal miners. Boys, youths, and old men (were they really old, or just toothless?) stood bareheaded, leaning on picks and shovels. Their small, smudged eyes (only the creases showing white), squat bodies, and tape-wrapped shins proclaimed them to be Slavs. It was impossible to tell from their swarthy expressions whether the sight of a presidential cortege moved them or not. Implicit in the stare of those eyes, the power of those knobby hands, was labor's historic threat of violence against capital."

Morris is comfortable with the ruling class (which is why he was chosen for the Reagan book), but he seems to share Roosevelt's point of view – willing to be a contrarian, and take criticism from the racists of his day. He was very much in the tradition of the socially conscious upper-class Republican; that – plus his addiction to the outdoors and rugged sport – made him an archetypal figure, a sort that today's upper classes do not aspire to be.

Though Roosevelt worried darkly about the immigrant unrest in the coal fields and large cities, he knew reforms had to come about, lest his fears of rebellion be realized. He was a pragmatist, and his abundant common sense was leavened with good cheer, a healthy mix. His views on race were, for his time, also progressive. He had Booker T. Washington, the famous African American educator, to dinner: the first black man to dine with a president in the White House. Morris writes: "The President felt entirely at ease. It seemed 'so natural and so proper' to have Washington wield his silver. Here, dark and dignified among the paler company, was living proof of what he had always preached: that Negroes could rise to the social heights, at least on an individual basis. Collective equality was clearly out of the question, given their 'natural limitations' in the evolutionary scheme of things."

The response of most of the common press to Washington's presence at the meal is shocking to read. Roosevelt consistently spoke out against lynchings and mob violence throughout his presidency, and, until its end, when he became embroiled in the Brownsville case, where he had a black regiment dishonorably discharged on trumped-up charges of rioting, he was seen as a friend to African Americans.

Roosevelt was one of the few true intellectuals to have become president. (And, when compared to the last, Bill Clinton, Clinton appears to be the palest of imitations.) *The Works of Theodore Roosevelt* "had begun to come out in 1900 and bulked as large as fifteen-volume sets of history, natural history, biography, criticism, memoir, and political philosophy." Roosevelt was the only president to earn "a living with a pen," before becoming president, unlike modern presidents who earn a fortune from a book after holding office.

One of Roosevelt's last Messages to Congress "included demands for inheritance and income taxes, national incorporation of interstate businesses, greater federal power over railroad rates, compulsory investigation of major labor disputes, wider application of the eight-hour day, and no fewer than four new battleships."

Roosevelt was a man of his times well ahead of his times. Morris's important, stirring biography deserves to be hailed as a major contribution to the scholarship of the period. What it skirts of the other historic currents of the time is more than made up for given all the brilliant light he sheds on Roosevelt as President. As Roosevelt habitually would say when greeting a new acquaintance, most readers will be completely, "Dee-lighted!"

First appeared in the *Chicago Sun-Times,*
November 18, 2001. Review of Edmund Morris,
Theodore Rex (New York: Random House, 2001).

Steve Neal: Happy Days Are Here Again

Steve Neal's posthumously published history of the 1932 Democratic convention is a public service and a parting gift. Neal leaves the nation and his city with a valuable document, pertinent to the times – given the two political presidential conventions to come this summer – and to the city he loved, detailing the role Chicago played in the beginning of FDR's road to the presidency.

The history of modern political campaign books usually begins with Teddy White's *The Making of the President, 1960,* on the JFK election. Back in 1932, there was a great deal of press coverage (and many more newspapers being published), but there weren't a host of insider-laced accounts of the presidential race appearing shortly after the election such as we've had since 1960, books that detail the ins and outs of the conventions. Neal reaches back through history and produces one for us. And it is remarkable history that he provides. FDR, given his four terms, has becomes such a keystone in American history that the image of him as president is the one most people carry. How he became the presidential nominee of his party for the first time has vanished from the collective memory. Neal's resurrection of just how it happened is quite an awakening, showing just how close FDR came to not being the nominee in 1932, a circumstance leading to who-knows-what, given all the momentous history that followed.

Neal covers not just the political emergence of FDR as a presidential contender, but also how Roosevelt recast modern politics and campaigns. The convention of 1932 was a clash between organization and personality: Roosevelt had the superior organization, and he fought for the nomination against a collection of gaudy personalities – not just the men who sought the nomination, but also their colorful supporters.

Neal's history, of course, profits from this cast of characters, all products of the Roaring Twenties, legendary figures in the facts and fictions of American life: William Randolph Hearst, Huey Long, Al Smith, Will Rogers, Joe Kennedy, and a host of Chicago characters whose names are found on street signs and buildings throughout town.

Before the '32 convention began, Roosevelt, then governor of New York, was the front-runner in the number of committed delegates, though short of the two-thirds majority he then needed. "To win the nomination," Neal writes, "Roosevelt would need a combination of luck and savvy political management. Louis McHenry Howe, sixty-one years old, and James Aloysius Farley, forty-four, were in charge of the Roosevelt operation in Chicago. Their war room was Suite 1702 in the Congress Hotel. The sickly and frail Howe, who had been promoting Roosevelt for the presidency for twenty years, would not leave this suite for the duration of the convention."

Luckily, a lot of action took place in the suites of various hotels: phone calls to the candidates and other power brokers, meetings and meals spent hammering out deals. Neal devotes individual chapters to the half-dozen candidates vying for the prize, beginning with Roosevelt: FDR's lead "was based on two decades of political activity.

He had already waged a national campaign as the 1920 Democratic nominee for the vice presidency. In this losing effort, the young FDR barnstormed in forty-two states, delivered more than four hundred speeches, and got to know the country."

But, beyond the nuts and bolts, Neal describes and the structural impediments to nomination that Roosevelt overcame; he shows how FDR had to deal with the personal issues each of his rivals brought to the convention. Al Smith, the former governor of New York and the unsuccessful Democratic presidential candidate in 1928, was the most ardent foe of Roosevelt. Smith wanted Roosevelt to lose even more than Smith wanted to win.

Neal's portrait of Al Smith is uncomplimentary: Smith, still bitter over his loss in '28 and the anti-Catholic bigotry it uncovered, hated Roosevelt's patrician background – though Roosevelt did more for the common man than Smith would have ever attempted. And when other members of the anti-Roosevelt forces in Chicago began to crack, Smith fumed more than anyone else.

Neal handles the complications of a complicated week in Chicago with great style. Chicago may have been the host of the convention, but Steve Neal is the host of this particular party, and he introduces each of the players concisely and with charm. On William Randolph Hearst: "The master showman of American newspapers was a mediocre performer on the stump and the most unlikely of politicians. He did not enjoy public speaking, hated small talk, and did not like most politicians. W.R., though, was shrewd in choosing issues that struck a responsive chord with the voting public. Franklin Lane, the California Democratic leader, said that the wealthy newspaperman 'knows public sentiment and how to develop it very well, and will be a danger in the United States, I am afraid, for many years to come. . . . He feels with the people, but he has no conscience.'"

Neal captures the stress and anxiety of the participants contesting for a great prize in a small space over limited time: everything is magnified, including the doubts of possible victory. Roosevelt's men are aware that there are small procedural votes their candidate can't afford to lose (or, at times, to win). They back off the battle to do away with the two-thirds rule (put in place as a sop to the Southern states to help preserve unequal civil rights), and, after Roosevelt's ultimate victory, the two-thirds rule is finally abandoned for all time. As Neal points out, since 1952, none of "the major political parties had gone beyond the first roll call" for their nominee.

Neal manages to infuse suspense into a story that has none. He involves the reader so thoroughly with the goings-on, that one is submerged in the intricate machinations between groups and individuals that Roosevelt's nomination does seem to be hung in the balance. Neal's depiction of the convention's first three nominating ballots, which go on round-the-clock, is especially riveting. When FDR's nomination is, at long last, secured, one is relieved that it has finally all worked out. There are any number of modern day lessons to be gleaned from Neal's history, such as how the 1932 controversy between the "wets" and the "drys" – those who favored prohibition and those who didn't – mirror today's political battles over the pro- and anti-gay marriage movements. And Neal shows how, despite conventional wisdom to the contrary, Roosevelt's physical condition was a convention campaign issue.

In an epilogue, Neal encapsulates the remainder of the campaign and the histories of the men we have gotten to know well throughout the book. And, in 1932, it was largely a man's world. Yet, Roosevelt's presidency was going to change that, and there are intimations of that new deal throughout. Frances Perkins, FDR's future labor secretary, pops up in a cameo role, and Roosevelt's children and wife, the influential Eleanor, fly with FDR to Chicago to accept the nomination, an exciting and tradition-breaking trip, and one that signifies the modern age to come.

Steve Neal's unexpected death in February is a loss the *Sun-Times* still hasn't recovered from. His coverage of the city was nonpareil, and the excellence of his new book is only further confirmation of that fact. Indeed, when Neal writes about the city in *Happy Days Are Here Again,* the writing becomes especially spirited. Many paragraphs are riffs on the city he loved: "During convention week, the musical *Clowns in Clover* opened at the Apollo, Randolph and Clark Streets. *Do Your Stuff,* an African American musical revue, extended its run at the Adelphi. Duke Ellington, billed as 'Harlem's Aristocrat of Jazz,' performed at the Lincoln Tavern in suburban Morton Grove. Joe E. Lewis, whose theme song, 'Chicago,' celebrated his 'toddlin town,' and Julia Gerity, 'queen of the blues,' were the headliners at the North Side's Vanity Fair. The Mills Brothers, the first African Americans to have their own show on network radio, had returned to the Palace on Randolph Street," and on and on, the words tapping their feet. I'm sure Neal meant *Happy Days Are Here Again* to be taken as a somewhat ironic title. But, for many, its ironies are far more dark and deep.

First appeared in the *Chicago Sun-Times,* July 4, 2004.
Review of Steve Neal, *Happy Days Are Here Again: The 1932 Democratic Convention, the Emergence of* FDR *– and How America Was Changed Forever* (New York: William Morrow, 2004).

Amanda Smith: *Hostage to Fortune:* The Letters of Joseph P. Kennedy

Joseph P. Kennedy, the patriarch of the Kennedy clan, was, for the Baby Boom generation, a silent man. He was the quiet, proud father behind his son, John F. Kennedy, at the 1961 inauguration. Then, by the year's end, an old man struck dumb by a stroke, which incapacitated him until his death in 1969. I can never remember hearing his voice.

Well, I've heard his voice now – clear, straightforward, astute – in the long compendium of letters, diaries, notes, and telegrams that his adopted grandchild, Amanda Smith, has put together, titled *Hostage to Fortune: the Letters of Joseph P. Kennedy*. But it is an incomplete title. The book is actually an epistolary biography, replete with the contemporaneous letters and writings of his children, his wife, and a variety of associates, linked together by five explanatory essays supplied by the young editor, a doctoral student in history at Harvard University.

The title comes from a radio address Joe Kennedy gave on behalf of Franklin Delano Roosevelt's third term presidential race, "My wife and I have given nine hostages to fortune," he said, endorsing FDR's reelection (while echoing Francis Bacon). FDR gave Kennedy his most public face, making him chairman of the Maritime Commission, a member of the Securities and Exchange Commission, and, most notably, ambassador to Britain. But, this volume makes the point that it was Kennedy himself, and his five doomed children, who were hostages to fortune.

The silence surrounding Joe Kennedy throughout the sixties is not completely broken by this book. Some of the controversies of his life are not settled in its 764 pages: his relationship with the femme fatal Gloria Swanson, ties to the mob because of his liquor business, tales of stock manipulation. Amanda Smith is a faithful granddaughter, insofar as she has done yeoman work discovering, compiling and preserving this trove of materials. Though she does display some distance on this wealth of information with judicious appraisal, she still defends her grandfather against some of the more infamous charges, one of which is that of pervasive anti-Semitism. "Nevertheless," Smith writes, after citing a few egregious examples, "he would always insist that his dislike was not categorical but individual."

Although he was very sensitive to slurs cast upon the Irish and Irish Americans, he could not step over some parochial divide and see his remarks about Jews as similar to those he so despised when directed at his and his family's origins.

Joseph P. Kennedy did not come from nowhere. His father, Patrick J. Kennedy, though not the dynamo Joe became (and relegated in this book almost exclusively to footnotes), was a man of modest substance, enough to send his son to Boston Latin, and then on to Harvard. (JPK's granddaughter is just the last of a long family history with that institution.) Smith reports, somewhat grandiosely: "One estimate has it that the family that Joseph Kennedy generated has itself generated more words than anyone or any phenomenon besides Christ and the War Between the States."

In any case, one has to go to biographies (such as Doris Kearns Goodwin's friendly *The Fitzgeralds and the Kennedys* (1987), and the not so friendly *The Kennedys* (1984) by Peter Collier and David Horowitz) for anything much before 1918, when Joe was twenty-nine. Kennedy's first letter in *Hostage to Fortune* is to his draft board, making a case for an exemption from service in World War I for working in management at the Fore River Shipbuilding Company.

Even by then, men of power and influence were speaking on his behalf, and his meteoric career was already well on its way. That nothing exists fit to print before Joe Kennedy was twenty-nine is an amazing fact in itself. The first and last entries of the volume are by his wife Rose, the first a reminiscence of "Early Life," and the last an entry entitled "Thanksgiving '61."

The first half of this epistolary biography is roiled by odd intrusions: interspersed with Kennedy's correspondence about business matters, largely in Hollywood (where he imposed, what would be called today, a "business model" on a fractious industry) and Wall Street (where the stock market crash left him "untouched"), are the children's writings, the youngest letters of Joe Jr., JFK, Kathleen, Rosemary, Bobby, Teddy, Eunice, Patricia, and Jean. Since there are so many Kennedy children, the kids' correspondence, which acts as an unsettling Greek chorus of the tragedies to come, keeps its youthful tones and subjects until quite late in father Kennedy's life.

There is the pathos of his daughter Rosemary's letters, burdened with mild retardation, and then the shocking silence, following the lobotomy she receives, on both her father's and mother's and siblings' part. She is never mentioned again; she just falls from the volume, and no one (other than the editor) makes note of it. One can only wonder what other unpleasant matters Joseph Kennedy edited so ruthlessly out of his life.

The most lengthy section of material covers his London years; the period of his ambassadorship from 1938–40 comprises nearly half the book. One marvels that a man so sharp and prescient in the world of business (had he been a young man now he would certainly be one of the IPO millionaires of the nineties) could have been so wrong about the history-in-the-making he was witnessing. It stems, in part, from the blindness that fueled his cultural anti-Semitism.

Joe Kennedy's isolationism and pro-German attitudes (he was for "getting along with dictators," as he put it, foreshadowing Ronald Reagan's UN Ambassador Jeane Kirkpatrick, who pushed making pragmatic distinctions between "authoritarians" and "totalitarians") are revealed in detail, and are somewhat self-explanatory. No one can charge that these remarks have been taken out of context, since Amanda Smith has labored so hard to supply context along with the complete record.

For a professional audience, this volume will satisfy a thirst for documentation, and fill out the histories of business, diplomacy, and politics yet to be written. What is more surprising is that it also fills out the biographies of his children. In all those that exist, of Jack, Bobby, and Ted, none capture the poignance of their young lives more than this volume. Indeed, for the general reader, *Hostage to Fortune* will doubtless serve as the most unlikely of Father's Day gift books, for it presents, as artifacts alone can, what Kennedy was like as a father to his children: encouraging, scolding, reassuring, steadfast, loving.

For those who wish to know just what it was like to grow up a Kennedy, this book shows it more than any other I've encountered. It certainly makes all the Kennedys more human – though, at this point, one wonders if that is necessary.

Amanda Smith discovered, in her research, a crumpled scrap of paper in Kennedy's handwriting, written a half hour after his daughter Kathleen's death (in 1948) in a plane crash, "No one who ever met her didn't feel that life was much better that minute. And we know so little about the next world we must think that they wanted just such a wonderful girl for themselves. We must not feel sorry for her but for ourselves."

Because of the time notation, one can wonder if this most private note was, itself, meant to eventually become public. Joe Kennedy wished his public life to be as public as possible; but he kept his private life private. As Amanda Smith writes in an Editor's Note, "I have come to regard privacy as precious and irretrievable." In that way, obviously, she is just like her grandfather.

First appeared in the *Chicago Sun-Times,* January 14, 2001.
Review of Amanda Smith, editor, *Hostage to Fortune: The Letters of Joseph P. Kennedy* (New York: Viking, 2001).

John A. Farrell: Tip O'Neill and the Democratic Century

John A. Farrell's new biography of Tip O'Neill shares more than a passing similarity with another Farrell's work, James T. Farrell's multivolume novel, *Studs Lonigan,* which detailed in gritty, street-wise prose, the wasted life and dissipated times of William (Studs) Lonigan, a lower-middle-class Irish-Catholic Chicagoan, from 1910 to the early 1930s.

Tip O'Neill and the Democratic Century presents us with the life and times of Thomas P. (Tip) O'Neill, Jr., a middle-class Irish-Catholic from Boston. Its author is the White House correspondent for the *Boston Globe,* and his penetrating and entertaining biography shows us the rest of the century through the rise and accomplishments of the consummate political man, Tip O'Neill.

It is not often that the publication of a biography of a deceased politician is a timely event, but this one is. Indeed, this illuminating work couldn't come at a more propitious moment, just as the Democratic Party enters a new century having lost the presidency and both houses of Congress narrowly to the Republicans. Whether or not the twenty-first century becomes the Republican century may depend on whether the lessons found within Mr. Farrell's book are taken to heart by the Democratic Party.

This is not the typical biography, but a more panoramic production, a newsreel of nearly three-quarters of the last century. We see Tip O'Neill compete with the startling events of his time, events he influenced or observed from the inside. Over and over, this volume serves as an antidote to the America malady of forgetfulness: here is our political past, presented clearly, and with style.

Samuel Johnson, quoted by James Boswell, said, "The Irish are a fair people; they never speak well of one another." Well, Farrell possesses some of that quality, but in the main, he can find good things to say about the anti-Vietnam War movement and Ronald Reagan's mad but successful plan to outspend the Soviet Union into financial (and governmental) bankruptcy.

Tip O'Neill is often described (by Farrell and others) as a "man's man," which appears to mean a guy who likes to spend most of his time with other men, but doesn't want to have sex with them. O'Neill was blessed (there's hardly any other word) to have had a devoted wife, Millie, who took care of him and their five children, and let the young (and then old) politician do whatever he wanted, whenever he wanted. It was a good thing O'Neill rewarded her devotion with a life of productive public service during interesting times.

Farrell's book is popular history, but of a superior sort: though the person of Tip O'Neill, he makes the nuts and bolts of governing, at the state and national level, fascinating and understandable. Hindsight is not always 20/20, but Farrell is even-handed surveying the controversies of the last half century – The Great Society, civil rights, Vietnam, Middle Eastern, Irish and Central American policies, The Greed Decade, Iran-Contra, etc.

Unlike the insider see-it-now books of Bob Woodward, Farrell's is a more straightforward narrative, with a wider range, free of Woodward's fly-on-the-wall, made-up dialogue.

O'Neill's early career in the Massachusetts legislature was marked by a certain provincialism, and close ties to the hierarchy of the Catholic Church. Farrell writes: "Massachusetts politics was, at the time, quite susceptible to theocratic intervention, especially when it came to lifting restraints on women." A proposed birth control bill was the center of controversy, in the spring of 1948, and "O'Neill fought the bill in committee, blasted Planned Parenthood and led the Democrats in voting against the legislation." O'Neill and other Catholic legislators "labeled the proposal a ploy to free women to pursue such idle goals as 'careers, cocktail parties and bridge games.'" A year later, O'Neill became the first Democratic Speaker of the Massachusetts House of Representatives.

But, when O'Neill was elected to the U.S. House of Representatives, in 1952, he began a slow evolution that paralleled the rest of the country's twentieth century march toward liberalism in matters of religion, race and social mores. O'Neill's district, North Cambridge, was the fiery furnace that shaped and reshaped him, since it was divided between ethnic blue-collar folk; immigrant-based Irish, Italian, and African stock; and America's premier intellectual center, the site of Harvard University, among others.

On one hand, there was O'Neill's steadfast loyalties and on the other, a never-extinguished intellectual openness to new ideas and change. The divisions in his district were a potent anvil and hammer, and O'Neill grew to faithfully represent and reflect these same tensions throughout the nation. His transformation, however, took time. During O'Neill's first term, "He opposed attempts to cut the House Un-American Activities Committee's budget, and continued to support its work for another fifteen years. . . . He voted to outlaw the American Communist Party; to increase defense spending; to ban Red China from the United Nations; and to add the words 'under God' to the Pledge of Allegiance."

The Vietnam War is refought in these pages, and Farrell captures the heat and horrors of the time, detailing O'Neill's long-coming change of heart, and his final opposition to the war.

Unlike our post-World War II presidents, who are term-limited, a member of Congress can embody the history of the country, and O'Neill was in elective office for 50 years, including five terms as Speaker of the House. In this chronicle, Presidents Eisenhower, Kennedy, Johnson, Nixon, Carter, Reagan, come and go, but O'Neill serves on until 1986.

The volume's 700-plus pages encompass a great deal of complicated history, and Farrell records it with economy and grace. He slights very little and seldom seems superficial, since his account unfolds through people's actions, as well as their words.

The portrait of our government that emerges is both alarming and reassuring. It is one of the most valuable accounts I have read of how the system works. And many of the same politicians and journalists of Campaign 2000 (with the glaring exception of George W. Bush, who appears not at all, unlike Al Gore) fill its pages (and most of them will find something to be embarrassed about). Indeed, the same issues contested back in O'Neill's heyday – Social Security, taxes, less or more government – are being fought over today, as if no one recalls what happened yesterday.

It is amusing to read about the early careers of legislators who are playing prominent roles in the ongoing, perennial Republican struggle to undo FDR's New Deal programs and to eliminate as many taxes the rich are forced to pay, while the Democrats attempt to preserve some safety net for the disadvantaged and the down and out.

For instance, John Breaux, George W.'s favorite tax-cutting Democrat, turns up in Farrell's book, during the second-term Reagan budget debate, thusly: "After the White House had caved in and restored the sugar subsidies demanded by John Breaux and three other Louisiana congressmen, Breaux joked that while his vote was not for sale, 'It can be rented.'"

As O'Neill became larger at the end of his life, the House of Representatives seemed to grow smaller in the person of Newt Gingrich. Farrell rightly pinpoints the influence of C-Span, and television in general, for the transformation. "Television was a perfect vehicle for Gingrich's plans: it poorly conveyed the subtleties of compromise and instead rewarded controversy, polarization, symbolic amendments and the repetitious presentment of partisan themes." But change was everywhere. Until the eighties, as Colorado's Pat Schroeder is quoted saying, Congress "was the planet of the guys."

Farrell seems to agree with O'Neill that a chief accomplishment of the Democratic Century was the creation of the modern middle class. O'Neill, shortly before he died in 1994, said: "In the country of my youth, there was no middle class as we know it today – only the very few rich at the top and the millions and millions of poor at the bottom, with a huge and terrible difference in between."

As Farrell notes, the Democrats' success caused their failure. Part of their base became middle class enough to begin to compare themselves to their betters, wealthy Republicans. Now, of course, at the dawn of what might be a Republican century, that middle class is finding itself stagnating, and the poor are poorer than ever.

If the new president were a reader, I would recommend that this book be the one he tries to get through this year.

First appeared in the *Chicago Sun-Times,* March 11, 2001. Review of John A. Farrell, *Tip O'Neill and the Democratic Century* (Boston: Little, Brown, 2001).

part three

the personal and the political and the literary

Raymond Carver: Hemingway Without Money

In November, 1993, I published a review of three books, all related to Raymond Carver, in my local hometown paper, the *South Bend Tribune.* In another context, I once claimed that reviews were eulogies for books no one reads, but that remark, like most, is never entirely true. In Carver's case, there will be, has been, an audience for *Short Cuts;* but for the majority of books, you can count on only one attentive reader – of the review, at least: the author. Obviously, I would not hear from Carver; but I did hear from his widow, Tess Gallagher, who took exception to something I wrote, an exception that is important enough to be discussed more fully in connection with the work of Raymond Carver: the subject of money. Since the book reviews in the *South Bend Tribune* are not indexed anywhere, our daily town paper being the proverbial fish wrap, it is not likely any present reader has read what I had to say. Below, one will find the original review I wrote, shorn of the local paper's editing and cuts.

Raymond Carver always struck me as Hemingway without money. But, since his death in 1988 of cancer at age fifty, it's become clear that even a quick assessment needs to be more elaborate. Carver is an American success story of a different sort; one of his editors, Gary Fisketjon, quotes Carver in *Remembering Ray,* a collection of memoirs and tributes that serves as notes towards a biography, "Nobody ever asked me to be a writer," and that makes him different than Hemingway, indeed. Becoming a writer was not on the list of possible occupations counselors recommended at high schools a guy from Carver's background attended in the early 1950s.

Throughout *Remembering Ray,* it is often said that Carver did something "new" in his short stories; one typical comment, by the novelist Lewis Buzbee: "He added to our literature an original body of work that gave voice to a world that had, until him, no voice of its own, a world of working-class tract homes and the quiet and powerless families who live in them . . ."; and another, his widow's, the poet Tess Gallagher, forgivable hyperbolic reaction: "Carver's stories had the kind of impact on American fiction that Einstein's theory of relativity had on science. We couldn't quite fathom how it worked, but it changed the way we regarded the lives of middle-class working people."

Part of the problem comes from the confusion, as expressed above, about "working class" and "middle class" – who was Carver writing about? And, despite Carver's considerable impact on American fiction, none of his classmates at the thirtieth-year reunion of his high school class in Yakima, Washington – that Carver and Gallagher showed up at – knew him as a writer (except the organizer of the reunion, who worked at the local newspaper and had read an article about him). Now, that says something poignant about the state of American fiction.

Carver seemed to be Hemingway without money because of his simple, most often called "accessible," prose style. Here is the beginning of his story "Vitamins," reprinted in *Short Cuts,* a collection of nine Carver stories and one poem, which serves as the basis and companion volume for the 1993 film by the *à la mode* director, Robert Altman: "I had a job and Patti didn't. I worked a few hours a night for the hospital. It was a nothing job." That simplicity is one reason Carver's style has been so emulated by young writers who have risen to that level of flat statement, without yet sinking to Carver's depths of understanding and feeling. But it is the early Hemingway stories that prompt the comparison, before glamour took over most of Hemingway's subjects. For Hemingway travel was international; for Carver it was up and down the West Coast.

Carver did begin to isolate, and speak for, something new in the culture, and it was at the heart of his odd generation: born in 1938, too young for World War II, too old for Vietnam (and missing as well the police action in Korea), a generation of smokers and drinkers, a lot of them dying early of lung cancer, like Carver. He married young and had two children. The poet Dennis Schmitz describes Carver's early adult life: "The small towns, seedy rentals, the piecemeal college study, the intermittent bursts of relative prosperity. . . . Ray understood the characters in his stories who were knocked about by circumstance because he was one of them."

Living in Northern California during the boom and bust cycles of the sixties floated a generation of white males with families through irregular jobs that still allowed them a semblance of "middle class" life. The West Coast-ness, the California aspect of Carver's stories, is important. Ted Solotaroff, the East Coast editor and writer, gives this very Manhattan summary of his view of Carver's characters before he met him: "I had respected his fiction rather than cottoned to it. His typically small-town isolates were of marginal interest to me; they didn't seem to see or feel or learn much beyond their insecurities, the bleakness of their prospects, the force of their streaks of envy, jealousy, cruelty, shame, dishonesty, or some other twisted energy that flared up like a chronic fever in a meager, congested life. . . ."

What Carver was tracking was a light-blue collar life, the shattering of pre-World War II middle-class verities that the post-World War II generation of parents and children would endure: the atomization of families, economic insecurity, the malling of America. Only someone from the East Coast like Solotaroff could refer to Northern California communities as "small towns" – that captures a myth that didn't survive in the places where Carver put down very temporary roots (feelers is more like it, not roots).

As the poet Morton Marcus more accurately describes it, "Ray and Maryann [Carver's first wife] were living in Cupertino, a suburban town thirty miles south of San Francisco and ten miles north of San Jose, the center of a middle-class residential area which in the late sixties and early seventies served the families of the burgeoning computer microchip industry called Silicon Valley." It wasn't so much Carver's jobs (or nonjobs) he wrote about, but his neighbor's. Like most writers who finally capture a large audience, Carver's early stories were prophetic: he was writing about the exception that was soon to become the rule.

And Carver did get lucky: he rode the ascendancy of the short story as the fashionable literary form throughout the late seventies and eighties, and, as one rememberer puts it, Gordon Lish, at that time a powerful editor at *Esquire,* took an interest in his "career." Carver's stories were recognized in New York publishing for what, in part, they were: an anthropological phenomena, a regional, non-Manhattan, West Coast, Sunbelt, shallow-rooted existence that was soon to become dominant in the culture, Reagan country coming home to roost.

As the short story writer Jay Woodruff puts it: "Most of Carver's characters voted Republican in 1980. As that Bull Decade unfolded, as Reagan's betrayal of working-class America became evident (scripted so skillfully that one might conclude the era's most influential writer of fiction was not Raymond Carver, but Peggy Noonan), Carver continued to remind anyone who bothered to listen that much of America remained on its back, prone on a sofa, out of work, numbing itself with television and beer, cigarettes and dope, while the house fell apart and the repo men pounded on the front door."

Again, the term "working class," as thrown about in these memoirs, means anyone who works, anyone who is one or two paychecks away from eviction, but otherwise Woodruff is on target. And the irony is that Carver was lifted out of the world he mainly depicted in his four volumes of short stories, *Where I'm Calling From, Will You Please Be Quiet, Please?, What We Talk About When We Talk About Love,* and *Cathedral* – from where the stories in *Short Cuts* have been taken. Well-published by Random House (both Knopf and Vintage), Carver caught the wave of trade paperback distribution for serious fiction, received grants and deserved honors, and, finally, the attention of Hollywood, where even "product" that originates on the West Coast has to pass through the bath of the East Coast to pick up its particular sort of sheen before being taken back home again, properly laureled. Enter Robert Altman; exit Raymond Carver. The screenplay of *Short Cuts* changes a number of essential things: location, professions, and class. Carver is about subtle gradations, whereas Hollywood is about vivid amplification. Selling vitamins in Carver's story becomes selling phone sex in Altman's movie. *Short Cuts,* the screenplay, is a classic comic book version of Carver, but Altman's images could likely become Carver's in the popular culture's mind.

However, it is Altman's film, however distorting, that occasioned a new burst of attention for Carver's work. *Short Cuts* collects some of the grimmest Carver ("Neighbors," "They're Not Your Husband," etc.), and its last story, "Tell the Women We're Going," is my choice for Carver's least worthy tale, one that's more exploitative than exploring. His fiction of the damaged and down on their luck deserves many readers, though through the eighties Carver was one of the few who benefitted from the general inflation and speculative fever of the decade, and caught for himself a good bit of surplus capital, enough to buy a Mercedes off the showroom floor for cash. As one of his characters might have said: "Beats all."

Altman's film might lure novice Carver readers to the earlier collections, where they can discover "Cathedral," and his homage to Chekhov, "Errand," and take note of the direction Carver's later work was taking, the final destination of which was, by his early death, taken away from us all.

It was the line, "Carver was one of the few who benefitted from the general inflation . . ." that Tess Gallagher objected to. She wanted me to know that Carver was in no way rich, and reminded me of the struggles he had with money over the years. I responded, telling her that she had my sympathies, and that I knew that it is often more irritating to have a loved one's life publicly picked over than one's own. I went on to point out that I wasn't under the impression that Carver had struck it rich, but that I was contrasting his early life, and his stories, with the circumstances he was encountering at the end of his life. The cliché "rags to riches" does contain the distinction: a person who makes that trip doesn't necessarily become rich, but every now and then he or she does come into riches (e.g., a Mercedes). I was making a point about the speculative Reagan-Bush years, when the inflationary fever hit publishing, and a number of writers I knew received six-figure advances for nonfiction books of various sorts, which no one is doling out these days, even for nonfiction, much less short story collections.

My remark about surplus capital referred not to Carver's, but to other individuals' – in this case, it appears, the film people Carlo Ponti and Michael Cimino (Gallagher had mentioned in her letter that the Mercedes money had come from them). Writers tend to get money in chunks – which helps confuse their class status – but when they do, it is somebody else's surplus capital they are acquiring. That's true with grants as well. It's different from getting a paycheck. That was the distinction I was aiming for. Near the end of his too-short life, Carver was coming into some extra money. Had he lived, he doubtless would have achieved (or remained in) that wished-for status often, understatedly, described as "comfortable."

The question of money and writing is not a resolved one. An article in the June 27, 1994, *New Yorker* about the novelist James Wilcox's checkered economic history managed to underreport a few things: chiefly that Wilcox was one of the few well-published writers of his generation who chose (at the point that it was possible) not to be employed full-time at a university, and this choice threw him upon the mercy of the publishing world, which, in his case, actually has shown a good deal of mercy. If one added up the various advances Mr. Wilcox's powerful agent got him for novels that didn't earn out, the money gets to the six-figures rather quickly, putting him in the top 20 percent of contemporary novelists. The problem is that even a forty-eight thousand dollar advance doesn't last long these days. And if the trend is down, book after book, rather than up, times get tough quickly. There are a number of Wilcoxes these days. After two or three novels, if they haven't acquired a large audience, publishers look elsewhere; there is more cachet in acquiring a new face than running an old one by for the third or fourth time. But the contemporary predicament for most serious fiction writers (it has been true always for poets) is that they do need to teach to write, and teaching often leaves them less time than they need. And for poets, these days, in the economic culture it is worse: *après* Rod McKuen, *le déluge*. There isn't, today, a "popular" (bad) poet captured in the greater public's bloodshot eye – though the author of *The Bridges of Madison County* may substitute.

Today, the amount of money you receive depends on the size of your audience. This has always been true (see Melville, etc.), but it is now truer. All the terrible things predicted for publishing over the last ten years have come to pass; they've hit the beach and litter the shore. Short stories, ironically, as I pointed out in my essay in *Short Story Theory at a Crossroads* a number of years ago (1989), are the fashionable literary form because they are now the nonpaying art form, rather than the belittled, high-paying commercial form of pre–World War II American periodical publishing.

Carver's work, indeed, has begun to carve out a place for itself in the popular culture. But at the end of his life, when things, happily, had finally become a lot easier, I don't think it un-coincidental that he became so interested in the world of the worldly Chekhov, or that "Errand" takes place in the very "comfortable" environs of a grand hotel – it is the atypical Carver setting, though pocketing the cork certainly is the typical Carver gesture.

First appeared in *Short Story,* vol. 3, no. 2, Fall 1995; © 1995 by SHORT STORY. Review-Essay of Raymond Carver, *Short Cuts: Selected Stories* (New York: Vintage, 1993); William L. Stull and Maureen P. Carroll, eds., *Remembering Ray: A Composite Biography* (Santa Barbara: Capra Press, 1993); Robert Altman and Frank Barhydt, *Short Cuts: The Screenplay* (Santa Barbara: Capra Press, 1993).

Michael Ryan: *Secret Life*

It is a strange fact of the nineties that publishing a confessional memoir, detailing subjects that the author considers "degrading" and "shameful," is a good career move. Michael Ryan's *Secret Life* is a very nineties product, insofar as it charts a conversion experience, and life of victimhood, that was caused by a defining event (in his case, molestation by a neighbor) that occurred when the author was five years old, and carried through his life, until his enlistment into a twelve-step program in his late forties. Ryan is in step with the times.

Ryan is, of course, an award-winning poet, and the subject of gossip in the small world of literarature (especially, the poetry) since being shown the door at Princeton in the early eighties. A practical impulse may be behind his desire to do this sort of autobiography: he is able to control, or redirect, the gossip. The result is an engaging read, though more conventional in execution than it might be, for the bulk of the book covers the years five to twenty-one in his life, and is, in consequence, very much a grammar school, high school and college memoir. He captures how a precocious teenager sees the world, but, after a while, it seems you are reading an account by a precocious teenager. The "adult" portions of the autobiography are the slimmest and most under-the-spell of the new conversion, whereas the earlier years are under the "trance" of sexual obsession. This is not, overall, an intellectual memoir; or, at least, I hope it isn't. How his life became his poetry is only hinted at.

Ryan claims to be a "sex addict" – and writes that it was "a disease nobody recognized then and still seems to some people like a joke. It determined what I thought and what I felt." I don't think it a joke, but I don't accept the disease analogy, either, since most addictions are solitary and that is not quite the sexual addiction Ryan has in mind. Also, it is difficult to claim such a malady without the echo of a boast accompanying it, since Ryan needs to enlist partners to participate in his "addiction"; they do a bit more than just "enable." "Sexaholic" is, perhaps, more apt a term, though it doesn't have the same dramatic ring; also, alcoholics in twelve-step programs aren't allowed to drink at all. What's the cure for sex addicts? No sex?

Ryan shows aspects of being an endorphin, or adrenalin, junky, in the way long distance runners are – waiting to, wanting to enter that state, that zone. Sex as a physical activity can generate what, obviously, is a condition one may wish to return to again and again. But there is very little pleasure described (and not much depiction of heterosexual sex) in *Secret Life;* Ryan appears more a "conquest" addict than a sex addict. His analysis – or presentation, there isn't much analysis – of his bisexuality will not do much for the nature/nurture debate, though it will fit in nicely with the moral majority's view of things.

His book carries a disclaimer – "The names, distinguishing traits, and places of most of the people represented here have been changed" – and one responds, oh, he's writing fiction. *Secret Life* does bring up the question as to whether fictional nonfiction is a separate genre. The mixture of startling candor and careful deception is often the seducer's cocktail of choice. Ryan leaves out his "parade of pretty wives" and that leaves a rather large gap when one is detailing sexual obsession. And it is strange that, in this childhood centered book, not one mention is made, or thought expressed, of why, after a number of marriages, he has no children, or even what he might think about that volatile subject, given his history. One could presume that he is all the child he ever needs to raise; empathy is not his strong suit.

The serious question looms: if one took "Bob Stoller" (the molester) out of his life, how different would Michael Ryan be? The molestation went on periodically over about a month's time. Those scenes are both terrible and effective. Though what went on in the years before, ages zero through five, that made him react the way he did, rather than "run away," as another little boy on the block did, creates an unhealthy fog around the question. Ryan's father was a major-league alcoholic; his mother an equally intoxicated soul, in the sense of seeing the world as she wished it to be, rather than as it was; his older brother, as portrayed, appears something of an odd duck, addicted to the more fetishistic aspects of the Boy Scouts well into adulthood; and there is an older sister, who Ryan thinks was also molested by "Stoller," but someone who became capable of "love." Absent of "Stoller," Ryan's family alone could bend (or not bend) any number of tender or not-so-tender reeds.

Ryan, by his own account, always wanted attention, and he doesn't seem to notice that his memoir is, in that regard, in complete harmony with his earlier attempts to get it, to place himself center stage. Early on he describes that, when he was in third grade, the class had "a good-deed contest." He writes, "whenever we did a good deed . . . we were to draw a snowball" next to a snowman each child had drawn previously. "It was on the honor system. Nobody would be checking on us." He cheats furiously, and soon "my paper was crammed with snowballs, as if my snowman had fallen backward into an enormous honeycomb." He won a prize. It is an instructive anecdote.

Near the close of the book, he writes, "There's a slogan in my twelve-step program that has helped me a lot: if you want to feel self-esteem, do estimable acts. (Not prestigious: estimable.) Every day, I have to do a few (small, modest) estimable acts, loving acts, preferably ones nobody knows about. This is now my secret life." Two things: One, secret!? oops, all those estimable acts are secret no longer; And two, he seems not to notice there is a connection between both of the "good deed" episodes. Narcissus seems to be blind to everything but himself.

Fired (oops, suspended with pay) from Princeton in 1981 for "sexual harassment," he has now, at U.C. Irvine, adopted a new style of teaching (no more sleeping with students). But, it is a style that demands duplication. He announces to them he is writing a memoir about being molested and requests that they do the same, though it doesn't have to be "shameful." I'll show you mine if you show me yours.

There are many curious, unexplored things going on in *Secret Life*. It is a first step in therapy; at least in getting to know whom he is – through memory recall – he might begin now to explore the topic a bit more fully, get under its surface. And the surface is fine. It is well written, though he is overly fond of a good sentence or description, since he tends to repeat them.

But, for me, the spookiest thing is that Ryan uses for a jacket photo the boyhood picture of himself that his molester took, the molester's first seductive advance toward him. That poignant picture is worth a thousand words, even if they aren't the thousands of words Ryan has supplied. *Secret Life* isn't dedicated to anyone. In some ways, it could be dedicated to the most important person in Michael Ryan's life, himself, or, by photographic inference, to the long gone "Bob Stoller."

First appeared in *American Book Review,* vol. 17, no. 2, December–January 1995–96; © 1996 by *American Book Review.* Review of Michael Ryan, *Secret Life: An Autobiography* (New York: Pantheon, 1995).

Philip Graham: *How to Read an Unwritten Language*

Michael Kirby, the narrator of Philip Graham's intriguing first novel, is a devoted storyteller – as is the author, whose previous volumes are a collection of short stories, *The Art of the Knock,* and a work of nonfiction, *Parallel World*. "I've always felt that the secret life is available," Michael begins, "whether on the chipped and lipsticked rim of a coffee cup or in a crumpled tissue's faint smell of sex, in the smudgy fingerprints of a child's frayed comic book or along the jagged flap of a crudely torn envelope. Even a single gnawed crescent of fingernail is a voice that might speak."

This is a memoirist's voice, as much as a novelist's, and *How to Read an Unwritten Language* hews to the memoir form, revealing its characters' secret lives, much as the poet Michael Ryan's recently published autobiography, *Secret Life,* does. Novels in memoir form raise a number of questions, for once the "I" is employed, all is possible, meaning the "I" can tell us anything. And a reader can become irritated when information is withheld.

Graham's narrative design is two overlapping vectors of time. One is the slow rate of growing up, adhering to the appropriate chronology, the other, the "present" moving at a much faster pace, over a short period of a few months.

Graham does childhood exceedingly well; these sections are touching, comic, and heartbreaking. The portrait of the three siblings, Michael, Dan and Laurie, dealing with a remote father and a going-crazy mother is, for all its literary familiarity, fresh and poignant, full of mordant observation: "Dinner abandoned, our parents locked themselves in their bedrooms, where they spoke in angry whispers, indecipherable even with my ear to the door. Dan and Laurie sat hunched before the television like defendants waiting for a jury to announce its deliberations. . . ."

Michael's life is exceptional in a number of ways, but he doesn't seem to notice it. And that stance of innocence becomes questionable, since he notices so much everywhere else. Early on, he shakes a woman's hand whom he has just encountered: "We stood silently, letting this grip linger perhaps moments too long, our palms both slightly moist. I imagined messages swiftly passing back and forth between our mingled beads of sweat: two private histories now one salty residue, an improvised petri dish growing something that might tell us what to do next."

First novels are often growing-up, family novels, and *How to Read an Unwritten Language* is not an exception. Graham's portrait of the father is both accurately intimate and aloof and, in the same way, Michael's brother and sister are rendered sympathetically, but standoffishly. When Michael escapes to college, his circle does not widen. He meets a young woman, Kate, an artist, and, upon graduation, they marry and, without too much difficulty, divorce not long after. Michael has begun to sell insurance and he continues to do that, never finding the economics of life to be overwhelming. His damaged mother instilled his habit of first eliciting and then telling stories. It was from her that Michael learned the erotic passivity of being a "good listener." She displayed what today would be called multiple personalities. Michael transfers the talismanic power of her story telling to found objects and, when those stories are released, they turn into found prose poems. Many are successfully provocative, in the manner of short short stories, like the enigmatic tales of Borges. Chapters are given titles taken from the stories: "Chiming Glasses," "Suicide Songs," etc.

The stories Michael hears are seductive and he, in turn, uses them to seduce. One character, an art gallery owner and chance encounter, is taken by Michael's stories and puts on a successful one-man show of Michael's quirky, but ordinary objects, with the stories as accompanying texts. "This serving plate once belonged to a sleepwalker, an elderly woman living with her son's family near the end of her life. Though once a devoted and accomplished cook, she was barely able to make a pot of tea. But at night, in a dream-like state, she set places for her family in the dining room. This silver plate was always in the middle of the table. . . ." The show sells out. But, despite that, Michael continues his solitariness, remaining disconnected from the art (or larger) world. The insurance selling, never substantial, now evaporates. Michael is fascinated by the inner world – his mother's feminized domain of hidden selves, and those that are publicly masked and displayed.

The woman he picks up at the novel's start turns out to be a married TV weather person and Michael, through his stories and objects, and two acts of violence, is able to separate her from her abusive husband. The novel ends the day after their new marriage begins. "Happily ever after" doesn't leap to mind.

The special strengths of the novel are its clarity of prose and the alert sensitivity on display throughout. Leaving a miserable fair with his first wife, Kate, toward the end of their marriage, Michael records: "We stepped carefully past dark puddles, the last, stray drops of rain falling into them like little explosions, and our reflections shimmered and shook to pieces all the way to the parking lot."

That Graham invents a narrator, who discovers that the telling of stories is illuminating and powerful, seems a superfluous task for a novelist. And, because of the first person voice, it is difficult to avoid the "Siamese twin-ness" of novelist and narrator, and accept the naiveté of one, and the sophistication of the other. *How to Read an Unwritten Language* is instructional and often pleasurable, though the many affecting, insightful lessons it teaches could profitably be absorbed by the author as well as the reader.

First appeared in the *Chicago Tribune,* November 19, 1995;
 Review of Philip Graham, *How to Read an Unwritten Language* (New York: Scribner, 1995).

Tim O'Brien: *In the Lake of the Woods*

Tim O'Brien is one of his generation's most deservedly acclaimed authors. O'Brien's writing career has recorded both hits, *Going After Cacciato* (1978), *The Things They Carried* (1990) and peculiar misses, *Northern Lights* (1975), *The Nuclear Age* (1985) – his novels set in America having alternated with, and fared less well than, books that use Vietnam as their subject.

The challenging and provocative *In the Lake of the Woods* follows that pattern in part. Coming after the widely praised, Vietnam-based *The Things They Carried*, the new novel is set in the States, but it combines both worlds – doing so with mixed, but ultimately satisfying, results.

The protagonist of *In the Lake of the Woods*, John Wade, is a middle-aged politician who had been a member of Charlie Company when it overran the number of small Vietnamese villages now collectively known as My Lai, killing almost everyone they found there – mainly, in descending numerical order: women, children, and old men. *In the Lake of the Woods* is Wade's biography, but the problematic premise of the novel is that it was written by a fellow veteran who has set out to discover the mystery of Wade's life: "Biographer, historian, storyteller, medium – call me what you want – but even after four years of hard labor I'm left with little more than supposition and possibility. John Wade was a magician; he didn't give his tricks away."

These interpolations, which come at the ends of chapters, are done by means of footnotes (other secondary source materials are also footnoted with standard bibliographic references). But O'Brien is giving away some fictional tricks with this choice, and it is hard not to question his methods.

The story, without footnotes, is in another tradition of American fiction, bringing to mind Dreiser's *An American Tragedy,* which also makes potent, criminal use of an isolated body of water. Lakes have played a metaphoric role in our literature that is both benign and malevolent – a medium always mysterious and unknowable, and O'Brien fills the novel with that quality:

"It is by the nature of the angle, sun to earth, that the seasons are made, and that the waters of the lake change color by the season, blue going to gray and then to white and then back again to blue. The water receives color; the water returns it. The angle shapes reality. Winter ice becomes the steam of summer as flesh becomes spirit. Partly window, partly mirror, the angle is where memory dissolves."

After losing a primary election for U.S. senator, Wade and his wife, Kathy, rent a cabin in the Minnesota wilderness: "They needed the solitude. They needed the repetition, the dense hypnotic drone of woods and water, but above all they needed to be together." Wade had become lieutenant governor of the state at thirty. He seemed to be a shoo-in for senator until his presence at My Lai was uncovered during the campaign. (It was a fact he had hidden from everyone since he had left military service.)

Wade's life unravels still more: His wife "disappears" near the end of their vacation, lost in the Great North. Or was she murdered by Wade? The unnamed biographer can't decide.

O'Brien has set two contradictory narratives forward: one a compelling mystery, the other an investigation into the nature of mystery, of knowing itself. They do conflict. Readers hooked on one are likely to be irritated by the other.

Wade is a compelling character; his wife, Kathy, is much less so. As Wade's life history is revealed, O'Brien recounts step-by-step the killings at My Lai. These pages are shocking after twenty-five years, even if one knows the facts. (O'Brien makes liberal use of a 1992 nonfiction book, *Four Hours in My Lai* [by Michael Bilton and Kevin Sim], which is equally unsettling to read.)

I suspect O'Brien's novel will be the first account of My Lai many younger readers will encounter. O'Brien, it appears, wants to place his fact-based fiction in the service of history (rather than the more usual history in the service of fiction), and he is for the most part successful. Even mainstream Hollywood, not especially reticent these days, has shied away from depicting My Lai.

After the carnage is revisited, O'Brien invents a most cruel and grotesque death for Kathy; he seems compelled to top the violence already described. "Finally it's a matter of taste, or aesthetics," the "biographer" informs us. In chapters labeled "Hypothesis" we get different versions of what may have occurred.

However, it is clear that O'Brien wants to understand violence, but not to exploit it. As hideous as the possibilities are, history provides Wade (and O'Brien and the reader) with contemporary counterparts. The controversially convicted Green Beret slayer of his wife and two children, Jeffrey MacDonald, floats unnamed (along with others) in the ether of Wade's darkest impulses.

And it seems O'Brien, in the eleventh hour, pulled back from the logic of his character's character. Reviewers were supplied with a rewritten ending for the book long after the bound galleys were distributed, a rare occurrence. The difference was small, a matter of a few lines, but the change leads the reader to favor a verdict of not guilty for John Wade.

O'Brien himself might still be unsettled about the matter. What is clear, however, is that he has written a risky, ambitious, perceptive, engaging, and troubling novel, full of unresolved and unresolvable energies and powerful prose, a major attempt to come to grips with the causes and consequences of the late twentieth century's unquenchable appetite for violence, both domestic and foreign.

First appeared in the Chicago Tribune, October 16, 1994; © 1994 *Chicago Tribune*. Review of Tim O'Brien, *In the Lake of the Woods* (Boston: Houghton Mifflin/Seymour Lawrence, 1994).

Peter Dexter: The Paperboy

Peter Dexter, the National Book Award winner for his 1988 novel, *Paris Trout,* is a no chapter author. His four previous novels (*God's Pocket, Deadwood, Paris Trout, Brotherly Love*) and now, *The Paperboy,* are all rapidly unspooling texts, their scenes, long and short, broken only by the briefest gap of white space (and, in the new novel's case, an addition of a tiny typographical decoration, a square) – just space enough to catch your breath and plunge forward into the headlong tale. Dexter doesn't seem to want to give you too much time to decide whether or not to proceed.

The Paperboy revisits some familiar Dexter territory and characters. Hillary Van Wetter, the novel's baddest guy, is a descendant, spiritually, if not literally, of Paris Trout, Mr. Dexter's best-known villain – just one more weak link down the cracker food chain. (I cannot squelch the opinion that naming him "Hillary" is some sort of not-so-private joke on the part of Mr. Dexter, given the present occupants of the White House.) And we are in northern Florida, up near the panhandle, the spongy bottom of the South, where everything and everyone is a bit fungoid and fantastical.

Though the form is the same as his earlier fictions, *The Paperboy* differs by being narrated by an I – Jack James, one son of the owner of the "Moat County Tribune," brother to Ward James, the father's favorite and the novel's catalytic character. Its first sentence is: "My brother Ward was once a famous man."

How Ward became famous, and how the Van Wetter family aids his advancement, is the center of *The Paperboy*. What's around the edges is interesting, too; Dexter's view of journalism – since he was a practicing journalist until the great success of *Paris Trout* – his views on prize winning and national recognition (for it is Ward winning a Pulitzer Prize that makes him famous), are subjects that hover over the story like the ubiquitous mosquitoes around the swamps of Moat County.

Dexter's narrator, Jack, is a late adolescent at the time of the novel's action, 1969, one who just lost his swimming scholarship at the University of Florida: "... I was expelled for an act of vandalism. Specifically, I drank a small bottle of vodka and drained the swimming pool, which, while childish, is more complicated work than it may seem from the outside. I don't want to get into the mechanics of it now, but let me assure you that you don't just pull the plug."

This voice (sophomoric it would be called in '69) gives *The Paperboy* a distinct boy's novel tone: everything is seen from a late male adolescent's point of view: slightly leering; dopey, yet arrogant; sex addled, but chaste; full of codes and strictures of honorable behavior, abundant hero worship (of brother Ward). In short, Jack is a pain in the neck.

Ward arrives back in Moat County on assignment from the "Miami Times," bringing along another reporter, Yardley Acheman, and one Charlotte Bless, a bombshell of sorts. Jack's first reaction to her: ". . . current shot through me six directions at once." Charlotte has rounded up the two reporters to help free her new boyfriend, the death row convict Hillary Van Wetter, for being "railroaded" for the killing of Sheriff Thurmond Call some four years back. Charlotte had initiated a prison correspondence with Hillary (she has an interest in killers), and he has become her fiancé, though one "she had yet to meet." Ward and Yardley quickly commence their backwoods version of Woodward and Bernstein.

Paraphrase of *The Paperboy* is in some way an injustice, since the novel itself is written as paraphrase. Dexter is of the lean and mean school. His, for the most part, gripping tale is cinematic and it is expertly sketched, not elaborated upon, and when he does pause longer than a sentence or two (say, in the depiction of Jack and Ward's father), psychological complexity does not arrive to shore up the additional facts and language. Ward and Jack's mother had left their father some years before, "moved to California with a drama teacher from Moat County Junior College," and hardly another word is thought about her by the abandoned male trio, past or present. The world of *The Paperboy* is a boy's world, Horatio Alger's domain – it's the Hardy Boys, only x-rated, guns and butter.

Jack tags along with Ward and Yardley – and Charlotte, for whom Jack's current is still strongly flowing. They meet with Hillary in the state prison, after confronting his local, ineffectual, attorney to receive permission. These scenes are riveting, though the jailhouse visits are mostly safe sex encounters between Hillary and the smitten Charlotte. Hillary's first guttural words to her capture his charm: "You look like your pitcher."

Ward and Yardley get the story, Ward being the leg man, the one who does the actual reporting; Yardley, a Miami man-about-town, is there for the writing. Dexter does seem to want to reinforce one particular cliché about journalism: that great reporting is best displayed by the simplest of language, and any fancy prose style engaged is just so much sticky icing that disfigures the cake.

But there is one bit of reporting that Yardley does (with the pliant Charlotte along) that Ward suspects to be bogus. Ward investigates the source in Daytona Beach, and is brutally assaulted by two sailors he has picked up in a bar. Given his other novels, especially *Paris Trout,* Dexter doesn't flinch at depicting old-fashioned ways of thinking. He tends to revel a bit much in the social mores of the times of his stories – it frees him to transgress against the politically correct. Here he seems to equate homosexuality with self-hatred. Yardley writes the story from Ward's notes. It springs Hillary from prison. It wins the Pulitzer Prize.

But there is a secret at the center of the story, beyond Ward's homosexuality (which does make brother Jack swallow hard, but at least checks his pontifications). Is there a source? Or, if there is one, is it a plant of Hillary's? Letting Hillary out of prison has about the same effect as letting Dracula out of his coffin. Dexter's handling of the various plot lines is skillful, though toward the novel's end, one begins to feel disappointed that there aren't enough pages left to adequately wrap everything up. Everything is – with the exception of old Yardley – wrapped up (though not adequately), thanks to Hurricane Sylvia, but it seems, at this point, Dexter himself is more impatient to be done than his readers might be.

The Paperboy is an out and out yarn, an entertaining story, full of a conflicting mixture of world-weariness and naiveté, told with a chip-on-its-shoulder, humble-pie braggadocio, but all its characters do become real and memorable in their outlandish ways, and I, for one, was sad to see them come to their unfortunate, and hasty, ends.

First appeared in the *Chicago Tribune,* January 29, 1995; © 1995 *Chicago Tribune.* Review of Pete Dexter, *The Paperboy* (New York: Random House, 1995).

John Updike: The Afterlife and Other Stories

When speculation is offered on which white male American fiction writer might next be awarded the Nobel Prize, John Updike's name usually comes up. The Argentinean Jorge Luis Borges, who died in 1986, never received one because of his politics (or, more exactly, his country's politics). One wonders, what would be denying Updike the honor? (Norman Mailer, perhaps, who also impatiently waits in the wings?) Updike is certainly international enough, with his novels set in foreign countries – *The Coup,* and the recent *Brazil.* But Updike's long, brilliant career has lacked one element which usually prevails in Nobel considerations: the humanity novel, the uplifting tract that is embraced wholeheartedly by some section of the reading and critical public. Saul Bellow was able to slide just past that line, aided by an ethnicity that is wired more directly into the tragic world.

And Updike always has been a little sour, a good wine just a bit off. Uplift has always been more of an aesthetic question, with Updike, than a social one. His just released eleventh collection of short fiction, *The Afterlife,* focuses clearly some of his virtues and his vices. Updike has been a rather reluctant experimenter in style and form, and when he has let himself become frisky, it is in the novel, not the short story, where he will gamble and reach.

Since the late fifties when Updike began publishing, through most of the eighties, he seemed to have a divided publishing life (at least in his fiction). He seemed to be split in two: two voices – the Rabbit voice (of the quartet of novels: *Rabbit, Run; Rabbit Redux; Rabbit is Rich; Rabbit at Rest*) and the one that conformed to his autobiographical self, and two publishing venues – the *New Yorker* for his genteel fiction and *Playboy* for his nongenteel (although now, given the changes at the *New Yorker*, that division is no longer necessary). The only other voices he would use would be colorful personas (Bech, for one), and these would be confined, most often, to the novels (with the exception of Bech's).

One thing that stands out about *The Afterlife* is how Updike's two principal voices are becoming one. As if, now that Rabbit is supposedly laid to rest (unless Updike produces *Rabbit Rots*), his voice – the middle class curmudgeon, the closest thing Updike has to a man of the people, the white male not part of any cultural elite – has blended with the upper-middle class voice of most of the short stories (and many of the non-Rabbit novels), the voice of a Harvard-educated, successful writer.

For *The Afterlife*'s stories are bathed not with the pale, simple nostalgia for the far away or long ago, but with a decidedly cold light thrown over those things "lodged deep in the transparent mass of lost time."

The twenty-two stories collected here are often meditations on adultery, and subsequent second and third marriages, and on a world utterly transformed: (from "The Journey to the Dead") ". . . those Fifties and early Sixties when you moved toward your life with an unstressed freedom no one could understand, now, who had not been young then. There was less outside to that world – less money, fewer cars and people and buildings – and more inside, more blood and hopefulness." Most of the stories have a male protagonist of around sixty (roughly Updike's age), and one theme keeps constantly surfacing: (from "Playing with Dynamite") "Things used to be more substantial. In those middle years, as Fanshawe gropingly recalled them, you are hammering out your destiny on bodies still molten and glowing." It is Updike's realization that, as he ages, he becomes less substantial, less here in the world, and this fact appalls him. So the afterlife these stories speak to is not necessarily the one that follows death, but what follows, not one's spent youth, but one's spent middle age: (from "Grandparenting") "He was a newly hatched grandfather, and the universe wanted to crush him, to make room for newcomers."

Updike is the true person of letters: writing and publishing the higher forms of magazine literary criticism, novels, short stories, poetry, plays and memoir. When the semi-informed bemoan the absence of literary journalists such as Edmund Wilson, one can point, among others, to Updike. One effect all his essay writing has had on his short stories is their diminished amount of scene and presentation. Rumination now dominates. His great descriptive talent, Updike being one of the best (again along with Mailer) metaphor makers in contemporary American literature, is somewhat muted in these tales, but it is still there: (from "The Journey to the Dead") "'I suppose. But a woman is like a spider, Marty. She has her web. She likes to feel the different threads vibrate.'" A woman dying of cancer is speaking, for there is a good deal of the usual sort of hovering afterlife in the collection. And (from "His Mother Inside Him"): "The store had been the classier though smaller of the two major downtown emporiums, both rendered defunct by the rise of suburban malls; inside the revolving doors, gusts of candy-sweet perfume had swamped his youthful senses. . . ." That verb, "swamped," is very expensive, and only a writer with Updike's wealth of talent can afford so many.

It is an easy thing to recommend *The Afterlife,* and I wholeheartedly do. I even would recommend its author for the Nobel Prize, but I wouldn't bet on him ever getting it.

First appeared in the *South Bend Tribune,* January 29, 1995;
 Review of John Updike, *The Afterlife and Other Stories* (New York: Knopf, 1994).

John McGahern and Colm Tóibín: *Collected Stories, The Heather Blazing*

On the heels of William Trevor's *Collected Stories,* Ireland sends us another: John McGahern's. That has something to do with the age of both writers (Trevor was born in 1928, McGahern in 1934), but it is also due to the Irish affinity for the modern short story. The daddy of them all, James Joyce's brief 1914 collection, *Dubliners,* has spawned generation upon generation of short stories in this country, as well as in Ireland.

There are a number of crucial differences between the stories of John McGahern and the more lionized William Trevor. Trevor's subjects are largely genteel, steeped with nostalgic disaffection (especially those with Irish locales), somewhat cosmopolitan, whereas McGahern writes about an Irish society so limited, so claustrophobic, so confining, the idea one could be nostalgic about it is a pipe dream.

Anthony Burgess once praised McGahern's work by claiming that no one else so well caught "the peculiar hopelessness of contemporary Ireland." That strange triumph may well account for the fact that McGahern's stories are less well known than Trevor's. Here is a case where, for American readers, the collected stories may well serve as a first introduction (in book form) to McGahern's short fiction. In the states, McGahern is known more for his novels, especially the 1979 book, *The Pornographer.* As that title might indicate, McGahern has had his run-ins with his mother country; his second novel, *The Dark* (1965), was banned in Ireland, and resulted in his being fired from a teaching post at an Irish Catholic school.

That nonlethal fatwa didn't deter McGahern, or empty his work of its sexual and religious subject matter. Reading the thirty-four stories here collected makes one understand why the tide of immigration from Ireland doesn't ebb.

McGahern's best stories are his longest – "The Country Funeral," "The Conversion of William Kirkwood," "Oldfashioned," "Doorways" – stories that amass a lot of close detail of Irish life, family connections, village-life interactions. These are not miniaturized novels, but stories more in the blunt, sociological vein of D.H. Lawrence than the well-honed lyricism of James Joyce. Long stories make up roughly half of the volume; a number of earlier, shorter stories are about, alternately, men alone, and men about to be alone. Read singly they are effective, but read together their repetitions become too apparent. Yet, since this male experience of solitude and disconnectedness seems so prevalent, McGahern has developed quite sharp sensitivity to it: (from "Along the Edges") "With all the casualness of the self-satisfied male, he kissed her goodnight and it caused her to look sharply at him before she went in, but he noticed nothing."

The portraits of father/son and mother/son relationships in McGahern's stories are daunting. In "Sierra Leone," a father wishes to sign over his farm to his son, in order to disinherit the woman he married after the death of his first wife: "'Are you saying to me for the last time that you won't take it?' And when I wouldn't answer he said with great bitterness, 'I should have known. You don't even have respect for your own blood,' and muttering, walked away towards the cattle gathered between the stone wall and the first of the walnut trees. Once or twice he moved as if he might turn back, but he did not. We did not speak any common language."

Most of McGahern's stories render the same verdict: (from "Old-fashioned") "During this time he made a few attempts to get on with his father, but it was more useless than ever." And just as sons have no common language to speak with fathers, and have given up all attempts to get on with them, they never are able to detach from their mothers, or the memory of them: (from "The Wine Breath," a story about a priest who dreams of death now that his mother has died) "But when he looked at the room about him he could hardly believe it was so empty and dead and dry, the empty chair where she should be sewing, the oaken table with the scattered books, the clock on the mantel."

McGahern's tales are utterly convincing, poignant and moving, and the writing is unflinching and spare, but I would not recommend reading more than a handful at one sitting. They are bitter pills, and you do not want to swallow too many at once, filled as they are with the potentially toxic knowledge, expressed in "The Country Funeral," of "the poor fact that it is not generally light but shadow that we cast."

The protagonist of Colm Tóibín's second novel, *The Heather Blazing,* shares with many of McGahern's male figures a similar emotional makeup: as a father he is cold and reserved, detached from his two children, remote to his wife, committed to the law (he is a judge), but barely cognizant of its human applications, and devoid of most tools of self examination.

Eamon Redmond, the judge, recalls one afternoon with his wife – a memory that comes to him after her death – when he tried to explain his detachment. Redmond's wife, Carmel, remarks:

> "You know, when either of your parents are mentioned you become strange. I don't know if you know that but your whole body changes. I feel there's a sort of pain in you I feel it even now that I've mentioned your father and mother."
>
> "My mother died when I was a baby."
>
> "How do you feel about that?"
>
> He was silent, sipped his wine; then he looked out of the window and back to Carmel who was still watching him.
>
> "She is just someone who wasn't there."
>
> "And your father?"
>
> "We managed together, I suppose. It must have been hard for him?"
>
> "And for you?"
>
> "It's hard to talk about it. It made me very self-sufficient. I can look after myself."

That dialogue, and sentiment, is typical of the novel. Tóibín is a younger writer (his first novel, *The South,* appeared in 1991), and he eschews the more directly autobiographical material McGahern and his generation employ. Tóibín has a plain style, and the novel's repeating structure (the last day of a year's session of high court is the starting point for every leap forward in time [three year's worth], whereas the rest of the story is recounted through flashbacks) reinforces the simplicity. Brief scenes from the judge's entire life are relived, and through them we view bits and pieces of post World War II Irish history, seen from the perspective of solid supporters of Eamon de Valera, prime minister of Ireland from 1951–54, and head of the Fianna Fáil party.

Eamon Redmond meets his future wife (when both are teenagers) at a political rally: "'And Fianna Fáil will follow on [de Valera's] good work – that's what I tell them,' Carmen said. 'But we're the party that respects the Church.' She sounded as through she did not believe what she was saying, as though she was trying out slogans on them, and Eamon moved away. . . ."

That postwar period is the most successfully rendered in the novel. For contemporary Ireland, you will need to have read other Irish writes, like McGahern – or seen films or listened to U2 records and Sinéad O'Connor – to provide a context. Unlike McGahern, Tóibín is dealing with almost exclusively well-educated people, but they, too, have immense difficulty finding a "common language," and have largely given up attempts to get on with anyone near them. The novel's title comes from a revolutionary song: "a rebel hand set the heather blazing/And brought the neighbours from far and near." And reading this very undemonstrative and elliptical novel of character, one can assume there is irony at work: the readers who are drawn to *The Heather Blazing* from far and near will view not the blaze, but the barely smoking ashes produced by the Republic of Ireland's current smoldering history.

First appeared in the *Chicago Tribune,* February 14, 1993;
 Review of John McGahern, *The Collected Stories* (New York: Knopf, 1993; Colm Tóibín, *The Heather Blazing* (New York: Viking, 1993).

Jim Crace: Signals of Distress

Jim Crace's new novel, his fourth, *Signals of Distress,* takes a step backward in time from his 1991 novel, *Arcadia,* from the twentieth century to the nineteenth. *Arcadia* was anachronistic in many ways, a quasi-allegorical tale of life and death, as well as a rich depiction of twentieth-century English commerce and culture, written in a style that seemed at odds with its more contemporary subjects. An award-winning English writer, Crace's prose is lush, lyrical, out-of-its-time, but in *Signals of Distress,* it fits the never-never land of period reconstruction (early nineteenth century) quite well.

The story's premise is simple: two ships put into the small coastal English village of Wherrytown during a storm. One, a coastal steam packet, struggles into the harbor; the other, an ocean-traversing barque, is beat-up and beached on a sandbar.

Aboard the coastal steam packet, Ha'porth of Tar, snug in the harbor, is Alymer Smith, its only debarking passenger and the novel's chief protagonist. Alymer is a member of a solid, soap-producing family, Smith and Sons, and, after weathering the storm, he falls asleep and dreams, somewhat prophetically, of "kelp and some young country wife, ensnared and going down, with Alymer drowning in the girl, the girl sucked under by the weed, the weed pitchforked like hay on tines of sea and wind."

Alymer "should have stayed at home instead of meddling abroad," and "abroad" means down the English coast, away from the city. Sundry entanglements ensue. Alymer and the author lay open Wherrytown for us like a ripe fruit torn by an eager hand. Aboard the beached and injured ship, the Belle of Wilmington, is a crew of "Americans" and a slave cook, Otto, whom Alymer indulgently frees. The idea of Otto, more than Otto himself, galvanizes the citizenry and begins to become legendary.

Crace writes historical fictions, and *Signals of Distress* shares a few contemporary antecedents (Hugh Nissenson's *Tree of Life,* for one, Douglas Unger's *The Turkey War,* another): history reimagined or viewed through a very late-twentieth-century microscope (or magnifying glass). What was it like? is answered, sort of, since the issues highlighted come from today's headlines, not necessarily 1837's.

Yet, individual consciousness from centuries past evaporates more quickly than does the architecture, or even the discovered remnants of what people ate once upon a time. How did they think? is still more of a puzzle than what they wore. And Crace is after more than that: he wants to illuminate how society creates itself, how it, early on, sends out its own signals of distress.

And what does the late twentieth century want to know about the early nineteenth? According to Crace, we want to know how chamber pots are put to good use; how many guests share cramped quarters; how the soap industry makes use of technological advances, and deskills, and lays off long-term employees; how food is eaten and prepared; how sex is carried off and endured; how wounds are dressed; how village life mends together and is controlled by a small trinity of people: minister, inn keeper, and hearty business-broker-about-town; how young girls acquire husbands and escape to the new world; how debts are paid, and revenge exacted.

Crace is especially good at describing work, letting it and the novel's characters evolve simultaneously. Here the "Americans" are helping haul in a record catch of fish, pilchards, overseen by the village's reigning businessman, Walter Howells, Wherrytown's CEO:

> The Americans would not get any cash from Walter Howells. He regarded them as volunteers, free labour, and not worth a fourpenny fig between the lot of them, despite their noise and swaggering. They were too clumsy with the fish and were a hindrance rather than a help. They teased each other and flirted with the working women. The splashed their skirts, or dropped a pilchard down their apron fronts, or touched the younger and prettier women unnecessarily while they helped to put the baskets on their backs. The women, happy to be flirted with, on such a high and zesty day, carried the pilchards through the snow and sand up to the salting hall, next to Walter Howells's house. Their baskets filled the lane, the yard, the courtway to the hall. Any living fish that jumped free of the baskets didn't stand a chance. They suffocated on the icy air. Or they were scavenged by cats and gulls and by the little girls whose job it was to grill them for breakfast on the beach fire. There wasn't any idleness. This was a working hive.

Crace's novel has the look of miniaturized Dickens, revved up and sleeked down for the nineties, or one of Gilbert and Sullivan's operetta sailing crews redone by Sam Shepard. The senses are the audaciously appealed to, and life's indignities are wonderfully rendered: "Both eyes were clear and moist. But everything below his nose was blue and swollen. His lips were a pair of overripe damsons, bloated, syrupy and sapped together by dry blood, with stripy wasps of scab feeding at the juice."

Signals of Distress is consistently enjoyable even as one wonders what it is: history? well, no, though a tidbit of fact here and there is doubtless more than accurate; story? yes, but there isn't that much, and one crucial plot turn quite foretell-able. It is more a novel of character, insofar as Crace's cast is to a man (and woman) vivid and compelling; even a small dog has an engaging presence and personality. Such a feat on such a rather small scale might be indigenously British.

Here is the Belle's Captain, after being rudely awakened to be told that the body of a drowned sailor has been found: "The Captain closed the bedroom door. He should have dressed and gone down to the pilchard nets. He should have shown his Captaincy. Instead he went to Mrs. Yapp and took refuge in an hour more of sleep. His head ached badly when he woke. His shoulders were like wood. Hard winds, bad luck, a bar of sand had beached his ship. His masts were down, the cattle lost, the African set loose; the ground was deep in snow; and every half-wit in the land was either staying at the inn or banging at his door in the middle of the night with more bad news. . . ."

For the reader it is a delightful stay in Wherrytown, regardless of the toll it takes on its other inhabitants, natives and transients alike.

First appeared in the *Chicago Tribune,* December 31, 1995;
 Review of Jim Crace, *Signals of Distress* (New York: Farrar, Straus & Giroux, 1994).

Robert Olen Butler: *They Whisper*

Robert Olen Butler's literary career illuminates a number of salient facts about our late-twentieth-century world of writing. Butler published six novels between 1981 and 1989, but it took his remarkable 1992 collection of short stories, *A Good Scent From a Strange Mountain,* which won the 1993 Pulitzer Prize, to make the literary world truly take note.

The Pulitzer prompted the *New York Times* to run a profile asking, "Just who in the world is Robert Olen Butler?"

With the publication of his new novel, *They Whisper,* that question may be more readily answered. Butler has always been something of an enigma. Not many young men who graduated with a master's degree in playwriting from the University of Iowa in 1969 rushed off to enlist in the Army as counter-intelligence special agents. Thanks to the Army's training, he became fluent in the Vietnamese language, and it is clear from what he has written that his experiences in Vietnam are ones he wouldn't have missed for the world. He left Vietnam in 1972, and from 1975 to 1985 he was editor-in-chief of a business newspaper in New York. He was married in 1972, and has one child, a boy.

These bits of biography are pertinent only because *They Whisper* is in the form of a memoir – and the life of its narrator, Ira Holloway, conforms in many ways to Butler's own – ending in 1980, a year before Butler's first novel, *The Alleys of Eden,* was published.

Read as a novel, without any knowledge of Butler, *They Whisper* is one book; read with some knowledge of its author, it is another, due to the nature of the memoir form. Memoir does not, as one might readily assume, stem from simple memory; the root of the word is memorandum, another idea altogether.

Memoirs are public documents in the sense that they are written by people who have been involved in important events. When one embarks on a novel in the form of a memoir, one needs to provide a context for the personal events depicted. If it is nonfiction, the context is there: it is history. If it is a novel, it needs to be invented or given to the characters.

The flaw with *They Whisper* (if one chooses to read it that way) is that there isn't much context here. But if you let the "nonfiction" leak in, the facts of Butler's life, it fills out what is missing, aspects of character that are never alluded to in the novel or put to question.

When, toward the novel's end, Ira tells us, looking through a massage parlor's (Vietnam's most successful export) two-way mirror at a roomful of available women, "I am weak with love for them all," we truly believe him, since after 298 pages it is quite a redundant observation on his part.

Ira has had a most peculiar sexual evolution for an American male. The early part of *They Whisper* contains charming, fresh, though not unfamiliar, tales of sexual awakening in, and around, Wabash, Ill., during the late fifties and early sixties – experiences with the aloof tomboy and the high school slut, Midwestern boyish yearning on humid summer nights, which Butler does as well as anyone.

After this mild preamble (somehow university experience doesn't figure much at all), it's off to Vietnam, and Ira, almost alone among the hundreds of thousands of men sent there, is equipped with a key to the hearts of Vietnamese women: their language. He is both a voice and a pen, intellectually and sexually.

Ira is a sensualist, and that he manages to make his instantaneous falling in love with a Vietnamese woman who is soon to be executed – thanks in part to his interrogation, which is purely seduction on his part – not monstrously out of place is a feat not to be taken lightly.

There is something preposterous about Ira, but not unbelievable. Vietnam is a cornucopia of flesh for him; whatever that war was, it mainly served as a horrendously costly procurer for Ira.

But then it's back to the States in 1972. Greenwich Village and Saigon are in most ways dissimilar, except he meets Fiona, his wife-to-be, on the street there. At this point, *They Whisper* becomes a bad marriage novel; Ira assumes the unlikely role (given his history in Vietnam) of battered spouse.

He is not a violent man, and his position as a linguist in Vietnam has limited the amount of carnage he has personally caused. Earlier signs of Fiona's instability, before marriage, gave their relationship an interesting erotic edge, but after marriage its progress renders him the numbed witness, a victim of her developing religious mania.

Butler never makes Fiona a character much beyond her body, in the sense that we never hear what they might talk about, or what he might have been interested in outside her body language. Ira, too, ultimately lacks dimension. Most notably, we never are permitted a sense of his ambition: it is just absent, or we need to take it for granted.

For, what is an articulate sensualist to be, but a writer?

Except it is never considered. His ambition seems to be merely employed – "I was writing some little ode to a handheld calculator" – at a company that allows him to meet a few interesting women. It is where the problem of fiction and nonfiction becomes most grating. We might presume Ira wants to become a novelist and win the Pulitzer Prize someday, but it is never mentioned, and what he thinks about the larger world, too, is kept eerily at bay.

There are only a handful of novels by contemporary male writers that tackle the subject of heterosexual male longing, and *They Whisper* presents a compelling and detailed view of it. The topic is often avoided at book length, not because of reservations about gentility, but because of how foolish an author can appear, so completely exposed. Regardless of all the talk about sex in serious contemporary novels, one discovers that there is actually not that much on the page, and when one finds it, there is usually more naming than description. Butler takes his time. We know women and eroticism are important to him. As a memoir, *They Whisper* is revelatory and dramatic; as a novel, it is frustrating, though always provocative.

First appeared in the South Bend *Tribune,* April 17, 1994; Review of Robert Olen Butler, *They Whisper* (New York: Henry Holt & Co., 1994).

Richard Ford: Independence Day

Richard Ford's brilliant, engrossing new novel, *Independence Day,* is, according to its publisher "the long-awaited sequel" to Ford's 1986 novel, *The Sportswriter,* though that novel did not seem to cry out for, or promise, a sequel. The new novel, *Independence Day,* most assuredly, does. *The Sportswriter* was one of the few successful attempts to "break out" a literary writer, give him a larger audience immediately, and this was accomplished by publishing the novel as a trade paperback original, skipping entirely a hardcover edition. It worked; it was widely reviewed, though *The Sportswriter* received somewhat mixed notices. There has always been a critical uneasiness about Ford's work as a novelist.

All the ambivalence disappeared, in 1987, with the publication of Ford's collection of short stories, *Rock Springs.* It was as if the vices detected in the novels (great minor characters, troubling major ones, for instance) became virtues in the short stories, since short stories are a matter of vivid minor characters. The praise heaped on Ford was unstinting and deserved. Just this year, he was named the winner of the Rea Award for the Short Story, given to writers who have made significant contributions to the form.

With the publication of *Independence Day,* Ford's fifth novel, following the largely unheralded *Wildlife* (1990), Ford begins to resemble – given that *Independence Day* is a sequel (and, most likely, a prequel) – an unlikely model: John Updike and his Rabbit series. Frank Bascombe, former sportswriter and short story-ist, five years older since we last left him, is becoming Harry "Rabbit" Angstrom, though Harry in the later phase of the Updike pentalogy, the upper-middle-class Harry of *Rabbit is Rich*. "I live happily if slightly bemusedly in a forty-four-year-old bachelor's way in my former wife's house at 116 Cleveland, in the 'Presidents Streets' section of Haddam, New Jersey," Bascombe reports.

There are crucial differences, of course, which seem to be generational. One of the most striking is the narrative voice Ford uses in both Bascombe novels, first-person, present tense, a point of view both contemporary and peculiar. Each novel covers only a handful of days, which allows for a good bit of past tense recollection, but the present tense is there, annoyingly in your face.

Ford wants us to accept a first-person, present tense narrator as a new convention – just go with it. I find the convention hard to swallow, especially when the narrator is a lapsed writer, as Bascombe is, who keeps telling us ("my long-ago and momentary life as a writer") that he won't be taking that up again. What does he think he's doing? He's not talking to himself.

Both *The Sportswriter* and *Independence Day* are in the long novelistic tradition of the memoir form. But what is this form in the present tense? a voiceover narrating the everyday, an outpouring of one's immediate thoughts and responses. The equivalent of this method is, unfortunately, talk radio. And a number of times it presents the reader and Ford with ludicrous situations (Bascombe narrates jauntily when occurrences depicted should leave him speechless – or at least, for a moment, at a loss for words), which color one's reaction to Frank and the entire novel.

How one reacts to Frank will dominate one's opinion of *Independence Day*. (Readers of the earlier novel will find no slackening of his charms.) He's popular with the ladies, has the kind of looks and gait most everyone finds appealing, is glib, and more than presentable, and fell into enough money (from the movie sale of his one and only collection of short stories) to be upper-middle class at the beginning of the eighties. The divorce from "X" (as she was called in *The Sportswriter*, now Ann, though no explanation is given for the new lack of reticence) has not reduced his circumstances (Ann has married someone older and richer than Frank, has custody of their kids, and is well housed on the shore in Connecticut). And Frank has now found the most faux-intimate profession, suitable for his voyeuristic tendencies: he sells real estate, expensive homes, though the boom has softened in 1988, the time of the novel, the July fourth weekend of the Bush-Dukakis election campaigns.

Late in the novel, one of the wonderfully sketched minor, very minor, characters (Ford does a knock-out job with these; this is a long novel, but it is stuffed, a veritable pomegranate, with small, gem-like portraits) pops up, Carter, a former neighbor of Bascombe's, which leads him to speculate, "Carter, I'm positive, couldn't tell me where I was born, or when, or what my father's job was, or what college I attended," and, though a very careful reader might be able to answer some of that list, it serves only to remind us of how little we do know of Bascombe's life before marriage, and his hollowed-out childhood contributes to the vacancy one can feel exists at the heart of Frank's character.

Arriving at his mid-forties, Frank has reached his "Existence Period," one of the themes of which is "that interest can mingle successfully with uninterest in this way, intimacy with transience, caring with the obdurate uncaring." Bascombe finds it easier to draw a bead on others, rather than himself, since he contends he is not "a man who believes life's leading someplace." Frank, in his way, strives to be ordinary, to be an everyman, though that seems to be more Ford's problem (in the sense that Ford is not ordinary, but wants his literary offspring to be a regular guy).

Updike had an easier time making Rabbit ordinary; he didn't make him a one-book, arty author to start with. But it's hard not to like Frank – who wouldn't like someone who makes fun of *Democracy in America* ("a book I defy anyone to read who is not on some form of life support") and people who have spent too much time in "addlebrained Vermont – picking berries, spying on deer and making homespun clothes using time-honored methods."

There are many pleasures to be found in *Independence Day.* The first ninety pages or so of house selling will be instructive and entertaining to most anyone, and Bascombe's wise cracking is often tartly wise. But, like Updike via Rabbit, it is the author's portrait of America as it, and his protagonist, evolve and change that Ford fixes so well: Bascombe might make fun of de Tocqueville, but that is what we get throughout *Independence Day* – what democracy looks like in America, the eighties in summation, the country palpably alive – for what distinguishes Frank as an American with a capital A is his love of life, energy, things and, however trammeled, his own free-wheeling thoughts, and his atavistic impulse toward independence.

There is not much story to recount (though there is a profusion of events). In *The Sportswriter* Bascombe's oldest boy, Ralph, has died in childhood of Reye's; in *Independence Day* the remaining son, Paul, now a teenager, is menaced by life and Bascombe's so-distant parenting. There is a visit with Frank's latest girlfriend, Sally, with whom he may, or may not, break up, and the ex-wife, Ann, in Connecticut, as well as brief encounter, there, with his young daughter. There are excursions with Paul to the, in order, Basketball and Baseball Halls of Fame. Race and class make interesting appearances. Minor characters are murdered, and a major character badly injured, but none of those strings is tied up. Perhaps they are there for the next go around. (There is a propensity for violence in Frank that flares up a couple of startling times, but is not acted on, though it might be if Ford does take Bascombe into the 1990s.) And, given the various strengths and compelling virtues of this important novel, I'll be, this time, waiting for the next one.

Harvey Jacobs: *American Goliath*

Satire often has two faces: one is Swiftian – savage – the other is Thurberesque – lovable. Among famous contemporary satirists, one might think of the face of, say, Andy Rooney, or, less well-known, the author at hand, novelist Harvey Jacobs. The Swiftian sort of satire is scalding: it wants to burn what it satirizes from off the face of the earth. The Thurber sort, the Andy Rooney sort, couldn't live without what it makes fun of, since it needs the material for its own humor, amusement.

Harvey Jacobs's new novel, *American Goliath,* is an entirely successful satire of the second sort. His novel mines the "true, incredible events" of willful mass delusion suffered by large numbers of the citizens of New York State soon after the close of the Civil War: the "discovery" on a humble farm of a buried giant man, thought to be a petrified person or a statue of great antiquity, one possessed of magical powers. *American Goliath* is a riot of dedicated humbug and slapstick denunciation. All historical fiction (Jacobs's novel starts in 1868 and ends, more or less, in 1870) is written to be viewed through a scrim of contemporary consciousness, no matter how authentic the costuming might be of the players cavorting on stage. Jacobs is following a traditional, and well-rutted, road; one often traveled, especially since E. L. Doctorow's *Ragtime* (1975); one frequented by contemporary writers as diverse as Jim Crace (*Signals of Distress*, 1995), and William T. Vollmann (the *Seven Dreams* series, begun in 1990).

One reason why today's authors are reaching back into the bin of history is the fatigue generated by our current media-drenched contemporary world, where the here-and-now is omnipresent and, subsequently, becomes quickly tired of: it fades on its electronic shelf, yellows around the edges. To find freshness, authors have donned pith helmets and have gone hacking through the thickets of library stacks (and past libel laws' statutes of limitations), looking for valuable morsels, the more ludicrous, and grotesque, the better. Artifacts, such as the giant stone man of Cardiff, N.Y., are at least long-gone, and their relative deadness gives them vitality as story material. The hackneyed, alas, is now the everyday.

As satire has two faces, there are two principal uses made of these historical finds: one is terror, the crime story resuscitated; some lesser known Jack-the-Ripper sort of character is exhumed, and his or her terrible deeds are put on display, hence the great success of Caleb Carr's *The Alienist* (1995), for instance.

Then there is the comic turn. Harvey Jacobs's fresh morsel "the Cardiff Giant," is, to quote how the Library of Congress delicately catalogues it, a "Forgery of antiquities," belonging to "New York (State) – History – 19th century." But not just any historical oddity will automatically turn into captivating and useful fiction: it does need to speak to our time. And here Jacobs has the late twentieth century, not the nineteenth, right smack in his crosshairs.

THE TABLOIDIZATION OF HISTORY

What is our present media age but a hoax of giants? Throughout *American Goliath* the contemporary parallels offer themselves up all-too-rapidly: our recent and current presidents, Nixon, Ford, Reagan, Bush, and Clinton (not to slight the merely vice presidential, Agnew, Quayle, and Gore), a crew all simultaneously alive and kicking until just a few short years ago. And the media's much improved (since the 19th century) ability to make mountains out of molehills (as the Cardiff giant was made out of a slab of Iowa granite), so that the words "news" and "hoax" take on complementary meaning, rather than their once, more sober, definitions. Are O.J., Princess Di, etc., more news than hoax, or more hoax than news?

So, Jacobs has both his curio, and his modern subject, and he runs with it. Jacobs is very much in tune with his times, since his career has made him something of a multi-media personality himself. He is a novelist (*Beautiful Soup* (1993), *The Juror* (1980), *Summer on a Mountain of Spices* (1975)) and short-story-writer (*The Egg of the Glak* (1969)), but even more pertinently, he is a television writer and dramatist, one who worked for ABC for fifteen years as director of industry affairs and satellite communication. *American Goliath* is indeed a novel, a literary event, but it is one that is shot through with larger media awareness and consciousness.

And Jacobs has his own informative website – www.americango liath.com – as well. As Jacobs makes the block of granite that becomes Goliath aware of the outside world, so too is the novel itself aware of the multimedia world it has been launched into.

RUSHING TO THE PAST

Another benefit Jacobs gets from rushing to the past is that he can bring to the page a florid style without seeming precious or anachronistic. The plain style of our electronic media age is always startled by any vocabulary or sentence structure that hints of the baroque. When such a style is assigned to "olden" times, it is tolerated, so Jacobs's wit, and somewhat fancy prose, can be safely enjoyed without being censured as out of step with the times.

One reason history revisited is appealing and potent today is the tabloidization of all news, brought about not by the tabloids, but by television. If we see all our news in our living rooms, and all our news is personalized through personalities, real people, we begin to be more interested in the people than the news itself. If we have an uncle, we worry about his impending divorce as well as his views on NAFTA. And television turns all public figures into relations for us: the American public, our one, big, happy family.

So, too, all the historical figures who populate *American Goliath,* Cornelius Vanderbilt, P.T. Barnum, Jim Fisk, Boss Tweed, and on and on, we get from belt (or below) level, but that is what we have come to expect and want from our public figures: the real story. The private has trumped the public, insofar as the medium (television) is a very private one indeed. If news is advertising, and if advertising creates desire, so news creates desire – the desire to know those who make it. Jacobs taps into this in an intense and winning way in *American Goliath.* His story starts with a short preamble by the block of granite that is to become the Cardiff giant (the preamble concludes, "Congealed eternity. I think I will sleep now. Or am I asleep?"), and then Jacobs introduces the erstwhile protagonist, George Hull, who "drifted through a dream, smoking himself. He turned into a cigar, a Partagas El Cid Corona: thick, mellow, and slow-burning."

George is the son of a successful cigar merchant, Simon Hull. (Here Jacobs is catching the recherché, pro-cigar, fashion wave.) George is married to a Civil War widow, Angelica, whose former husband was paid to take George's place in the ranks: one provision was that should he die George would marry his widow and produce a child, an heir-not-so-apparent.

What George does produce is his scheme of the Cardiff giant, a scam and a hoax to show up the religious poseur, Reverend Mr. Henry Turk, who is engaged to George's sister, decamped from the ancestral home in Binghamton for the empty wilds of Ackley, Iowa. Brother George's impulse is to defraud the hypocritical (it is the Rev. Turk, who, along with grotesquely converting the Indians out west, is preaching from Genesis that: "There were giants in the earth in those days," and that earth was the United States of America. Imagine someone wanting to play a hoax on Jim Bakker, or Pat Robertson, or Jimmy Swaggart, or Jerry Falwell – well there was Larry Flynt trying to do something to upset Rev. Falwell.

In our day and age, satire can seem rather toothless, since nothing upsets anyone: the hypocritical can be revealed and emerged enhanced rather than diminished (pick your candidate from the religious above, or, say, the secular political consultant Dick Morris). Fame enlarged is fame preserved. Jacobs's novel makes sport of our sad, present-day, phenomenon.

A DUEL OF CHARLATANS

George and his extended family's penchants fill the early pages of the novel. (George regularly visits his sister-in-law Loretta in her morning bed, while his brother Ben, Loretta's husband, an early riser, has gone off to roll cigars. George views the lubricious Loretta: "There were her feet, toes curled, ten startled witnesses to an unfolding crime.") Jacobs keeps up a sustained level of bawdiness throughout the novel ("Breasts with nipples like pussy willow destroyed all restraint"), part of the overall tone of enjoyment throughout, shared enjoyment of human foibles and pratfalls.

After the Hull family, and its domestic complications, we have the social world, the avatar for that being Barnaby Rack, ace reporter for the New York *Clarion*. We meet Rack on our most famous battlefield: "His managing editor, John Zipmeister, told him to trundle his ass to Gettysburg before the bodies buried there cooled to oblivion. 'I don't want a war story,' Zipmeister had said. 'I want a postwar story.'" Following his assignment, Rack selects a name from a grave and goes off to track down the dead man's story (as it happens, Angelica's former husband), and, so innocently, the private and the public are braided together. Before Rack exits the cemetery, he runs into P.T. Barnum's favorite dwarf, Tom Thumb, and the other crucial modern element, show business, is entwined: "'May I ask why Tom Thumb is in Gettysburg?' 'To pay tribute. As a General to his troops. Though this battle was none of my making and I'm glad of that. The carnage, the carnage. Why must the future be built on blood? And you?'" The potent American trinity is formed: the private, the public, and the promoter – a powerful combination. Rack's last sight of Tom Thumb that day captures Jacobs's effective use of atmosphere and comedy: "Barnaby saw General Thumb rise over the horizon, spinning like a fragile pinwheel, dodging fire, still singing anthems to his audience of skeletons."

George Hull and company reenter on the way to Iowa to visit his sister: "George appreciated the mobile miracle provided by the Pullman Company, a splendid example of technology in the service of affluence." Angelica remains "unimpregnated," but the idea of the giant is hatched: "George Hull's swollen brain uncurled a worm. . . . Giants they wanted? Giants they needed? Should such a gigantic appetite be ignored?"

Implementing the hoax requires a cast of comic minor characters, and Jacob does each of them superbly. Though not speaking blank verse, they are the clowns, knaves, villains, and grave-diggers taken from Shakespeare's local repertory company.

The giant is fashioned, carted, buried in New York State, discovered and exalted. America is given what it wants, and needs, unsettled from a Civil War and President's assassination – something to believe in. (And what have we been given of late: Angels in America? Septuplets?) And Goliath is not just a stone behemoth, a "fossilized" man of gigantic proportions, but more importantly, a cash cow.

P.T. Barnum can't stomach an amateur having all the luck, so he quickly fashions a competitor, "the only, original," giant, named Titan, to compete with Hull's "Goliath." Both are brought eventually to Manhattan for the novel's climatic battle, a duel of charlatans.

HUMBUGS TO ORDER

American Goliath is a portrait of America's origins, and it attempts to travel all the streams that overflow their banks today. One is our indigenous anti-Semitism, which Jacobs handles, as he handles everything, with a comic touch. The Borscht belt includes New York State, but it also runs through the territory of the novel. Aaron Bupkin is the book's catalytic character, a dowser, "the famous Jew water witch." Aaron is leavening throughout the story, both inside and outside of the action, the town, the community. He has heard about Reverend Turk's tract that "made the case for America as the Holy Land where Biblical giants once frolicked like rabbits. Its author, a Christian evangelist named Turk, presented a premise entirely absurd but surely intriguing. Riding to Cardiff, Aaron speculated that if there were giants in Onondaga County, a few of them must have been Yids. He imagined an enormous

Jew breaking through the trees, blocking the trail, waving a staff, proclaiming in thunder: 'Shema Yisrael Adonai eloheinu Adonai ehad!' Hear, oh Israel, the Lord is God, the Lord is One. So tell me, is this the best road to Syracuse?"

No character is wasted in *American Goliath*; all of them interact, overlap, before the final page is turned. Having a dwarf (Tom Thumb), a Jew (Aaron), a Hull (George), and assorted other archetypes and symbolic personages, Jacobs is able to map a lot of present-day American cultural cartography.

The manner of the novel is intelligent comic melodrama and its form is hundreds of short scenes, dated and placed, which reinforces the play-like drama that is unfolding. (Think of Stephen Vincent Benet's *The Devil and Daniel Webster.*) *American Goliath* is up to date with its short bursts of story, which seem to understand the late-twentieth-century lure of short attention spans (never be boring), but also hoping for the rare readers with a long attention span with which to knit the scenes together. Throughout the novel, Jacobs employs a superior kind of superficiality, with offhand descriptions such as, "'He's the color of ice. I see through to his bones,'" which is Angelica's first glimpse of Aaron Bumpkin, a meeting soon to further complicate his life and hers.

Jacobs can't shake his apparent innate good-naturedness, or escape being the sort of satirist that loves what is being satirized. He is no Swift – perhaps because he believes that the folly around him can't be burnt off the face of the earth, except by the ultimate folly of the most absurd fools themselves. *American Goliath* is a delightful trip through the rise and fall of a phenomenon. Here today, gone tomorrow. By way of resolution, Jacobs has Barnum say to Hull, when their scams are revealed, and, more importantly, their attractions' audiences have dwindled, "'The crowd makes its humbugs to order. If we hadn't been there to give them their giants then we'd have cause for guilt. But we were and we did. A pair of *American Goliaths* clumping out of the fog with hope in their hearts. . . ."

A satirist with hope! As one of the talking stone men might have said, "Look what we all have come to."

First appeared in *The World & I,* vol. 13, no. 2, February 1998, a publication of the Washington Times Corporation and is reprinted with permission. Review of Harvey Jacobs, *American Goliath: Inspired by the True, Incredible Events Surrounding the Mysterious Marvel Known to an Astonished World as The Cardiff Giant* (New York: St. Martin's Press, 1997).

Thomas Keneally: American Scoundrel

Thomas Keneally likes to write about rogues with hearts of gold, bounders who do well by their fellow citizens in times of great crisis. Keneally's Booker-Prize-winning novel, *Schindler's Ark,* which became the basis of the film *Schindler's List,* made this clear. His rollicking, captivating new book, *American Scoundrel,* focuses on Daniel Sickles, the indefatigable son of corrupt Tammany Hall, who was notorious when young, and whose fame only grew greater as he lived to a very ripe old age (ninety-four). But, as bright as that fame was, it cooled more rapidly than any contemporary would have guessed. Now Keneally brings Sickles back to life, in every colorful and scandalous detail.

Keneally takes the less traveled road to great events. Schindler was his oblique path to World War II and the Holocaust, and Sickles's amazing life leads to the Civil War and reconstruction, up past the dawn of the twentieth century.

Unlike the last major attempt to popularize him, W. A. Swanberg's 1956 biography, *Sickles the Incredible,* which deals with Sickles's first wife Teresa sparingly, Keneally takes pains to give her, if not equal time, equal status in the narrative.

For it was her affair with Barton Key, the son of Francis Scott Key, that made Sickles a thoroughly infamous figure of his time. He shot and killed Key a few blocks from the White House in what was called, in the nineteenth century, "broad daylight," leading to a scandalous trial, the O.J. courtroom drama of its day.

Indeed, Keneally's version of Sickles life gains its remarkable clarity and bite because it is filtered through a very contemporary lens. Its treatment of Teresa and the social mores of the country as it heads, inexorably, toward civil war is made vibrant and modern with Keneally's own sympathy and understanding, tempered, in a provocative way, by his Australian roots.

Here is a very American story, written with a dash of distance and skepticism, by a prolific novelist who wields his outsider's perspective effectively. American academic historians usually do not make fun of Abe Lincoln, and his wife, Mary Todd Lincoln, as well as other iconic American figures. Keneally's irreverence is both refreshing and enlightening. We learn why no one ever quotes Lincoln's first inaugural address, only his second, and why South Carolina still clings to the confederate battle flag.

Though Sickles's role in the battle of Gettysburg is how he has hung on to his place in history (then, as now, war was the vehicle of rehabilitation, which let Sickles be treated seriously once again, after being dismissed by a large part of the public as a troublesome lightweight), and is featured in the book's jacket illustration, it is over two hundred pages until we get there. The book's early chapters detail Sickles's sexual history and peccadilloes, though much more gracefully than, say, the Starr Report chronicles Bill Clinton's.

Keneally tells us that, as a teenager, "Dan had been considered by his parents, George Garret Sickles and Susan Marsh Sickles, to be sufficiently unsettled and in need of special tutoring that they arranged for him to live in the scholarly house of the Da Ponte family on Spring

Street, New York." As Keneally reveals: "It was a household like few others in that hard-handed, mercantile city."

The household's head, Da Ponte, the librettist of Mozart, oversaw a domestic enterprise that outdid any opera known to exist. Sickles met his future wife, Teresa, as an infant there, and married her when she turned fifteen.

Throughout, Keneally's novelistic impulses are in charge. Not that he, evidently, invents anything, but his interests lie in the realm of experience and sensation, of facts set in the context of the messiness of daily life, the material a novelist's imagination usually brings to the page.

He captures the textures of New York City and its male-drenched, close-knit, friendship-oiled politics of the period deftly, and shows how Sickles's prodigious gifts and life-force bound people to him, both friends and foes.

Luckily, some of Sickles's friends became presidents of the United States and when Sickles murdered Barton Key, one eyewitness fled to the White House to confer with President Buchanan about what he should do. Buchanan told the young man: "He should leave Washington straightaway, and return home on indefinite leave. Hence an American President, often referred to as the Chief Magistrate of the Republic, urged a witness – for all he knew the only witness to the murder – to flee from his legal responsibility."

By that point, midway through the book, one is well aware that Keneally has made a mistake: his title should be plural, not singular, American Scoundrels, not scoundrel.

During the last decade, we heard much tsk-tsking about mixing the personal with the political, that what one did in one's private life did not affect the public side. If that were true, this engrossing, entertaining history could not have been written, for Keneally shows how deeply interconnected the personal and the political are.

Keneally boldly steps forward in his narrative, writing: "In describing Civil War campaigns of the kind in which Dan was involved and for whose resolution Teresa waited, a writer runs the risk of bamboozling the reader with geographic names and terminology that tell everything except the human feel of events."

And Keneally is no bamboozler. He delivers, in spades, the human feel of events. And it is not so much that Dan Sickles was larger than life, but, in Keneally's brilliant telling, life was larger then.

First appeared in the Chicago *Sun-Times*, April 7, 2002.
Review of Thomas Keneally, *American Scoundrel: The Life of the Notorious Civil War General Dan Sickles.* (New York: Nan A. Talese/Doubleday, 2002).

John L'Heureux: *The Miracle*

John L'Heureux is a member of an endangered species. He was born in 1934 and has been a fairly prolific writer throughout his life. His first book was a volume of poems, *Quick as Dandelions,* published in 1964. Sixteen other books have followed, mainly fiction. L'Heureux was ordained a Jesuit priest in 1965, and he left the order in 1971. Those dates, more or less, mirror the time span in his new novel, *The Miracle.*

None of that biography should mark him as an endangered species, except that L'Heureux is the epitome of the mid-list author. Throughout the years, he has regularly published novels with commercial presses, and, though none have been exactly bestsellers, big publishing has stuck with him, for a variety of admirable reasons. His career as a writer is not likely to be duplicated by later generations. His cohort is the last to benefit from publishing's age of gentility, which has come almost completely to an end.

L'Heureux has been able to profit from being a niche author, and to chafe at the restrictions at the same time. He fits, not entirely comfortably, among a number of Catholic writers – James Carroll, Eugene Kennedy, ex-priests who have turned to fiction, as well as priest authors like Andrew Greeley. L'Heureux does not write large, sprawling, commercially successful potboilers, as do those three authors, but rather short, spare novels, ones most often composed in a prose described relentlessly as "deceptively simple," or, as the language of *The Miracle* already has been dubbed by the reviewer for the *New York Times Book Review,* "prose of unaffected simplicity."

LITERARY SPARENESS

Such spareness gives L'Heureux's work a decidedly literary cast. His novels have been both praised and damned by critics, but there has been enough good press to offset the bad, and to leave ultimate literary judgments an open question.

But, overall, there is an unsettledness about his work, both in general, and in particular. It pops up in most of his books, and it certainly does in *The Miracle.*

It's seems hard for L'Heureux to be completely serious. The novel that most tasked that impulse was the harrowing *The Shrine at Altamira,* published in 1992. In that novel, a father sets afire his young son in retribution for his wife's leaving him. There have been bits of horror in L'Heureux's other novels, but none other lingers over it so reverently. This terrible maiming, this hideous crime, seems to transfix L'Heureux so much so, that in this novel, alone, is he able to leave aside the occasions of silliness, the itch to make fun, to be facilely satirical, that show up elsewhere in his writing.

Including in *The Miracle.* Its story is not ripped from the headlines, as was the tale of *The Shrine at Altamira,* which I think is his best, most satisfying work. That novel contains an odd prologue, a cautionary note, which states: "We hear stories like this on television but we do not look, and when they turn up in newspapers, we glance away. . . ." But, *The Miracle* was doubtless well underway, if not finished, before all the latest dirty laundry of the Catholic Church has been aired out in the press.

Indeed, L'Heureux attempts to shut out most of the contemporary world in this small book. The novel takes place, briefly, in South Boston, and at length in a never-never land of a small seaside New Hampshire town, in an amorphous time frame, the very early seventies, which was a quite noisy time, but is not much heard in the village, which is hardly named, and referred to most often as the parish of Our Lady of Victories.

The Beatles tune, "Hey Jude," is said to be new, though that would make it 1969–70, though the Vietnam war has come to an end, which would make it 1975, or later. But L'Heureux is not exactly a social novelist, since there are other odd mistakes, like over-the-shoulder seat belts being used, which hadn't yet come into general use back then. He's more after tracking down social mores, than social material.

THE OLD SIN SANDWICH

Father LeBlanc – he is not so much whiteness as he is a blank – is exiled to this quaint town, because complaints have been lodged about his downplaying birth control restrictions and other Church sex-related dogma. About hearing confession: "The old sin sandwich: put the easy stuff at the top and bottom and then slip masturbation into the middle where it might not be noticed." Father LeBlanc is lenient and understanding. So, too, with birth control: "'Why do you mention this in confession?' he asks. And then he talks about it slowly, carefully, helping each one realize it is her own conscience she has to live with, not the pope's."

His bishop, it appears, is wisely sending Father LeBlanc away to confront the central question of whether he wants to be a priest, or not. But Father LeBlanc never has this thought. It must be inferred. Even L'Heureux doesn't seem to have had it.

The Miracle not only employs a simple prose style, but it is a cinematic one, too. Lean as a screenplay treatment, it zips along with scenes seldom longer than a page or two, as if the reader's attention span will be taxed with too much contemplation if we stay overlong in one place, or with one set of characters.

This lightness has its appeal. We're being told a story, by whom seems unimportant even to its author, about this good man with spiritual doubts. Father LeBlanc is sent off to help a dying priest, Father Moriarty, the most charming character in the novel ("Father Moriarty has ALS, which the nurse calls Lou Gehrig's disease, though he himself calls it amyotrophic lateral sclerosis. 'It's my own goddamn disease, not some baseball player's.'"); LeBlanc becomes involved with the old priest's housekeeper, Rose, a young, single mom who doesn't seem young, until we're told she is, though we are informed Father LeBlanc sees her as "pleasant. A little overweight. Pretty, he supposes."

It is her teenage daughter, Mandy, who is the miracle in question. Rose returns to her attic apartment above the Clam Box and finds her daughter – more or less – dead of a drug overdose. Time elapses, enough to allow the summoning of Father LeBlanc; Sal, the Clam Box proprietor; and Dr. Forbes, the village's alcohol-challenged physician. All, including the doctor, pronounce her dead and gone. But Rose cannot accept that. After an ambulance is summoned, she forces them from the room and prays to, or, rather, orders, the Virgin Mary: "You've got to be quick, she says, you've got to do this right away. The ambulance will be coming and they'll take her and then she'll be dead. I want her back, she says. I want her now. Do you hear me?"

At the same time, bedridden Father Moriarty, "eyes closed and gazing at the ocean, sees the surface break and a face appear, then a whole head, and thick hair fanning out on the dark water. It is a young girl, laughing carelessly, abandoned. Her face is shining. She is a vision, but she is full of life and she will never die."

Father Moriarty, he being the holiest fellow available, as well as dying from ALS, saves, it appears, Mandy. He is God's vehicle for intercession – or the quartet of personnel on hand failed to detect a blood flow, however faint, which still pulses. Mandy's eyelids flutter, she revives, with only a headache to show for her momentary otherworldliness.

Father LeBlanc considers it a miracle, though. Dr. Forbes is grateful that he hasn't been made to appear foolish. Rose is grateful and attends mass everyday, as she had promised the Virgin, but such proximity to Father LeBlanc only leads her to even closer contact after Mandy's original resurrection is rudely revoked.

NO WEEPING STATUARY

L'Heureux manages to make this mumbo-jumbo fall within the boundaries of willing suspension of disbelief. His lean, reportorial style does not overload the system with conflicting data that spoils the suspense, or makes the unlikely preposterous. Three amateurs and one alcoholic doctor can all make a mistake, right? Right.

Luckily, this is no weeping Long Island statuary, or leaking portrait of the Madonna, no public shrine announcing in neon MIRACLE, MIRACLE! Only the four have seen Mandy raised from the dead, and none of them make that much of it. The feat remains private, almost.

Father LeBlanc finds a new interest in Rose, however, since he thinks she was the agent of grace, rather than the infirm Father Moriarty. Father LeBlanc wants to possess, to know, the source of such power, the woman who "loved" her daughter back to life. And, eventually, he possesses Rose, the first woman he has ever made love to.

L'Heureux's sexual depiction has something of a first-time-ever quality about it, too. "They move in unison. They thrust. They ache. Finally they come together and dissolve in each other's arms. It is a kind of worship." There is no jaded roué at work here.

Complications ensue. Another woman, more appropriate in education and class, becomes interested in Father LeBlanc, having been taken by his good looks, strong physique, and an especially heartfelt sermon he has given based on, but not alluding to, Mandy's revival – and Jesus raising Lazarus from the dead. "'On the last day we will be asked the only question that matters. Not were you good or bad. And certainly not were you successful, were you popular, were you rich. But this, only this: 'Whom have you loved back to life when they were dead?'"

Father LeBlanc becomes, as he puts it, this woman's "vocation."

The novel's opening epigram is from Deuteronomy 30:19: "Choose life." It is also Father Moriarty's last words to the woman who pursues Father LeBlanc. It is also, obviously, L'Heureux's chief admonition, and point of the novel.

It is Father LeBlanc who is the foremost recipient of this life choice, though. He manages to win, whereas Rose loses twice, and Mandy is not allowed second miracles, though Rose is visited by a spiritual moment not unlike a Stephen Spielberg UFO encounter (lights, a car, shaking). Father Moriarty's death wraps up the novel's loose ends.

Every successful novel has to be something of a magic trick. We can't see how the strings are pulled, or how the rabbit either vanishes, or appears. L'Heureux, despite a clumsy moment or two, manages to pull off a rather neat trick, a story delicately balanced between soap opera and seriousness. It's good-natured, as he seems to want it to be.

Though this book was doubtless conceived of, and written, before the recent Church unpleasantness – scandals now multiplying because many bishops forlornly (and feloniously) tried to prevent scandal – *The Miracle* does have one direct connection to all of that. It does manage to point toward what caused so many heterosexual clergy to leave the priesthood in the 1970s. Some critics claim it was that exodus which led to the current scandals, since so many fathers who remained were too sympathetic to the largely homosexual indiscretions that came to light during the last three decades.

In *The Miracle*'s case, there is a happy ending: a priest pleased with his laicization, his reduction to the lay state, a mere civilian, with a good woman waiting for him after his release.

And, if there were still an Oprah Book Club (as there was when L'Heureux began this book), L'Heureux might have escaped his endangered species status, his confinement to mid-list hell, and, because of this entertaining and warm-hearted novel, may finally have had his career visited by the miracle most writers wish for: fame and fortune, yes, but, best of all, legions of readers, too.

First appeared in *The World & I*, vol. 18, no. 3, March 2003, a publication of the Washington Times Corporation and is reprinted with permission. Review-Essay of John L'Heureux, *The Miracle* (New York: Atlantic Monthly Press, 2002).

Toby Olson and Ellen Akins: *At Sea, Public Life*

These two novels demonstrate two levels of ambition: One, *Public Life,* gears up; and the other, *At Sea,* gears down.

Widely praised young writer Ellen Akins, now living in Cornucopia, Wisconsin, leaps upon a very large stage in her third novel, *Public Life*. It is replete with social issues and full of national and international intrigue, all explored through the private life and career of Ann Matter, media adviser to Henry Anderson – a U.S. presidential candidate who wins the race.

Toby Olson, who teaches at Temple University and is a past winner of the PEN/Faulkner award, investigates the much more circumscribed world of Provincetown, Massachusetts in his sixth novel, *At Sea*. He portrays a few short months in the life of Peter Blue, a policeman tilling the rotating crops of drugs and violence in the small patch of earth that makes up the tiny resort town on the tip of Cape Cod.

Ann Matter and Peter Blue both toil in one of the few growing industries in America – the service sector. They are members of the guard class. Peter Blue guards property and people, and Ann Matter guards the reputation of her employer, the president.

Public Life and *At Sea* are set in the vaguely recent past, and both count on the world seeming pretty much as it is, which creates interesting problems for their authors.

In Olson's novel, the national calamity of AIDS has not yet put its indelible mark on Provincetown, making *At Sea* seem more historical than contemporary.

But Akins has the more difficult time, since *Public Life* competes with – well, public life. Her campaign, and her president, can hardly hold a candle to the display of public self-exposure the country witnessed during the '92 presidential campaign, and, for all of Henry Anderson's charm, he's no Bill Clinton.

What he is is a combination of many previous presidents: the good intentions of Jimmy Carter, the populism of Ronald Reagan, the Texas background of George Bush, topped off with a dash of the earnestness of the current commander-in-chief. Anderson is a stew of familiar attributes, with Bush providing the dominant taste.

Akins has Matter consider: "He was so inept, and yet his character came shining through, and suddenly she felt protective, as if she were not the one who wanted to fix his hair, his grimaces, his hectic gestures and erratic speech, halting, then running on; as if his ineptness might be the key to his charm."

But the primary story of *Public Life* is Ann Matter's. She is the indispensable aide, part sounding board and part Peggy Noonan, who was Reagan's speechwriter and master of the eternal high school valedictorian prose style. The president tells Matter in an anguished moment, "I thought you were representative of the American public, the American psyche. . . . But you're not the public after all, are you? You're MY public."

But Matter has a non-public life, secret even from the president – an early marriage, a skittish ex-husband and a young child she has abandoned, who comes back, at the novel's implausible climax, to literally haunt her.

Public Life is a commendably ambitious novel, underpinned by a narrative method more sophisticated and delicate (multiple points of view intermixed with flashes both backward and forward) than can adequately support the rougher, soap opera-ish elements of its story. Though Akins makes a number of salient points about image creation and political life, she does seem to place (as doubtless do the practitioners) too much importance on the public relations aspect of running the government. One looks in her novel for where the real power lies, beyond that which flows from the images media people create.

Olson's *At Sea* makes good use of its wonderfully ambivalent title. Peter Blue is truly at sea, a handsome man with problems, the sort of fellow who has no shortage of people (both male and female) who want to help him solve them.

Olson is an exemplary writer. His earlier novels have won praise and deserved awards. *At Sea* borrows its form more directly from popular genre fiction: police procedurals and detective fiction. Rather than embellish and embroider those models with postmodern flourishes, as he has done in his earlier novels, such as *Seaview* (1992) and *Utah* (1987), here he restrains himself and lets up on digression and reflection, allowing the story to rush forward.

Peter Blue is investigating a rape while still involved in an ongoing narcotics case. He kills a local boy during a drug bust, and that, along with the later mysterious murder of the rape victim (and the death of his own marriage), sets the wild, dune-buggy-ride plot hurtling into motion.

As befits an author who has published fifteen volumes of poetry, Olson's work is textured with metaphor, a palpable sense of place, and rich complications of language that produce insight and wonder.

After the fatal drug bust, Blue observes:

> There was some light. He stood now at the edge of an old wooden dinghy, his fingers touching the smooth, oar-worn gunwale at the lock. It was starlight, and when he looked up and could see the stars, he felt it right that the town lights on Commercial rendered them invisible from there. Busy people didn't need stars. But here, where he was, the sea, and not artifice or commodity, marked each thing, held it in influence. And the stars, too, he thought, their influence. This dinghy, a boat bridge, to go out to the sea, then to go farther out, to have only the sea around him, only the stars over him.

The whodunit aspects of the plot stay fresh until the end. And how one investigation solves others is neatly played out.

When Blue's ex-wife leaves her bow and arrow in his closet, we know as well as Chekhov that we'll be hearing its twang before closing time.

Unlike Akins's novel, Olson's narrative remains straightforwardly dramatized. His characters all enter our lives three-dimensionally, whereas Akins's remain flat, but colorful, images projected on to the television screen to which so many of them owe their lives.

First appeared in the *South Bend Tribune,* June 27, 1993;
 Review of Toby Olson, *At Sea* (New York: Simon & Schuster, 1993); Ellen Akins, *Public Life* (New York: Harper Collins, 1993).

Pinckney Benedict: *Dogs of God*

First novels, traditionally, are sensitive reads – more than vaguely autobiographical, saddled with protagonists who bear a shouting distance resemblance to the authors. This first novel, by the young, gifted short-story-writer, Pinckney Benedict, recipient of the Chicago Tribune's Nelson Algren Award, among other prizes, could be one of the first of a trend initiated by a new generation of twenty-something male writers (Benedict was born in 1964). The new trend is to skip over the sensitive stage and go straight for the commercial jugular: let the blood flow, the flesh rend, the gunpowder burn – Generation X becomes Generation XXX.

Like last year's *A Simple Plan,* by another novelist in his twenties, Scott Smith, *Dogs of War* is an adventure tale written by a talented young writer with a feel for sinewy prose that is so drenched in violence that its panting eagerness for a large audience is as intense as the gleeful sadism of its characters.

And Benedict doesn't hold back on characters: the misfit posse is rounded up, all grotesque *isolati,* ready to mingle, headed inevitably for the showdown where everyone comes together with a bang. When something weird makes its appearance – a pack of wild dogs, for instance, headed by a crazed malamute – you can rest assured it will figure in the novel's climax. But Benedict is very impatient to get to a climax; *Dogs of God* is practically all climax, as if "cut to the chase," rather than say, "make it new," or "be interesting," is the new generation's most prized literary axiom.

Benedict makes use of flamboyant violence in his two well-received collections of short stories (*Town Smoke* and *The Wrecking Yard*), but violence in the short story form can be made to implode, rather than explode, be surgical rather than wholesale. At novel length, the excess begins to smell as much of crass exploitation as it does of cordite and burning flesh.

Benedict has degrees from Princeton and the University of Iowa Writers' Workshop, and displays a sure hand in conjuring both a sensory world and colorful characters. Goody, the designated protagonist, an amateur fighter with no known history, except a history of "sixteen and oh" bouts, is our moral compass, busted up as he is. The novel's prologue gives us his description of how he killed a man in an irregular, but arranged, fight in a machine shop. Goody is the novel's good guy (given the crew to chose among), but only as good as the diminutive "Goody" implies.

At the beginning, Goody mysteriously arrives in a rented house at the edge of a truly godforsaken cane field, the house being the site of a wife-killing by the previous tenant, intricately recounted, and Goody quickly discovers a dead body, vividly described, in the cane field. Goody stumbles on to drug capitalism at its ugliest, and the chase is on. Nothing in the landscape is not malignant; it's a world where Hawthorne and Poe meet Harry Crews, and the suspicion that *Dogs of God* may be an MTV version of an old-fashioned ghost story is hard to set aside.

But Goody is there to give Benedict license to describe a lot of connoisseur violence. He has a flair for description and sense of place.

In competition with the popular culture, what writing can do, that the camera cannot, is be articulate. The dead fighter, as regarded by Goody: "His left eye is closed, but the right is open wide; a frozen wink. He looks surprised to be where he is. The pupil covers most of the hazel iris of the open eye, and I am near enough to see that it is ragged at its edge, not smooth like you would expect. It is the dilated pupil that gives him his startled look. He has a slight smile on his lips. Blue shadow fills a deep rectangular dent in the exact middle of his forehead."

The publisher compares *Dogs of War* to James Dickey's *Deliverance,* but Benedict's novel doesn't mix the ordinary with the extraordinary. Everything and everyone in *Dogs of War* is extraordinary: Goody; his landlord Inchcape; Dreama (as in dream on, I suppose), the novel's one female character who is given more than a paragraph or two (this is what used to be described as men's fiction); Tannhauser, his name conjuring either Nazis or a Christmas carol, a self-styled backwoods drug lord with twelve fingers; two "transnationals," Bodo and Toma, who are the sinister foreign arm dealers and drug entrepreneurs come to do business with Tannhauser; two "Mingos," who are the murderous black employed protectors of Tannhauser; Yukon, his second in command, who loses the bare-fisted barn fight with Goody, enslaved laborers from south of the border who toil at "El Dorado," the former prison/resort/government installation that now is the site of marijuana cultivation and wholesale slaughter – all being churned into murderous motion by the arrival of one (one!) DEA agent in a helicopter, which will come to its end with the only other aircraft (prettily named Dakota) in the story's vicinity. All of this goes on in a small corner of West Virginia, its geography grotesque in itself, filled with endless, bottomless caves, and mysterious Cold

War civil defense facilities destined for high government officials, which prompts the only social comment in the novel, by one of the DC-3 contraband pilots, "'What do you imagine they want to save the President and Congress for anyway?' the pilot asked. 'If they got us involved in a nuclear war, it seems like time they took a look at retiring anyhow. Don't you think?'"

How much you enjoy *Dogs of War* depends on your taste for savagery and a good prose style. Benedict does imbue his characters with enough woolly life that some of their sadism does seem positively good natured; he is a superior writer, and his garrulous miscreants do grow, well, likable (Benedict being a more generous soul than they are), but I tend to back off when imprisoned children are feeding their quarters' plentiful supply of baby rats to starving wild dogs for everyone's general amusement.

But it has to be surmised that Benedict is not competing with past literature, but current cinema, not so much the magical realism of Marquez, but the special effects of the Indiana Jones Spielberg. A segment of the younger generation has seen the future and it is literary violence. Having missed the Vietnam War, they are stuck with the drug war. When Goody has his fated boxing match with Tannhauser's henchman, Yukon, even though Yukon is forty pounds heavier and a foot taller and meaner than the rabid malamute, we know Goody will beat him. It is often the fantasy of educated men that precision and knowledge can overcome those odds – David and Goliath lives on.

As one finds in movies, the bad guys never simply kill the hero (Goody has been snatched by Tannhauser's Mingos after leaving Yukon shattered and senseless) when they have the chance (though everyone else is being killed at the drop of a hat), but hold off executing him to allow the story to proceed, and for him to make his escape. Goody, at the novel's end, does escape, very much the worse for wear, so much so it seems that Benedict's dark and fertile imagination has only then finally flagged, and he has no idea what to do with him next.

First appeared in the *Chicago Tribune,* February 27, 1994;
 Review of Pinckney Benedict, *Dogs of God* (New York: Nan A. Talese/Doubleday, 1994).

Rick Bass: Platte River

Rick Bass's *Platte River* is a collection of three longish stories – not novellas, as the publisher claims – which have been previously published in the *Mississippi River,* the *Quarterly,* and the *Paris Review.* For what those three quarterlies cost, they are now available in a single volume, handsomely produced by Seymour Lawrence.

Bass, though young, in his mid-thirties, had published three collections of largely natural history essays (*The Deer Pasture, Wild to the Heart, Oil Notes*) before a prize-winning collection of stories, *The Watch,* appeared in 1989. The nonfiction shares some of the same locations as his stories, and the same interest in the land, animals, the adversity of extreme climates, and the isolation of men and women.

Russell Chatham's painting for the cover of *Platte River* does echo the book's tone: awe-inspiring nature, a sky-dominated landscape, country where the environment is in the foreground, and man is in the background. As Bass himself renders it early in the volume's first long story, "Mahatma Joe:"

> It had been a hard winter in northern Montana, so hard that ravens sometimes fell from the sky in mid-flight, their insides just snapping, it seemed, and like great ragged clumps of black cloth they'd fall into the woods, or into a pasture, landing a few weeks shy of spring.

> The stave-ribbed horses – those that the coyotes and wolves had not gotten – would go over and pick the crows up with their teeth and begin eating them, chewing the shiny black feathers.

Mahatma Joe is an itinerant preacher who migrates to northern Montana, a region where: "Everyone knew there were dangers still left to living up in Grass Valley. There were mountain lions, wolverines, bears, and wolves; it was one of the only places like that left." Mahatma Joe "had always imagined the little valley, ringed by snow and glaciers even in the summer, as a new place to build something, a new place to get it right." He had gotten it wrong in Alaska, and had come down to the Canadian border with his Eskimo wife, and put a stop to Grass Valley's spring celebration, "Naked Days, where no one wore clothes at any time, not even when they went in for groceries, not even when they went into the saloon. People fed their horses naked, slept naked for the first time in six months, and checked their mailboxes naked."

It doesn't take long for Mahatma Joe to accomplish this cultural change; he just sows a little self-consciousness, and, at least in town, the citizens put back on clothes. Now, there is something a little more than fanciful going on here in Grass Valley, a place where both Jack London and Tom Robbins would feel right at home. Bass is fashioning a new sort of western myth-making for gullible city slickers: strong men, strong women, strong drink, and strong emotions. But as one can see from what's quoted above, it's a tangible world; Bass feels his flora and fauna down to his toes. A young, single woman, one who had left the most selfish man in the world back in California, arrives in Grass Valley and, eventually, she and the sixty-eight-year-old Mahatma Joe hook up, after his wife slips under the river's ice and doesn't reappear again until early summer. The pleasures of Bass's story come from the soundness of his prose, and his ritualistic descriptions of nature and its extremes, rather than the new romanticism of his outsized individualists, who accomplish physical tasks that would task a company of marines.

The second story, "Field Events," extends the outsized quality. Its dominant male, A.C., most often referred to as "the big man," is big enough to dance with a cow on his shoulders. He also manages to build a shed as long as a football field out of trees surrounding the abandoned farmhouse he occupies. A.C. is first sighted by two young men, high school discus throwers, "swimming upstream, doing the butterfly stroke. He was pulling a canoe behind him, and it was loaded with darkened cast-iron statues."

The boys more or less adopt A.C. and bring him into the bosom of their family, in residence near Glens Falls, in northeastern New York. The two boys have two sisters, one, Lory, "was thirty-four, a teacher, and beautiful: she was tiny, black-haired, with a quick, high laugh not unlike the outburst of a loon. Despite her smallness, her breasts were overly large, to the point that they were the first thing people noticed about her and continued noticing about her." She and A.C. are mutually attracted. "Field Events," like "Mahatma Joe," is not a realistic story. Both seem to be parables absent of fresh morals, and yet their straightforwardness is somewhat hypnotic, and they can be enjoyed for their decided lack of tongue in cheek. Both stories possess a child-like quality; they are, in fact, children's stories for grownups. There is something beguiling about the amateur pageant quality they both share: simple, earnest playlets put on for the appreciative town folk. Both tales applaud individuals triumphing over adversity, done in clear prose, full of the smell of the earth, if not redolent of the more acrid stink of the mind.

"Platte River," the title story, shares a number of superficial similarities with the first two. The same outdoor accoutrements are here: the rushing river, strenuous activities, nature versus man, but its man of prodigious strength is not a citizen of never-never land, but a former NFL star, named Harley, "strange looking, as plain as butter, huge," who lives with a former model, named Shaw, in "an abandoned hunting lodge, large and airy, with the stuffed heads of deer and elk, moose and bear, staring down at them from the walls – ancient heads from animals shot fifty and sixty years ago. It's such a fairy-tale existence, Harley thinks," and one is quick to agree, but Shaw is leaving him, and Harley has the pedestrian task to visit a friend, a former college football-playing buddy, "the Wolverine," who teaches at an art school somewhere in Hemingway Country, near Traverse City, in upper Michigan. "It's sort of a scam that the Wolverine has been able to hire his old blocking buddy to come out to the art school and talk about football: fifteen hundred dollars for the weekend." And the weekend is mainly spent fishing with Harely's buddy, the Wolverine, and a handful of his friends, one, a determined suicide-to-be, named Nick.

Naming him Nick might be a joke on Bass's part (after Hemingway's Nick Adams stories), but, once again, "Platte River" is done straight and serious. A fish, a steelhead, is caught: "It's the most beautiful thing Harley's ever seen come out of the water – fluorescent red, emerald, stony black, chocolate brown, and moon silver." That is either a little too much color, or just right, depending on your taste.

Whereas "Mahatma Joe" and "Field Events" already have staked a claim to the world of illusion and make believe, the real in "Platte River" does transform itself into the magical, rather than begin with it. Harley is both the object of the classroom lecture as well as its subject. The Wolverine tells his students: "'This man is strong, stronger than any of us will ever be,'" and "pointing to Harley as if he's diagramming a poem – talking about its structure, perhaps. 'He's got talent, too, but mostly he's just strong. I thought we'd show you what this man used to do for a living. He was so good at it that in two years of doing this, he made enough money – not that money is any kind of measurement – to last him, if he's frugal, the rest of his life.'"

And the reader and the class get to see what Harley did and does and is. By the story's end, we don't quite learn about what happens to the suicidal Nick, we don't even quite learn what will happen to Harley, but in "Platte River," all of Bass's considerable gifts have arranged themselves so agreeably that we learn again what he is capable of doing – as he demonstrated in his stories in *The Watch* – so well.

First appeared in the *Chicago Tribune,* March 20, 1994;
 Review of Rick Bass, *Platte River* (Boston: Houghton Mifflin/Seymour Lawrence, 1994).

Michael Stephens: The Brooklyn Book of the Dead

A handful of years ago, novelist Mary Gordon published a piece in the *New York Times Book Review* lamenting what she calculated as the small number (actually none, excepting herself) of Irish-American novelists among her contemporaries.

Letters to the editor followed, citing a couple dozen Irish-American writers of fiction born around, or after, 1945 that she had overlooked. One of the most prominent, on the longer, more generous list, was Michael Stephens, whose first novel, *Season at Coole,* established him as one of the youngest and most perceptive voices surveying Irish-American territory.

In a way that would further mystify Gordon, Stephens went on to become the least parochial of writers; since 1972 he has published more than a dozen books of poetry, fiction, and criticism. His titles include *Lost in Seoul* (nonfiction) and *After Asia* (poems), which are volumes with a distinctly international flavor.

The University of Georgia Press has just issued an award-winning new collection of essays, *Green Dreams: Essays Under the Influence of the Irish,* which returns the globe-trotting Stephens to Irish-American subjects.

Season at Coole, republished as the second title from Dalkey Archive Press ten years ago, also helped launch that successful Illinois-based small literary publishing house, which has its own vaguely Irish air.

Stephens's new novel, his third, *The Brooklyn Book of the Dead,* returns to the first novel's cast of characters; the Coole progeny. Sixteen in all, they assemble nearly a quarter-century after we left them last in *Season* for the funeral of their father, who, though he died in Florida, has been transported back to Brooklyn, as was his wish, for services and burial.

The "action" in *Brooklyn* is limited to the comic and inspired yakking and reflection of the brothers and sisters as they contemplate their newly dead father's, and their mother's (deceased some years earlier) lives and legacies.

If there is a hallmark of Irish-American writers, it might be an overdeveloped fondness for using funeral parlors and saloons – all claustrophobic rooms – as fictional settings.

Sixteen voices are certainly enough for a chorus, and Stephens does a remarkable job in keeping their collective requiem aloft. "If the family had a gift," he writes of Emmett, one of the Coole boys, now middle-aged, "it was this art of the pontificating knuckle-headed know-nothing – a specialty, you might call it – especially to a roomful of brothers who could not verify anything he said, could not prove the veracity of any historical or imaginative facts Emmett of the crime waves cared to put forward to them in their grief and cups."

Stephens's novel quickly becomes a form of chamber opera: dour, yet humorous, schmoozing by the brothers and sisters punctuated by knowing arias on family bonds and that fabled place, Brooklyn, the borough of immigrants:

"After all, the Cooles were once the black Irish of this burg, the black pigs and green niggers of Marion Street, and the musical strains of this hellhole fit their temperament – and maybe still did – as much as any ethnic group that ever commandeered the broad vistas of these ramshackle streets."

Stephens is able to fashion myth out of sociology as we get the biographies, the scraps of lives, of each of the siblings – Nora, for instance, who chose to stay at home:

"Let Augusta and Eileen work in their dress shop and sweater factory; Nora would sweep the floor – not cook – but stoke the coal fires in the basement, wash the dishes and make the beds, and anything she needed to know about the outside, she'd find out later in the day when one of her sisters brought home the Daily News, whose pages were proof enough that Nora had made a wise decision."

We also get relatives:

"Uncle Jack was the first person, either on the Moody or the Coole side, to join Alcoholics Anonymous, though he was not yet in the program. This was a dry run. He was not drinking; he white-knuckled it, boring in on the television and the baseball game, trying to avoid the sounds emanating from the backyard, those drunken laughs and shouts, the pawing and hoots."

Brooklyn is, indeed, a singular Irish wake, and the reader might be a stranger stumbling in blindly to the service, but by the time he or she departs, having watched the old man finally put into the ground, the whole prodigious Coole family – its hopes, dreams, pasts, present, and likely futures – delicately and forcefully has been made indelible on our own memories:

"They would drive off in all directions, back out to the Island, to Newark and the airport, across Highland Park and through Cypress Hills, into the vaporous wonders of Ozone Park, into the safety of Queens and the 'burbs or into Manhattan and Jersey, up into the Bronx, at any rate, except for Brian, away from Brooklyn."

Stephens's powerful and tenderhearted novel is tour de force eulogy; it praises not just the dearly departed, but also the dearly living, and the toll death takes on us all.

First appeared in the *South Bend Tribune,* May 22, 1994; © 1994 The South Bend Tribune Corp. Review of Michael Stephens, *The Brooklyn Book of the Dead* (Normal, IL: Dalkey Archive Press, 1994).

Graham Swift: *Last Orders*

The title of the English writer Graham Swift's new novel, his sixth, *Last Orders,* echoes moodily down a number of different dark paths. It has three meanings, at least. The first is the novel's inert, diseased protagonist's (butcher Jack Arthur Dodds, whose cremated remains are delivered on the novel's first page and disposed of on the last) last death-bed request, his final orders, to hurl his ashes into the sea; the second is the military meaning, insofar as the three contemporary friends (Ray, Vic and Lenny) who accompany Jack's adopted son on the funeral trip, are duty-bound, given that they are all veterans, like Jack, of World War II; and, third, the humblest meaning, the pub call of "last orders" that the proprietor of the men's haunt ("They calls it the Coach and Horses but it ain't never gone nowhere"), has used so often over the years, bidding the men to have just one more of the same all around.

And Graham Swift, in a number of ways, is having his own just one more of the same, since *Last Orders* is replete with familiar Swiftian (small s) fictional elements, both in form and content. There are the recurring variations on foundlings, defective children, entwined histories, mature narrators, death as a structural device, that fill his five earlier novels.

Swift is best known in this country because of the great success of *Waterland,* his third (1984) novel, but the first one to be published over here. Swift found a happy blend of setting and situation in *Waterland,* and his didactic tendencies seemed appropriate (and desirable) given the voice of the history teacher/narrator. Swift had had some good success in England before *Waterland* with his first two novels, *The Sweet-Shop Owner* and *Shuttlecock,* but not enough to lure an American publisher.

Waterland was short-listed in England for the Booker Prize when it appeared in 1983 and it won the Guardian Prize for the best English novel. That was enough to soften up our own literary-public-relations complex; *Waterland* reached a larger-than-expected American audience, and was made into a film, starring Jeremy Irons, now available on home video cassette.

In critical circles, *Waterland* is used as a benchmark. Though it was Swift's third novel, he was viewed in the U.S. as an instant success, since *Waterland* was the only novel at hand. (The earlier two and a short-story collection, *Learning to Swim,* though, were quickly enough brought out in America.) But the two novels that have followed *Waterland – Out of This World* (1988) and *Ever After* (1992) – received a mixed reception, and neither ever achieved the popularity of *Waterland.* That novel still casts its long shadow over all subsequent critical comment.

Remove *Waterland* from the mix, and it is likely that American audiences might not be reading Swift's intelligent and affecting novels at all, though, by force of his output (perhaps he will become the British version of Joyce Carol Oates, having turned out six novels in twelve years), American publishers might have finally deigned to publish him.

Similar career paths have occurred in America. There are many examples. Here are two: Robert Olen Butler, the author of the Pulitzer Prize-winning *A Good Scent from a Strange Mountain.* His many previously published novels had left him sufficiently obscure until the collection of short stories won that prize (the equivalent of the Booker and the Guardian combined) – so, too, the career of William Kennedy, who was laureled late.

The paradox I am getting to is not that all writers need to write one "breakthrough" book, but that such a book allows readers access not only to the well-known book, but, also, to other books, never, until then, available for a larger readership.

Last Orders may be far enough away from *Waterland* not to gather Swift many new readers, and that would be a shame. He deserves new readers. Though Swift's recurrent themes and elements are present throughout *Last Orders,* what is also present, in greater measure, is the quality of affection for all the characters.

A FAITHFUL SON

No son has been a more faithful chronicler of his father's generation, even if there are no fictional portraits of his own father (or his own self. Swift seems to have an aversion to confessional autobiographical writing. In that way, his role in contemporary English literature seems to be that of an antidote to Martin Amis, his autobiographically inclined and enhanced contemporary who also sports a famous last name – and, in Amis's case, bloodline – of British literature.)

The old men of *Last Orders* (for an American audience) are an invigorating mix of the familiar and the strange; one of them, Lenny, describes them this way: "There's Ray and Jack who go back to the desert, same desert as me, Gunner Tate, except I never knew either of them then. There's Vic and Jack who had pitches opposite for the best part of fifty years, Dodds and Tucker, steaks and stiffs. And there's Jack and Vince, one in a bag and one off his rag." The shorthand is filled out in the narrative. Vic and Jack had shops opposite one another in the small town of Bermondsey, in the south of England – one a funeral parlor, the other a butcher shop. Jack is now cremated and is in a plastic jar and Vince, Jack's adopted son, is the younger generation figure who acts as the novel's catalyst, an angry young man of Thatcher's England, tired of pulling himself up by his bootstraps.

But the fathers, including Vince's dead one, are a different lot. *Last Orders* reminds us, as does the Dole campaign, that the generation that came of age in World War II will soon be gone, and *Last Orders* does supply a moving eulogy for it.

Like their counterparts in the states, as a generation they were men of unquestioned competence. They knew how to work, did their jobs well, and their own complaints did not deter them for getting things done.

Shopkeepers are, indeed, the heart of England. But Swift seems particularly gloomy about his own post-war generation, for all the older men's children are damaged and footloose. One daughter has gone off to Australia, another has been brain impaired since birth and has lived fifty years in a home (a tip of the hat here to the national health). Vince, Jack's adopted son, has spurned the family meat business and has turned into a shady used car dealer, not undisposed to pimping his own young daughter in order to secure a sale.

There is also Mandy, a young runaway, whom Jack had taken in as a surrogate daughter and who eventually marries the adopted foundling Vince; she contemplates the way she avoided the fate of other young vagrant girls, considering: "But now when I think of it, now when I see them huddled up in shop entrances and archways, in smelly blankets, I think, I was lucky." Swift's point seems to be that Jack and his pals have a strong sense of community and lifelong friendships, whereas Vince's generation and Swift's have only lifelong problems.

Water may have been the element of *Waterland*, but in *Last Orders* it is ash, by way of fire. Its epitaph from Browne's "Urn Burial" alerts us to that, "But man is a Noble Animal splendid in ashes, and pompous in the grave." The novel is full of its color: "The sea's the colour of desertion. It's the colour of wet ash . . ." and ". . . the paint on some of them weathered right off, the woodwork underneath all grey and feathery." Swift shows us, as his characters move through their world, the long but short trip from ashes to ashes, dust to dust.

ATTENTION PAID

One of the interesting aspects of Graham Swift's career is his use of narrative form and voice. In some ways, he shares aspects of the English novel associated with nineteenth-century storytellers, which has led to comparisons to Dickens, and the admonition by one critic, MacDonald Harris, that Swift is just what the doctor ordered, ". . . for the reader who is getting bored with the contemporary American mode of fiction and turns back, now and then, to Trollope, Hardy or George Eliot."

But Swift is not immune to interpretations of postmodernism, complete with the dozen buzzwords of contemporary academic criticism flying about his head (closure, foregrounding, problematicalness, etc.). For a writer of his generation (Swift was born in 1949), he has been the subject of a fair amount of scholarly interest. Narrative voice in fiction is a subject often of much more interest to critics (and other novelists) than it is to readers, but it is hard to avoid when dealing with Swift's work, especially *Last Orders.*

The baby boom generation in England doesn't go by that name. That concept, that sort of sociological focus – the youth culture as a cultural and marketing phenomena – is not a commonplace label (and obsession) in the U.K. as it is in the States – more respect for their elders, perhaps. The English do treat childhood differently, it seems – more consideration bestowed, but less attention paid. The Beatles may have influenced its generation of American youth more than it did Britain's. Youth culture was more an export than an import. Regardless, Graham Swift doesn't afford his generation much respect, or play, in his novels.

Yet, Swift does speak for his generation in an oblique way, through form, since he employs a very baby-boom-generation way, very post-World War II way, of narrating. All the narrative presumptions changed after World War II. The idea of "omniscience" took a drubbing after Auschwitz and Hiroshima. Narrative modesty began to take hold in writers. Who could know everything? Who could be godlike? Who could be Tolstoy? Who could be, even, a fly on the wall? Jacqueline Suzanne could, Harold Robbins, Tom Clancy, John Grisham could, that's who. Commercial writers never abandoned omniscience or the godlike narrator, but those loosely called "literary writers" gave it a lot of thought over the recent decades past, and a number of them came up with the first person solution: have "individuals" narrate, since they represented their own slice of knowledge, their own philosophical view, and could be trusted. Novels appeared where most every major character would give his or her view of events – say, Craig Nova's 1982 novel, *The Good Son,* for one.

Readers read whatever's there, especially if it is a novel, fiction, since they're after the "story" being told. Readers have not entirely grown comfortable with the multiple-first-person method of narration, but they have made accommodations to it. In this way, in the late twentieth century, form has become, well, formatted. As movie videos announce, "the film has been formatted to fit your television screen" and so too has narrative fiction been formatted to fit our time.

Last Orders has a baker's half-dozen of narrators, each given sections (hard to call them chapters, since some are but a page long) labeled with their names: Lenny, Ray, Vince, Vic, Jack, Amy, Mandy. One series of sections is named for places, and each of these is narrated by Ray, who acts as the default protagonist, since Jack is dead in the present parts of the story. And the story (a simple trip is its spine) is received piece by piece, like pages of evidence handed, one at a time, to a witness on the stand. Patterns emerge, the story fills out in time-lapse fashion, the relationships of a lifetime are explained, secrets uncovered and kept.

Jack and Amy's damaged daughter, June, causes a permanent rift in their marriage, which Ray ends up bridging for a time. Vic, the funeral director, learns this secret, but, as he says: "What you learn in this business is how to keep your mouth shut." Ray owns a scrap yard, which he sells to Vince, helping him start his own business. Of the men, Lenny's is the most peripheral voice; his daughter, Sally, was taken up by Jack and Amy as another surrogate for their institutionalized daughter, and she has her own history with Vince.

Swift uses the device of the quest (more than pilgrimage) to energize the narrative. The men's goal is the resort town of Margate where Jack has asked to be deposited into the sea. As one of Vince's used cars (a plush Mercedes) hurtles them toward the English coast, a number of way-stations are encountered (they stop for a meal and Vince announces to the barmaid, "Three old codgers to look after, and one extra who ain't eating"), including the cathedral at Canterbury. But, there is a task at hand (literally, the jar of remains). And we do wonder if their mission will be accomplished, and we hear the voices unhurriedly tell their stories. We are in the travelers role, listening to our haphazard companions explain themselves.

This contemporary use of the single or multiple first person narrator Swift employs is actually drawn from poetry. Chaucer's *Canterbury Tales* provides more structural parallels than thematic in *Last Orders*. Throughout, Swift leavens the story with the men's ordinary and hard-won wisdom. Vic muses: "Pride's a queer thing. It puffs a small man up but that's nothing to a big man who's afraid of looking small." Ray looks around as the men near their destination and reports, "The seagulls are whizzing around the sky like they're either having the time of their lives or they wish they'd never taken off." It also describes the condition of the men as their task is almost completed.

Multiple voice novels are, by definition, choral. And Swift's *Last Orders* is a rousing and rowdy small church choir. And what it sings, of course, is a threnody, a song of lamentation, for Jack and all their lives. And it is a lovely and moving one, indeed.

First appeared in *The World & I*, vol. 11, no. 10, October 1996, a publication of the Washington Times Corporation and reprinted with permission. Review of Graham Swift, *Last Orders* (New York: Knopf, 1996).

Bob Shacochis: *Swimming in the Volcano*

Bob Shacochis has been regarded as his generation's expatriate chronicler of the Caribbean ever since his American Book Award-winning collection of short stories, *Easy in the Island,* was published in 1985. Another strong collection, *The Next New World,* followed, but Shacochis's many fans have been impatiently awaiting the appearance of his long-promised first novel. That novel is *Swimming in the Volcano,* and I am happy to report that it fulfills one's highest expectations.

In these days of fast-food prose and predigested fiction, *Swimming in the Volcano* provides a feast; it is a book heady with language and thick with story. Given merely its plot, we seem to be on familiar ground: young, white and American, Mitchell Wilson is our man in St. Catherine. He works for the local Ministry of Agriculture, having taken up employment in this out-of-the-way (and fictional) remnant of the British Empire after a bruising breakup with an apprentice femme fatale named Johanna (Mitchell calls her Johnnie), who, after a period spent sharpening her skills, comes to St. Catherine and proceeds to raise the emotional and political temperature on an already very hot island.

Besides this troubling old flame, other staples of post-colonial Third World fictions pile up dockside; rival political factions that invent and invite revolution, drugs and tourists, do-gooders and degenerates, and the CIA. If you wondered what life was like in, say, Grenada, before the U.S. invaded, *Swimming in the Volcano* will provide more than a clue. But if the elements of this novel are not entirely fresh, Shacochis's handling of them certainly is.

Things get rolling quickly, but plot isn't the driving force of *Swimming in the Volcano*. Instead, it is Shacochis's language, his heart and his understanding that leave the reader feeling exhilarated.

Here, for example, is Mitchell Wilson, nose broken during a careening ride down a mountain in a brakeless taxi, on the way to the airport to his "unsolicited reunion" with Johnnie:

"Mitchell slumped back behind the seat, licking warm blood from the fountain in his nose, wanting to wreck right now and get it over with, arrive at the airport in an ambulance (though he had never seen one on the island), collect Johnnie, plead her onto the gurney next to him, commence the nursing process without delay, submit to the truce of medical crisis under which old animosities could be justifiably ignored."

At the airport, entering a souvenir stall to replace his bloodied shirt:

> Mitchell walked under the grating sheepishly, aware of the impropriety of his shirtlessness. The people of St. Catherine expected their guests to honor a code of respectability. The code was straightforward and universally known, not unlike the standard Mitchell was raised by in Virginia: a sound appearance is a great comfort to everyone's nerves, particularly when among scoundrels. A tastefully dressed crook with a shine to his wing tips, a pederast who drives to the Fairfax Hunt in a Jaguar and spreads an eighteenth-century carpet on the lawn for lunch at the rail – these were citizens one could depend on not to disturb the public peace, wholly preferable to a state's attorney who purchased suits off the rack at Woodies and licked gravy from his butter knife.

Male characters like Mitchell are not new to literature. One that readily comes to mind (and not just because of the similarity of the novels' titles) is Geoffrey Firmin of Malcolm Lowry's *Under the Volcano*. Both books share the same powerful combination of the serious and the sensual, the same palpable rendering of place, but here the expatriate functionary is not a burned-out alcoholic, but a man in his mid-twenties, alert and possessed of amazing stamina. And he needs it.

Getting through customs, Johnnie creates a scene (one of many in the book that will center around her):

> "Improper border behavior," Mitchell explained. "You don't grab things out of a customs officer's hand."
>
> "Perhaps," she said. She smiled in a way he knew too well – a suck on the lemon of irony. She raised her arms and flopped them against her sides. "I didn't know what else to do. I have five grams of coke taped to my diaphragm."
>
> He stood staring at her, stunned by her audacity.

We have here a portrait of a sensible man and a wild woman. But it is Mitchell's scrupulous hesitations that bring about most of the novel's fatalities, while his sense of superiority and entitlement, however justified, is hard to take at times. One has to remember, though, that all the principal expatriate characters are twenty-seven years old or younger.

Male, female, old, young, black, white, rich, poor, everyone in *Swimming in the Volcano* walks onto the scene full-blown, vivid and disturbingly distinct. Indeed, Shacochis rivals Dickens in his lengthy portrait of one of the novel's catalytic figures, Cassius Collymore – a kind of Cinderella in reverse, who was returned to his poor fisherman father as a young boy, after he had been brought up by a stable family.

> Nostalgia was the same for [Collymore] as starvation, and he could not endure its deep, inner pressures. And he avoided what

was, in his mind, the great human commerce and communion of the public dock, because even on an impoverished island where rags and clothes were too often synonymous, his were the most offensive, his body itself was an obscenity of neglect, and he was rebuffed for his crudity and for being the simpleton that the brilliance of the sun out on the water had made of him, framing his thoughts and feelings in a perpetual stupor. Truly, he became accustomed to this state, recognized it as his nature, inescapable, and so was able to provide himself with life's most austere comfort and permitted himself to believe that he deserved his downfall.

Swimming in the Volcano is set in the late 1970s during the brief Democratic interlude of the Carter administration – a period that, late in the novel, is summed up thusly by a disgruntled agent of our government: "The president had pardoned the draft evaders, was going to give back the Canal to a gang of greaser narcotraffickers and . . . was conducting formal negotiations with Havana for the first time since the Bay of Pigs." Mixing the political and the personal, Shacochis might be described as a counter-culture V. S. Naipaul, given his deft handling of the many-layered issues of race, nativism and power.

Shacochis doesn't drive stubbornly forward with his story; instead, he keeps tracking back, convoluting the narrative (especially toward the novel's end) with flashbacks and flash-forwards. Some will question that strategy, but Shacochis is a writer who takes his time and expects the reader to do likewise. *Swimming in the Volcano* is the finest first novel I have read in many years.

First appeared in the *Chicago Tribune,* April 25, 1993;
 Review of Bob Shacochis, *Swimming in the Volcano* (New York: Scribner's, 1993).

Willie Morris: *New York Days*

American journalism during the 1960s and early 1970s enjoyed a golden period. Willie Morris's valuable new memoir, *New York Days,* captures that time of literary fecundity, before it withered under the pitiless glare of television, and was smothered by the creeping vines of VCRs.

One often overlooked reason for that flowering of nonfiction was the redoing of obscenity laws in the 1950s and the early 1960s – thanks mainly to fiction, but ultimately nonfiction was the more affected genre.

By the 1960s, writers (additionally aided by libel law decisions) realized they could write what they wanted – not that four-letter words began to flood the pages of magazines and newspapers (though some did), but the style and subjects that established publications could consider seriously loosened up.

When Morris ascended to the helm of *Harper's* in 1967 at age thirty-two, its youngest ever editor-in-chief, the magazine was furiously playing catch-up. The sixties saw the birth of the "underground" press, which soon grew into the "alternative" media. Frisky journals of various sorts were starting to gain readers and influence.

Those were heady days in American writing: the novel was being dethroned as the crown of letters and replaced by the much jauntier cap of what is often erroneously lumped together as the "New Journalism." What was new (and soon to end) was the hyper-literacy of the public in the sixties and seventies – back then the phrase "reading public" did not mean a special interest group.

New York Days is many books at once: a sketchy history of American journalism, a portrait of the "Sixties," a romantic memoir of a young man's love affair with New York City, and a meditation on "the complexity of remembrance."

Each part succeeds and fails here and there, but Morris does give the reader an engrossing insider's view of how the world of intellectual life and publishing operated in those days.

One of the memoir's many ironies is that *Harper's*, the oldest continually published magazine in the country, an East Coast monument, was owned and operated during Morris's tumultuous tenure by a very Midwestern family, the Cowles of Minneapolis, "For the first time in its long and eminent history, *Harper's* was the property of interests other than the book publishers. . . ."

"This meant," Morris goes on to write, "that the magazine, in essence, had become the minuscule facet of a Midwest-based empire basically of moneyed absentees extending from the Atlantic to the Pacific."

The Cowles purchase of *Harper's* in the early sixties was an avatar of the corporate buying and selling mania that climaxed in the eighties, a type of behavior wilder and more unstable than any attempted by the counterculture.

And money plays a big role in *New York Days.* It shows up most floridly in Morris's love affair with the city. Much more candidly than in his first memoir, *North Toward Home,* Morris tells his story of coming to the big city. Morris, Mississippi born, graduated from the University of Texas and was a Rhodes Scholar (like Bill Clinton who, before going off as a Rhodes Scholar himself to Oxford, put in an appearance at the offices of *Harper's* to ask advice of Willie Morris, two upwardly-mobile sons of the meritocracy crossing paths), and became the editor of the *Texas Monthly* in 1960.

Young Willie had caught the eye of John Fisher, then editor of *Harper's*. Fisher offered him a job, dangling the promise of being editor-in-waiting. Morris, like our new president, had a talent for soliciting the attention of older, more powerful men. He repays them by being charming, bright and destined to run something.

Harper's did catch up with the rest of the fast pack of magazines, and it beat everyone else by more than a nose in one particular race. It published 90,000 words of Norman Mailer's *Armies of the Night,* titled, "The Steps of the Pentagon," in the March 1968 issue. As Morris notes, it "was the longest magazine article ever published." *Harper's* did best them all – in length – and letting writers write long had many consequences. It allowed writers to develop. However, one thing *Harper's* did not do was discover new talent. It gave space to a number of established writers.

Speaking of William Styron, Morris writes: "As with Norman Mailer, Bernard Malamud, Robert Penn Warren, Walker Percy, Philip Roth and others, my early young man's reading of his work made me promise myself that if I ever became editor I would purposefully seek him out for the magazine's pages."

Editing as hero-worshiping can work, especially if you have talented heroes. Those who were not well-known novelists crossing over to the nonfiction field (such as Truman Capote) that he printed were established journalists like David Halberstam.

It was left to magazines like *Rolling Stone* to uncover a new generation of writers; it did so because of length, too. *Rolling Stone* let writers write long because they had to add columns of print to offset their many pages of electronic equipment and record ads.

Another thing Morris neglected was the women's movement – or, more correctly, it was one thing he just did not get (as it is put today), since *Harper's* published a number of articles on the women's movement, most notably Mailer's "A Prisoner of Sex." Morris's depiction of his failing is both poignant and blockheaded. He still wonders why his wife wouldn't find his "own demanding yet animating life in the fulcrum of American letters and journalism . . . sufficiently stimulating for her." The years of his editorship ('67–'71) were the noisy hinge that opened the door to many social upheavals, and, for all the tumult he describes, being the editor of a national magazine often left him in the calm eye of the storm.

The times were changing and Morris resigned in 1971, not liking the direction the magazine's owners wanted to take *Harper's:* shorter, rather than longer articles, upbeat rather than downbeat, and the tricky business of giving the readers what they (according to surveys and studies) want to read, rather than what the editor-in-chief wants them to read.

Morris returned, subdued, to Mississippi to teach and to write. Since he never felt as if he truly belonged in New York City, it was easier for him to leave. But his New York days are now preserved in amber – his prose at times does have a slightly sticky quality – but within the pages of the memoir is the glitter and glamour of those years, their excitement and drama, a time when so much seemed possible to a young man from Yazoo, Mississippi.

Any sympathetic reader is likely to share his regret when he returns at the memoir's end to the imperial city he once bestrode and concludes: ". . . the direst of recognitions began to spring in my poor psyche that I had not made the slightest ripple on this place, for New York somehow obliterates you, and especially the outlander."

First appeared in the *South Bend Tribune,* January 23, 1994;
 Review of Willie Morris, *New York Days* (New York: Little, Brown, 1993).

Forward to the Past: The SLF Album

A full history of literary festivals and readings has yet to be written, but with her book, *The SLF Album: An Informal History of Notre Dame's Sophomore Literary Festival 1967–1996,* Linda DeCicco contributes one small portion. And I expect a complete study to be written one day, since there now seems to be an appetite in the academy for this sort of historical work. See, for instance: Gerald Graff, *Professing Literature* (1987); Andrew Levy, *The Culture and Commerce of the American Short Story* (1993); and D. G. Myers, *The Elephants Teach* (1996).

The rise of creative writing, along with its trailing literary festivals and visiting writers, has been a subject of conflict in academic settings over the decades, since it highlights the pedagogical divide often found in English Departments – the competition between living literature and supine texts, practice and theory. As D. G. Myers writes in *The Elephants Teach,* a history of creative writing in universities since 1880, "A devotion to literature has aroused suspicion (and stirred contempt) on the part of literary scholars for a hundred years and more." And the foregrounding of literacy, rather than orality, is thrown into confusion when writers read; it's forward to the past.

When one considered "readings" in academic settings pre-1960, one usually thought of poets and poetry. Consulting the record catalogues of the time (Caedmon's, especially) to see what sort of writers were offered on vinyl platters – poets overwhelm the list – confirms this impression. Poets read their verse aloud.

Some novelistic exceptions come to mind: Twain, Dickens, Faulkner. In most American towns there was a remnant of the lyceum tradition, part of the adult-education movement of the nineteenth century, related to Chautauquas, where the famous and not-so-famous personages declaimed from a public stage. There, prose writers would turn up. There are histories of the Chautauqua movement (see, for instance, Harry P. Harrison and Karl Detzer, *Culture Under Canvas* (1958)). The well-known Lincoln-Douglas debates were part of a larger public cultural scene; not as well known is that their length rivaled how long Elizabethans stood in the pit during one of Shakespeare's plays.

The growth of literary readings, "festivals," of one sort or another at universities, grew alongside the mushrooming, during the seventies and eighties, of graduate creative writing programs. Before then their history is spotty. Notre Dame had two summer writers' conferences, involving English Department faculty writers and professors such as Ernest Sandeen, Lou Hasley, John T. Frederick, John Frederick Nims, and Richard Sullivan, among others, in the 1950s.

When I was an undergraduate in the 1960s, in Kansas City, Missouri, Allen Ginsberg and a small entourage (Peter Orlovsky, Gregory Corso, I recall), read in a local bar; they had agreed to read at someone's home, afterward, to accommodate the youth (myself included) who were too young to be admitted to the bar. Ginsberg was used to such haphazard venues. The San Francisco poetry renaissance was chiefly an oral phenomenon, readings in cafes and small bookstores leading the way – casual, unorganized, quasi-spontaneous, a lot like the poetry that got read.

That Ginsberg "reading" may have been the first poetry reading I ever attended. There weren't that many at the state university I attended in the mid-sixties. The Jewish Community Center in Kansas City had a series (a service such centers provided in many towns), and I did go to those. It brought literary culture to the wider community; there wasn't a lot of competition at the time, though one of Kansas City's own had just won the Yale Series of Younger Poets prize, and that had been reported locally (James Tate, *The Lost Pilot* (1967)). This was in the mid-to-late sixties, quite near the start of Notre Dame's SLF. I'm sure the young students who started the SLF were reacting to the same things at large in the culture.

In the Midwest, this was "new," rare, seemingly in opposition to the dominant atmosphere of getting and spending, conforming and coping: poetry for free, or almost.

And poetry led the way (except at the SLF). I've been trying to recall the first writer of fiction I ever heard read. I had heard Edward Dahlberg read, but never any of his fiction. It may have been myself, insofar as when I was a graduate student at Columbia University, in 1968, we were expected to give a public reading, and I drew the short stick to read first. Erica Jong followed, reading poetry. That was in 1968, the glorious *annus mirabilis* of the Festival at Notre Dame, when everyone attending was a "big name."

Columbia brought in writers to our classes, but they did not read: W.H. Auden, Isaac Bashevis Singer, Robert Penn Warren. They talked, but did not read. None of our teachers read then, either (Hortence Calisher, Richard Elman, Lore Segal, Jean Stafford), which now I consider strange – and Calisher and Segal have both read at the SLF in the 1980s.

All my teachers were prose writers so it didn't seem strange back then, at the end of the sixties. Poets read; prose writers were read. That we could, should, read their work was taken for granted. One recorded exception was when Katherine Anne Porter was "writer-in-residence" at the University of Virginia in the late fifties and she gave a public reading of her short story, "Flowering Judas." Genre played a role here. Short stories might be read. The transformation of the oral culture into a literate one (especially in the academy) was almost complete. But our entire culture is now becoming, largely, an oral-aural-visual one, reversing the process. One of the singular hallmarks of the 1968 SLF was that all the famous writers in attendance were writers of prose. Poets did not show up at the festival in force till 1970.

So, though I wasn't at Notre Dame when the SLF began, I was of the age that was present at the creation, the time when readings started pollinating across the land. Students were getting used to gathering together to hear the known and the not-so-well-known speak – and read. It was, also, the era of protest against the Vietnam War. Teach-ins led to read-ins.

Another institution was in its infancy at the same time as the SLF: the National Endowment for the Arts was in its early stages when the stages at Notre Dame began to fill up with contemporary writers. Notre Dame received money from the fledgling NEA for the 1969 SLF, but one drawback of reinventing the wheel each year, of minting a brand-new sophomore to run the festival, was the absence of any long-range planning, which would have allowed for the festival to apply for ongoing grants, back when there were grants to apply for. Now the NEA is sputtering, trying to live on despite the cold water the newly Republican-controlled congress of 1994 is pouring on it.

The dust has settled from that earlier period of cultural explosion; most of our explosions these days are of another, less metaphorical, sort. The times have changed, and so has the festival.

I have noted elsewhere in print that the end of the sixties and most of the seventies was a golden age for literature. Not necessarily for the literature that was produced (though quite a bit of it shines), but for the nature of the audience. It was golden.

In 1978, the number of first novels published was roughly that of the number of first novels published in 1962 (Library Journal has been keeping count) – slightly more than a hundred. During the sixties, the number of people in institutions of higher learning increased dramatically. It tripled. That period – from the early sixties to the late seventies – was a golden age of readers for serious fiction. There were many more readers being educated during those years, while the number of first novels published was being held constant. Student aid expenditures also more than tripled during the sixties, from around a half-billion to over three billion.

Now, over three hundred first novels a year are published. That increase is a result of the tripling of the number of people who went on to some form of higher education during the sixties (and beyond). But, there is no longer the happy surplus of readers. That bountiful ratio has changed quite a bit.

So, the golden age of readers helped beget the golden age of readings. Notre Dame sophomores were there at the forefront.

The first festival I attended was in 1982. The President of the University, Father Ted Hesburgh, introduced Czeslaw Milosz. Nobel Prize winners were not neglected by the administration. During a workshop the day after his reading, Milosz gave this bit, among other bits, of geopolitical advice to the gathered throng: "Everything the Russians say about America is true. And everything the Americans say about the Russians is true."

By 1982, the literary world had begun to change: the atmosphere of the sixties and seventies was being overtaken by the new president from California. The greed-is-good decade was underway. As John Barth put it (one of the "big names" of the 1969 festival – as well as

1980) in 1987, "SATs down, VCRs up? Books out, cassettes in?" The age of Reagan and the spirit that had initiated the SLF were at odds and the period of spontaneous combustion throughout the literary world was now flaming out.

The teaching of creative writing (especially at the graduate level) had changed, too, over the years. When I attended Columbia University back in 1968, the generation of writers who taught me was still functioning in the older "writer-in-residence" model. Even the pleasant odor of the title, "writer-in-residence," bespoke the lack of emphasis on classroom teaching and the desirability of learning more through bodily osmosis, personal contact, simple talk. The newer generation of creative writing teacher has a different work ethic – the irony is that writers employed today are functioning as old-style new critics with their students, pouring over their manuscripts, rather than offering primarily the sublime conversational generalizations of those who had taught them.

At the SLF in 1983, Richard Brautigan became symbolic of the era going-going-gone when he gave what turned out to be his last major reading before his suicide in 1984. He was subdued, melancholy, and seemingly disheartened, when, in the question-and-answer period following his reading, he seemed put out at the assumption embedded in a student question that he was a "commercial" writer. He wanted to be seen as an authentic hippie, one who did nothing for money. He didn't "sell out," as his generation would have it. Fortune had come his way. He was lucky. Though his luck, it appeared, was running thin.

But that distinction, between "serious" and "commercial" was being used more often in the early eighties, separating writers on the basis of audience size and, hence, income. That tension was always at play during the eighties and beyond, the sophomores always looking for "big names," dreaming often of inviting Stephen King and other such luminaries. And now, since King has published in the *New Yorker* (yes, the *New Yorker*), and has had the same story reprinted in the O. Henry Awards volume for 1996, he is certainly certified as "serious." Those changes mark the end of another literary era, when distinctions such as serious and commercial have begun to loosen.

In 1984, two African American writers were at the festival. Before that, the festival had been a very white, and mostly male, entertainment. Here, too, the times were finally catching up. Ralph Ellison had come in 1968 and the festival was stamped forever in the history of American race relations, insofar as Martin Luther King, Jr. was killed while the festival was on, but Ellison stayed to read. From all accounts (including Linda DeCicco's), it was a moving week, marked by many things, but it did link the SLF forever to African American history, even though the festival didn't acknowledge the connection visibly for a more than a dozen years. (Though what is not completely known is who was asked and wasn't able to come to the festivals during those years.)

When Ellison was here, Ernest Sandeen has recounted, he was attending a party given by himself and Eileen Sandeen and a local young African American roared up to the house on a motorcycle and cornered Ellison in the living room. Though Sandeen could not overhear the entire animated conversation, Ellison came up to him after the young man left, shaken, asking Sandeen in a distressed voice for reassurance that he wasn't an Uncle Tom, that he wasn't selling out his race.

In '68, those sorts of confrontations and those sorts of questions often heated the air. In 1984, one question that was in the air of Washington Hall was asked by a young white male student of the author of the theater piece, *For Colored Girls Who Have Considered Suicide When the Rainbow Is Enuf,* Ntozake Shange, "How does it feel to be a member of a minority?" Her reply: "Considering the population of the world you are in the minority and I am in the majority," was emblematic of the new times, the heyday of affirmative action, when cultural diversity was seen as a given, not an exception to be wished for.

From '84 on, the festival was able to arrange (and increase) the number of women writers who came to Notre Dame. Until then, it was one a year, at most two. Carolyn Forché, who came in 1987, personified another era-ending condition. Stories going around at the time marveled at the number of readings Forché had done and the amount of money she had earned doing them. By the late eighties "readings," "festivals," had become completely professionalized and institutionalized, and the sophomores found themselves dealing as much with literary booking agents as individual authors. And, by the nineties, "readings" have become part of the usual marketing of a book, and one is as likely to encounter an author appearing at a local super-bookstore as at a university.

In 1992, Harold Brodkey lent his elegant presence to the festival. At a party afterward, we talked about a number of literary matters, but also about diets, he suggesting the name of a macrobiotic master in Manhattan I might contact. (We had been discussing the subject of cardiac health.) I wondered, at the time, what he had and a few months later he announced, via the *New Yorker,* he had AIDS (would that he had used his appearance here to announce that!) and he died of the disease early this year.

We had talked about his long, long awaited novel, *Runaway Soul,* and I asked if he thought he waited too long, missing by about a decade the appetite for his rich, lyrical sensibility. No, he thought not. He seemed to have no regrets, only literary certainties, especially about his own writing's merit.

Even the no-shows of the festival, over the years, were interesting. Often someone canceled at the last minute, and usually it wasn't the last minute, but a week or so before, and a replacement was found. In 1983, Edward Abbey had introduced himself to the crowd in the library auditorium: "I am Mary Robison." Sara Vogan, the novelist, had an excuse in 1990, but offered it only over the phone to the sophomore who called after meeting her plane from San Francisco and finding her not on it. "Oh, I am painting my apartment." Her excuse became more poignant and apparent when she committed suicide not too long after. Reginald McKnight, the next year, 1991, got on the wrong bus from Kalamazoo where he was teaching at Western Michigan University and ended up in Chicago the night of his reading.

Each year, the sophomores want to have "big names" to attract audiences and what is odd is that the big names of 1968 when the festival truly began are the same big names now: Vonnegut, Mailer, Heller. Mark that up to good health-care and also the chief fact of the literary world of the eighties and nineties, the general winner-take-all society that we live in. But the writers who became well known during the golden age of readers described earlier have remained well known.

The economics of both fashion and commerce are the same: it is a lottery – the greater the number of participants, the larger the reward for the few. This doesn't dissuade people from participating; far from it – it actually increases the desire – the more writers writing and publishing, the bigger the payoff for the handful of writers who get lucky today.

The poet Derek Walcott came to the Festival in 1989. Not a big name then to the sophomores, but a big name to those who paid attention to contemporary poetry. He became a bigger name a couple of years later when he won the 1992 Nobel Prize for Literature (no one from the administration had introduced him in '89). His was the only reading I have attended in the Stepan Center, which the filmmaker, Michael Moore, referred to a few years later as "the Jiffy Pop dome."

It did give Walcott's reading a refreshing populist atmosphere, despite the atrocious acoustics. But every year there is the search for big names and what that means today is slightly different, for even the literary "big" names today have relatively small audiences, and name recognition (unless their books are turned into movies, authors remain, by and large, outside of the popular culture).

But one way to know a new big name is by the size of the fee requested. In 1995, the sophomores wanted to have Jamaica Kincaid read at the festival. Astounded though they were by the size of her requested "honorarium," they balked only when first-class travel and door-to-door limousines were tacked on. Writers are odd sorts of celebrities, since (the winner-take-all business) they can have very financially rewarding careers and yet not be familiar names to the student body at large. In 1993, Edward Albee was the big name and, it goes without saying, that his big name-ness came from his work in the 1960s, when the other culturally important big literary names were forged.

When T. Coraghessan Boyle came in 1989, the younger generation did not show much awareness of his work, though, once on campus, his rock star persona carried some word-of-mouth weight. But, in 1993, Albee's year, Tim O'Brien was actually the big name, since his books (or portions thereof) had been read and, more importantly, taught in high schools and university courses. His overflowing student audience seemed to have the most familiarity with O'Brien's work.

The word itself seems quaint today, given all the changes in the cultural scene, but in the sixties, "happenings," ersatz-spontaneous events fashioned into performances, became an art form; through the seventies a new genre rose up: the performance artist (and, during the same period, the proliferation of grant categories began at the NEA), and during the eighties the "PA" became a well-known art form thanks to Jesse Helms and the anti-NEA crowd, via Karen Finley and others.

Poetry, too, had left the genteel page and hit the rowdy stage during the seventies and eighties; it was the prose writers, as mentioned earlier, that were newly muscling into the scene. Poetry has a way of staying alive in the popular culture, if not through one identified poet (say, a Dylan Thomas, Robert Frost, or a Rod McKuen), but, principally, through song. The other Dylan, Bob, had the youth of his generation singing in the wind, but he flowed out of the tradition of Rimbaud, Whitman and the beats, the culmination of ever-evolving free verse. During the last ten years, African American rap music has helped to create a new audience for poetry, though its form is more elemental, dependent on rhyme, with its bawdy doggerel, half-limerick, half-Sprechstimme, roots.

But the writer as celebrity took a toll on literature, since the seventies and eighties were the decades of celebrity. And the festival was not immune to this: the writer as celebrity, writers as performers, writers as curiosities, writers as spectacle.

The personalities of writers are often contradictory. They can be seen, paradoxically, as intensely private exhibitionists. And readings sometimes are wrenching experiences, especially for prose writers. One example of this is the comic strip done by the novelist Rick Moody for *Details* magazine, in which Jonathan Franzen points out, in *Harper's* magazine (April, 1996), "a young author named Rick Moody hires a body double to do his bookstore readings for him. In the strip, Moody is making art of the torment that many young novelists feel at the pressure to market the innately private experience of reading. . . ."

The existence of the SLF has had a variety of important effects on our university. It was one cause of the formation in 1990 of the Graduate Writing Program in the English department, offering a week of contemporary writers on campus provided by the sophomores. There is often a concurrence of the visitors to the SLF and undergraduate class assignments, especially in the Core Course and Freshman Writing Program (the soon to be, doubtless, First Year of Studies Writing Program). Often this works almost too well, as my colleague Sonia Gernes, has reported: "Once I came early for the Sharon Olds reading, but, like many English majors and faculty, I couldn't even get near to a door of the library auditorium."

Even as the literary culture has declined nationally, been buffeted by the unspooling vortexes of video, VCRs, and cable, so too has the festival been cut back in both the number of writers and the number of days. It had been a week, then it went to six days, then five (and for the last two years, it has been supplemented with a night of student readings). Part of this is because the budget allotted for the festival has not kept up with inflation, and because of the disparity of fees between the writers. One of them usually would take home a large portion of the budget him- or herself.

Also, since the late-eighties, the Student Union Board and Student Activities has exercised more direct control. And, in 1992, the festival was put under scrutiny by a Student Government Review Committee, and asked to justify its existence; one of its primary faults, ironically, had been deemed "too much faculty involvement," according to the *Observer*, the student paper.

These changes were not just local; it was part of the rise of business ethos throughout the country, a bottom-line approach, the culmination of the greed-decade, that puzzled over the efficacy of living literature in the marketplace, just as commercial publishers have been retrenching, downsizing, and coalescing in the bigger world of corporate control.

But the festival has survived, and for the last two years the sophomores have kept attendance numbers high. And there is, for good or ill, less faculty involvement. (Indeed, few faculty members attend the festival at all, from the mid-eighties on, not a glorious endorsement of the importance of contemporary literature in the culture.)

But it is significant that the poets Bob Holman and Miguel Algarin, both from the New York City bar and poetry slam scene, kicked off the 1996 Festival, their movement being a fresh retreading of the poetry out loud movement as a public art.

So, it does not stay the same, but the SLF is a mirror held up to the literary culture, and one can see in its history what has transpired elsewhere. And, in one important respect, what was true in 1968 is true now: each year students at Notre Dame get to see accomplished writers alive and writing, celebrating the literature of the here and now.

First appeared as "Foreword" in Linda DeCicco, SLF *Album: An Informal History of Notre Dame's Sophomore Literary Festival, 1967–1996* (Notre Dame, IN: The University of Notre Dame Press, 1997).

Andrew Levy: The Culture and Commerce of the American Short Story

The first prose one encounters in Andrew Levy's study of the culture and commerce of the American short story is an anonymous description, part jacket copy, part abstract, of the book: "Since 1980, the American short story has undergone a renaissance of sorts. . . ." The rest of the paragraph is more factual than analytical, but it brought to mind some recent remarks of Tobias Wolff (found in his "Introduction" to *The Vintage Book of Contemporary American Short Stories* (1994) and somewhat paraphrased in an interview in the *Washington Post Book World* (January 8, 1995): "Most of the stories gathered here were published during the last fifteen years or so, during the period of what has been termed a short story 'renaissance' in this country. To judge by the respectful attention this renaissance has received from reviewers and academics, you would think it actually happened. It did not. This is a rhetorical flourish to give glamour, even valor, to the succession of one generation by another. The problem with the word 'renaissance' is that it needs a dark age to justify itself. I can't think of one, myself."

Wolff is wrong. Something did happen, and it wasn't merely "the succession of one generation by another." It is interesting how writers who don't currently teach or write much literary journalism (and some who do) often set up, as straw men, "reviewers and academics." Such designations are usually a matter of economics, and are the sites of the last battlefields of the "can't do, teach" wars.

But something did go on during the last fifteen years, brought about by the culmination of large forces prowling about the culture for a few decades. The short story went from being a reigning popular culture, commercial magazine form, to a reigning noncommercial, literary art form. There is a great deal of evidence for this. One of the easiest to discover is found in the backs of the two principal "best" short story annuals, where they list the magazines consulted. In the thirties, the list is short and made up, predominantly, of the well-paying slicks. During the last two decades, it has lengthened considerably and consists almost entirely of nonpaying, or token paying, literary magazines.

The commercial turns into the literary when no one will pay for its production – at least, not directly. The "renaissance" that occurred did not occur because of the writers of short stories, it occurred because of the consumers (the publications) of them, the demand side rather than the supply side. The "renaissance" had to do with the ascendancy of the short story as the literary art form most prized (in more ways than one) by our late-twentieth-century critical apparatus, which includes literary journalists and the academy and the mostly noncommercial publications that print short stories.

But twenty, thirty, years ago, it was a "dark age," very relatively speaking, for the short story, given the lack of critical caché the genre then carried. Wolff to the contrary, it has little to do with "succession."

Some of what it has to do with can be found in Andrew Levy's most pertinent and insightful volume.

Levy is not interested in defining the short story. Indeed, that moment may have passed. Lohafer and Clarey's edited volume of essays, *Short Story Theory at a Crossroads* (1987), which Levy slights – mentioning it in only one unilluminating footnote – may have been the apex of those defining tendencies.

Levy writes, about his own book: "The purpose of this work is to describe the birth and the construction of the short story as a literary form, and to describe the development of the social contract that guided the writing, teaching, and publishing of the short story in America."

He hints at the point I have made above (and elsewhere) when he states: "The workshop system currently provides a remarkable confluence of writerly authority and middle-class respectability – it allows for thousands of individuals to write fiction that deliberately eschews popular values, and to be remunerated for the activity. It institutionalizes the marginal voice." Here is one place where Levy and I differ: in matters of "remuneration." For most contemporary short story writers the remuneration is indirect – no one these days writes short stories for the "money," in the way F. Scott Fitzgerald claimed he did. The publishing (as opposed to the writing) of short stories will help you retain or secure a teaching job, raise your name in the critical realm, warm your heart on a cold day, but it will not earn you a living – or at least it won't earn a living for literary short story writers, beyond the world's two or three exceptions.

About a third of Levy's study discusses graduate creative writing programs and their effect on the literary situation. The volume's postscript is titled "Iowa City." Levy finds it hard to resist the current workshop-bashing that goes on in most critical circles. Though these commentators (often graduates of, or teachers in, writing programs themselves, as is Levy) tend to see the phenomena as a cause, rather than the effect that it most certainly is. Universities are the last refuge of hyper-literacy (among some of the professors, if not all of the students).

Levy isn't the most egregious basher, because he supplies a lot of entertaining evidence that, from its inception, the short story form was "taught," the genre always used as a veritable springboard for self-help and career promoters of the times. Graduate writing programs are, by and large, the institutionalization of a perennial ferment percolating throughout the culture. The Famous Writing School (of Bennett Cerf fame – who [of the baby boom generation] can forget the picture of the purported "faculty"?!) came before the proliferation of graduate writing programs throughout the land. Levy does a commendable job showing how these get-rich-quick handbooks – teaching how to construct the commercial short story – indirectly formalized the pedagogy of a lot of the teaching of writing.

"It is my belief that the historicist viewpoint tells the story of the genre in the most sympathetic manner possible," Levy tells us. And I share his viewpoint. Matters of production and reproduction are given their due, and Levy more or less succeeds at his advertised task, when he states: "The purpose of this work is to describe the birth and the construction of the short story as a literary form, and to describe the development of the social contract that has guided the writing, teaching, and publishing of the short story in America." His book "is devoted to individual and institutional visions of the short story. If Chapters 1, 3, and 5 describe how individuals responded to communal rules and expectations, Chapters 2 and 4 describe how the community itself transformed those individual responses into the foundations of new consensuses on the genre."

Levy is in a good position to examine these aspects of the American short story, since he is a graduate of a graduate writing program who went on to get a Ph.D. in literature, and did so while working for an East Coast-based magazine, *Boulevard,* which published short stories. He also writes short stories (and has just recently edited a textbook anthology of short stories).

Though Levy sees the situation as cyclical, insofar as a self-inflicted "amnesia" overcomes succeeding generations of short-story producers and distributors, he doesn't see it as schematically evolutionary as he might: the short story, Levy points out, is a product both useful to academia and the larger culture; but what marks his generation and mine is that it is a form that is produced by writers after they had actually, in formal settings, studied it as a purely literary form, not a commercial one.

What is new (in terms of sheer numbers) is that literature is being reproduced not by mere lovers of literature (which can be claimed by most writers), fellow readers, but by students of it. (The situation that apes the earlier commercial huckstering of the short story is the writing of "romance" novels. They, too, are largely an oral form – though one committed to the page – and, like the early-twentieth-century short story, the oral form will more quickly attract the amateur writer for money, than the *ars gratia artis* student sort.) This change is largely generational and evolutionary: Levy's study provides a lot of necessary data and, in many ways, complements Gerald Graff's *Professing Literature* (1987), by revealing how succeeding generations of students were exposed to the teaching of literature and what role the short story played in that instruction.

As the term "Counterculture" was coined, and, as the great growth period of higher education began in the sixties, one overlooked fact looms: what was "marginal" in the culture has become mainstream. As high school was to the culture in the 1950s, college was, is, in the seventies, eighties, nineties. The "literary" book audience is now the college "educated" audience.

The short story has become an art form rather than a commercial form because there is no perceived commercial audience for it – except in its most commercial oral forms: the sketch; the comic monologue; advertising, both print and TV; the half-hour, or the hour series; or the oral-based romance novels, see above. (Take the example of the new *New Yorker*: since Tina Brown became its editor a couple of years ago it publishes a single story an issue, or none, and serves up more than one only in a special summer "reading" issue – its own tony beach anthology.)

New journalism, so called, of the late sixties and early seventies, was more than cross-dressing genres. The commercial form of the short story today is the nonfiction article, profile, and "piece." There are no heated genre wars going on in nonfiction, no searches for what is an "article" or isn't an article. (What battles that rage are in courts over the matter of truth and falsehood – see, for instance, the work of Janet Malcolm.)

Levy's short (a common, form-induced brevity?) study is admirable and essential; he is a new generation writer and scholar (b. 1962) looking backward and forward and, for that, is a bit sketchy here and there. But his book is both useful and provocative, a combination that should even appeal to students.

First appeared in *Short Story*, vol. 5, no. 1, 1997;
 Review of Andrew Levy, *The Culture and Commerce of the American Short Story* (New York: Cambridge University Press, 1993).

Acknowledgments

I would like to thank all the editors involved for their willingness to allow (where needed) the reprinting of the pieces in this volume. The pertinent information of their origin is given at the end of each individual article. But, I would like to thank the following by name (somewhat alphabetical): Paul Baumann at *Commonweal;* Rich Heffern at the *National Catholic Reporter;* David Hoppe at NUVO; Henry Kisor and Steve Huntley of the *Chicago Sun-Times;* Greg Mitchell of *Editor & Publisher;* Steve Tomasula of the *Electronic Book Review;* Don Wycliff, Elizabeth Taylor, and Marcia Lythcott of the *Chicago Tribune;* Jaimy Gordon and Rachel Swearingen of *Third Coast;* the late Rochelle Ratner of the *American Book Review;* Lou Harry, *Indy Men's Magazine;* Clark Munsell, *The World & I;* Barbara Hanrahan, Rebecca DeBoer, and Harv Humphrey, Notre Dame Press; Gayle Dantzler and Andrew Hughes of the *South Bend Tribune;* Liz McMillen of the *Chronicle of Higher Education;* Mary Rohrberger and Farhat Iftekharuddin of SHORT STORY; and Linda Oblack, Nancy Lightfoot, Angela Burton, Bertolt Sobolik, and Rhonda Van der Dussen at the Indiana University Press and Cynthia Landeen, indexer extraordinaire.

In addition to editors, I want to thank these individuals, some connected to Notre Dame, some not. Magdalena Nerio, Agustin Fuentes and Notre Dame's Institute for Scholarship in the Liberal Arts,

Corinne Demas, Maura Stanton, Valerie Sayers, Christopher Fox, David Black, Ed Zuckerman, Charles DeFanti, Diane Abrams, John Matthias, Craig Nova, Irini Spanidou, Betty Signer, David Matlin, Jay Neugeboren, Kevin Coyne, Alice Elman, Joan Harris, Janey Skeer, Robert Kareka, Zane Kotker, Ilona Kelly, Marsha McCreadie, Harry Mark Petrakis, John Wright Stevens, R.D. Skillings, Dorothy Baker, Susan Blum, Lionel Jensen, Sam Hazo, and R. Jess Lavolette.

Index

In this index fictional characters can be found indexed under their first names.

WILLIAM O'ROURKE is the author of four novels, *The Meekness of Isaac, Idle Hands, Criminal Tendencies,* and *Notts,* and five works of nonfiction, *The Harrisburg 7 and the New Catholic Left, Signs of the Literary Times, Campaign America '96, Campaign America 2000,* and *On Having a Heart Attack: A Medical Memoir.* He is the editor of *On the Job: Fiction about Work by Contemporary American Writers,* and he co-edited the collection *Notre Dame Review: The First Ten Years.* He has received two National Endowment for the Arts fellowships and a CAPS grant from the New York State Council on the Arts. He was the first James Thurber Writer at the Thurber House in Columbus, Ohio, and the founding director of the University of Notre Dame's graduate creative writing program. A fortieth anniversary edition of his first book, *The Harrisburg 7 and the New Catholic Left,* is to appear in 2012.